BROKEN

a call to restore the house of Humanity

As a team of ten photojournalists, we set out to experience the world, to immerse ourselves in the cultures and people of every inhabitable continent in hopes of having our eyes opened to the stories that go untold. After traveling to over thirty countries in fifteen months, a common theme began to cry out for our attention. Everywhere we went, we discovered that nearly all social injustice issues stem from the brokenness of the family, the brokenness of the home. In a world of much diversity, the most universal longing of the human heart is to have a place to call home: a place of safety, love, and acceptance.

Never before have we seen such an increase in homelessness, prostitution, human trafficking, orphans, and domestic violence as in recent decades. Never before have we seen such a breakdown in the family unit. The very foundations of humanity, the building blocks of society, are crumbling and the result is a myriad of injustice issues that seem to only be gaining momentum. Family is the cornerstone, the origin of a healthy and functioning individual and society. If we want to see the end of social injustice, we have to start at the root - we must restore the family.

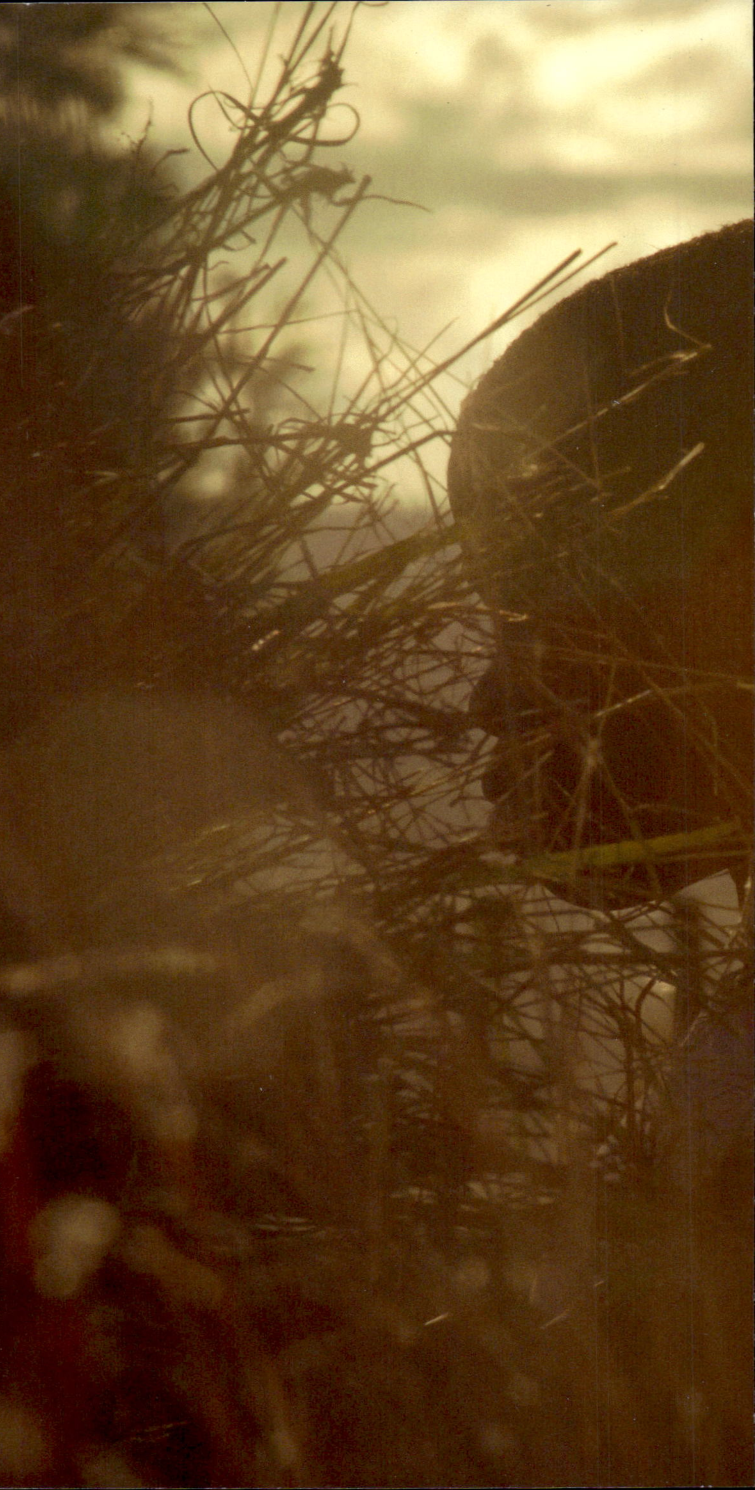

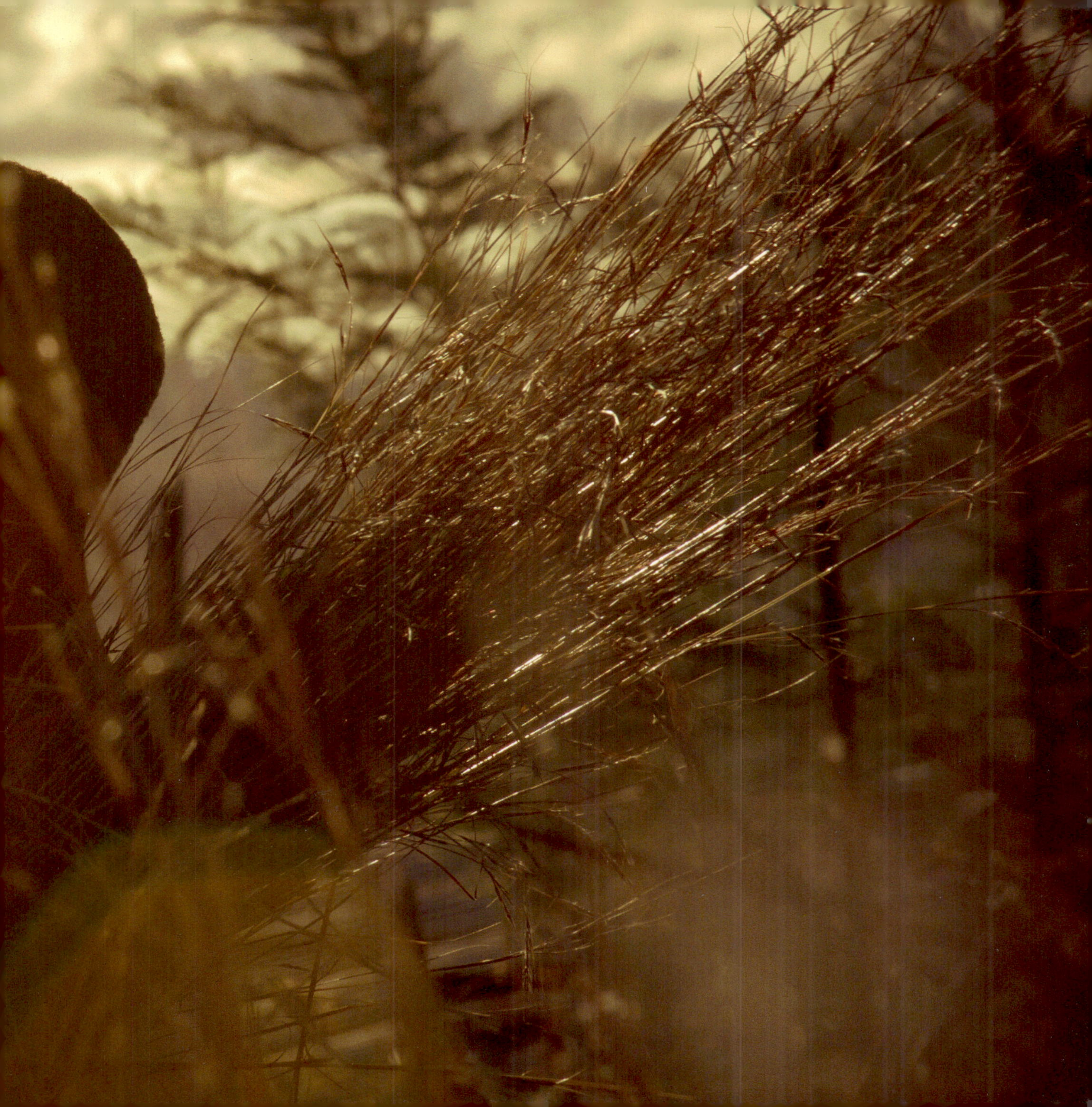

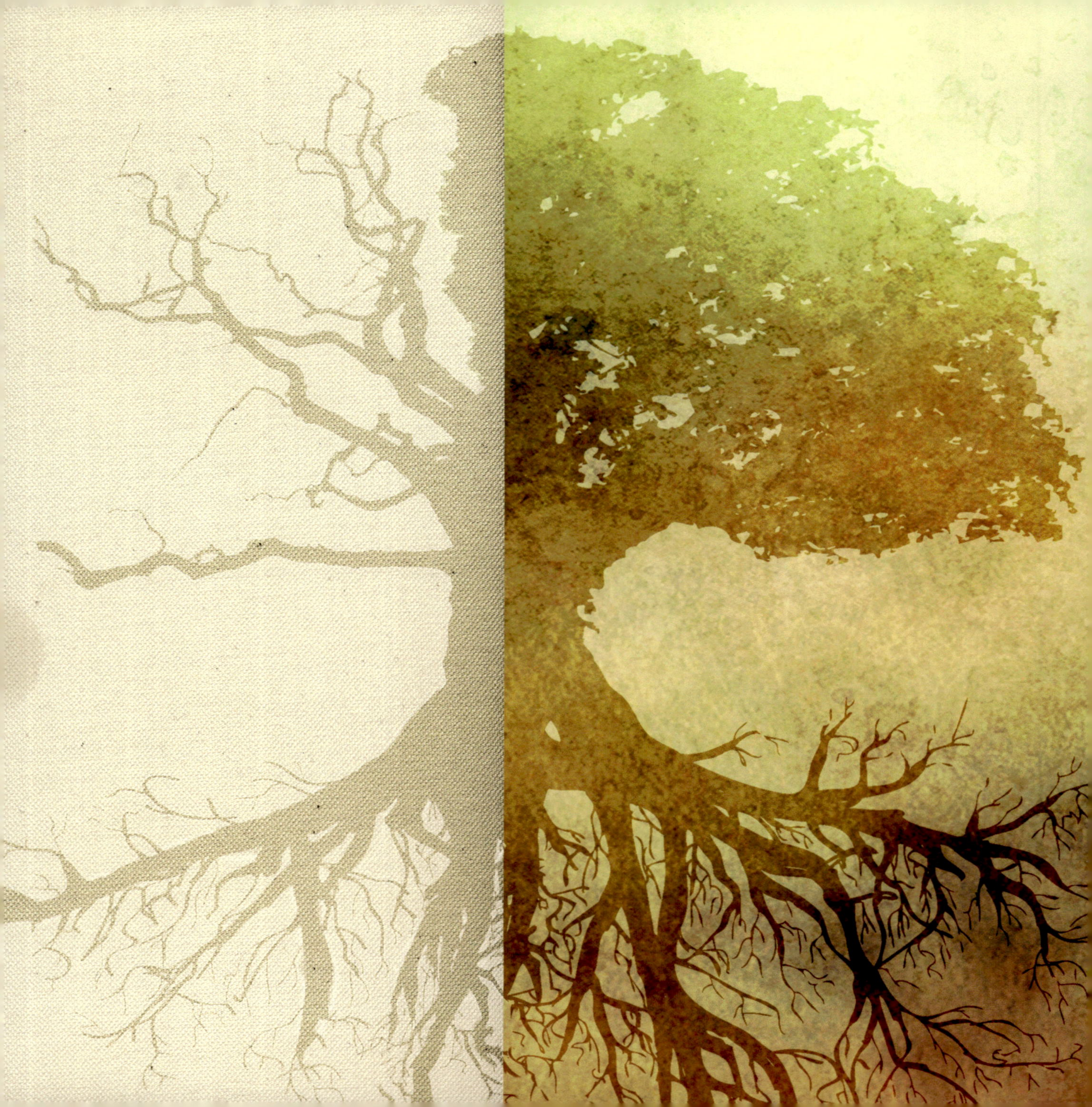

Like a tree consisting of roots, a trunk, and branches that bear fruit, so is the nature of our human condition. The roots of humanity begin within our family structure. Our trunk is the home where we hope to find stability and our lives bear fruit according to the soil in which we are grounded.

Generally, if we are rooted in infertile soil, our trunk will be weak and our fruit will be spoiled. However, if our roots are planted in nutrient rich soil, our trunks will be strong and our fruit healthy.

Around the world, people are increasingly being rooted in infertile soil - in brokenness, abandonment, isolation, hatred, anger, and exploitation. Their homes are flimsy and unsafe and they end up victims to social injustice.

Or·phaned

a child deprived of one
or usually both parents;
lacking support, care or
supervision

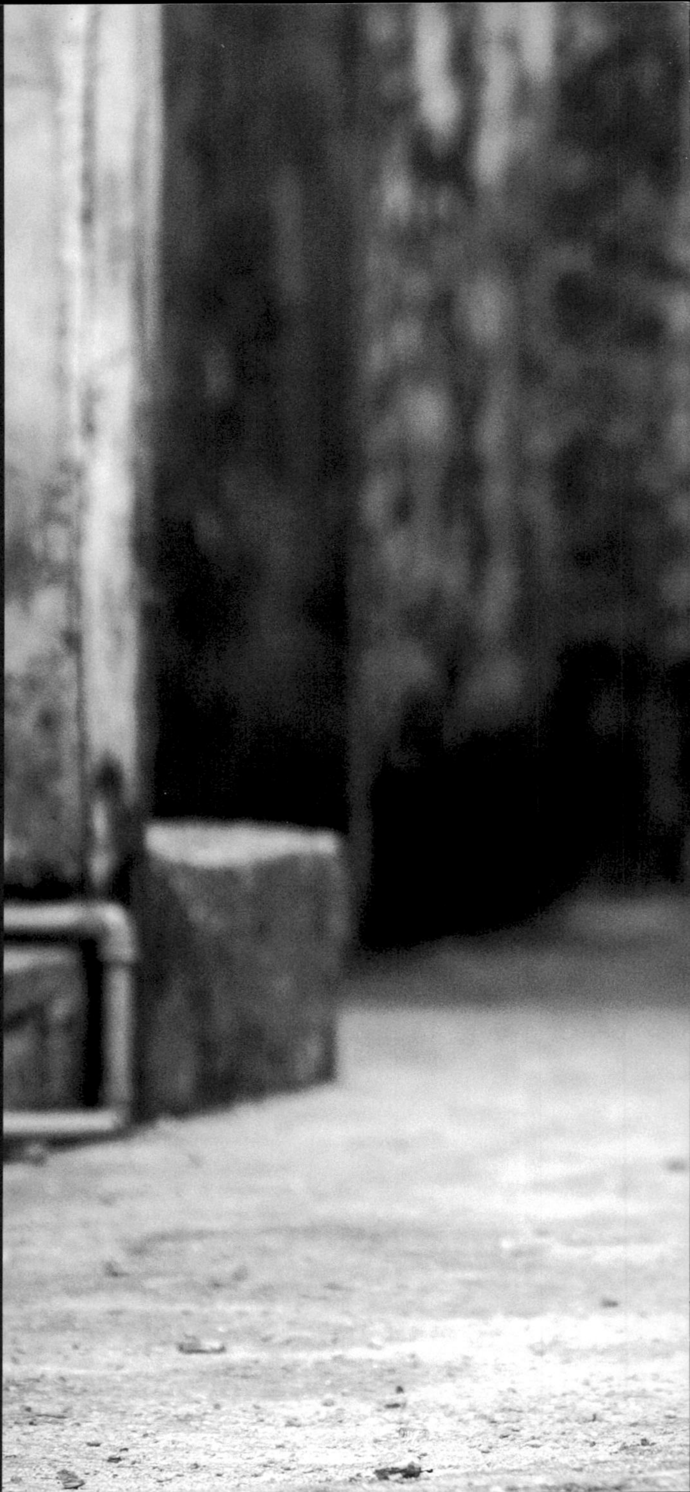

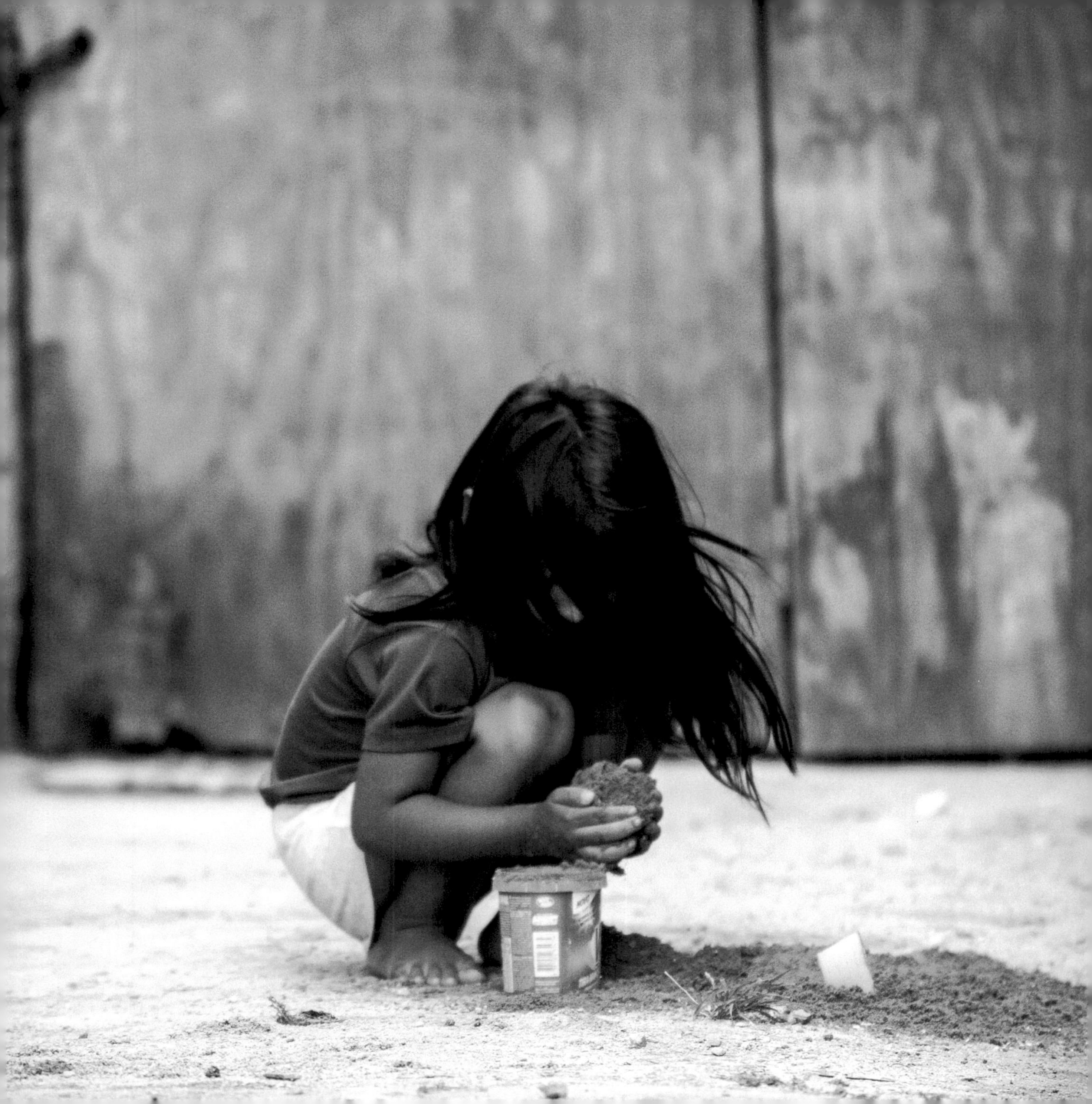

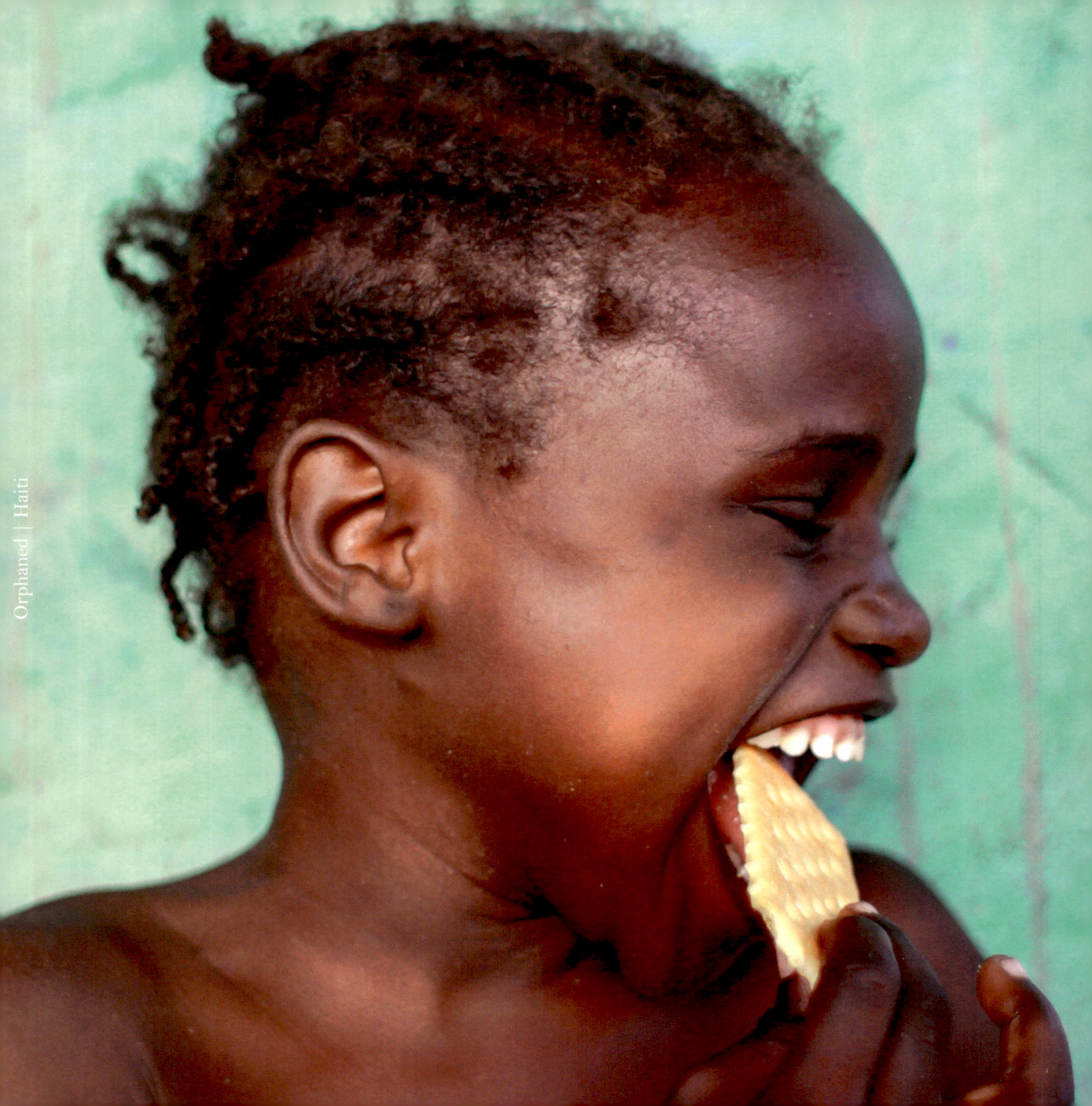

Orphaned | Haiti

Stumbling over the crumbled remains and stones of a fallen building in Port-au-Prince, Haiti, a scene of wounded survivors in the aftermath of the devastating 2010 earthquake begins to unfold. The sick lay on dirt floors and under canopies that shield the blazing sun: a makeshift hospital that is in desperate need of supplies and medical equipment.

As an increasing number of survivors arrive, the situation appears hopeless. We gravitate towards the section of tents that houses babies ranging in age from newborn to twelve months. Upon entering, we meet an elderly woman who is caring for her little granddaughter - a child without a name whom she just calls "Baby."

The grandmother holds the child, explaining that Baby is about four months old and lost both of her parents in the earthquake. She refuses to name her, believing that the infant will die well before her ability to speak or understand her own name. Baby is innocent, vulnerable, and nameless - dismissed as already dead.

We hold Baby's tiny, precious hands, peer into her empty black eyes, and begin speaking to her about her true worth. She smirks and giggles the more we speak, those beautiful eyes beginning sparkle. Eyes that know she is worth a name and has a calling despite her situation or possibly short life - a life intended to flourish.

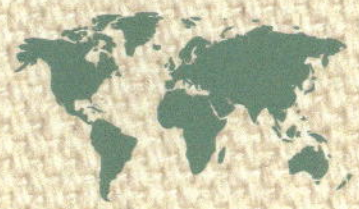

Worldwide an estimated **153 million children** ranging from newborns to age 17 have **lost one or both parents**.[1]

"Safety and security

don't just happen,

they are the result of

collective consensus

and public investment.

We owe our children,

the most vulnerable

citizens in our society,

a life free of violence

and fear."

- Nelson Mandela

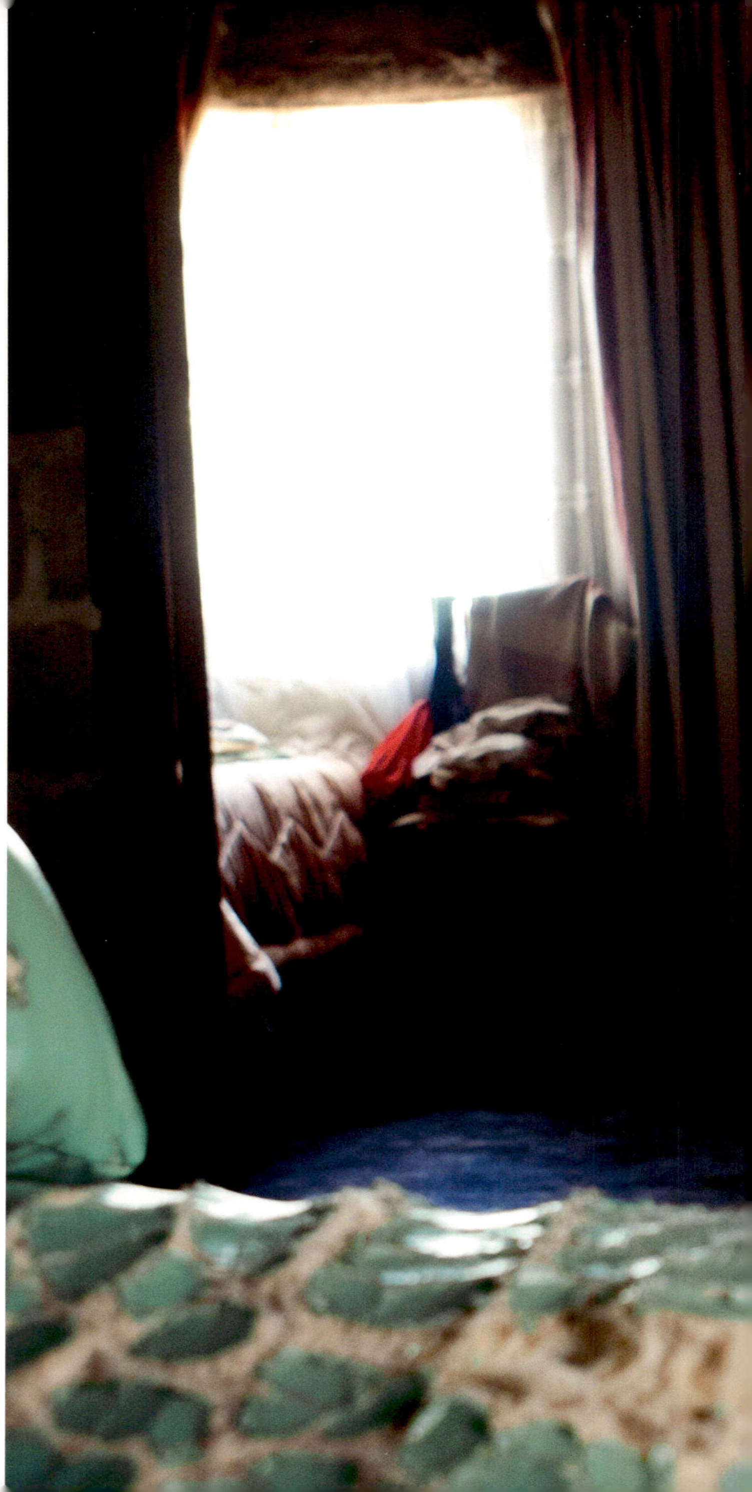

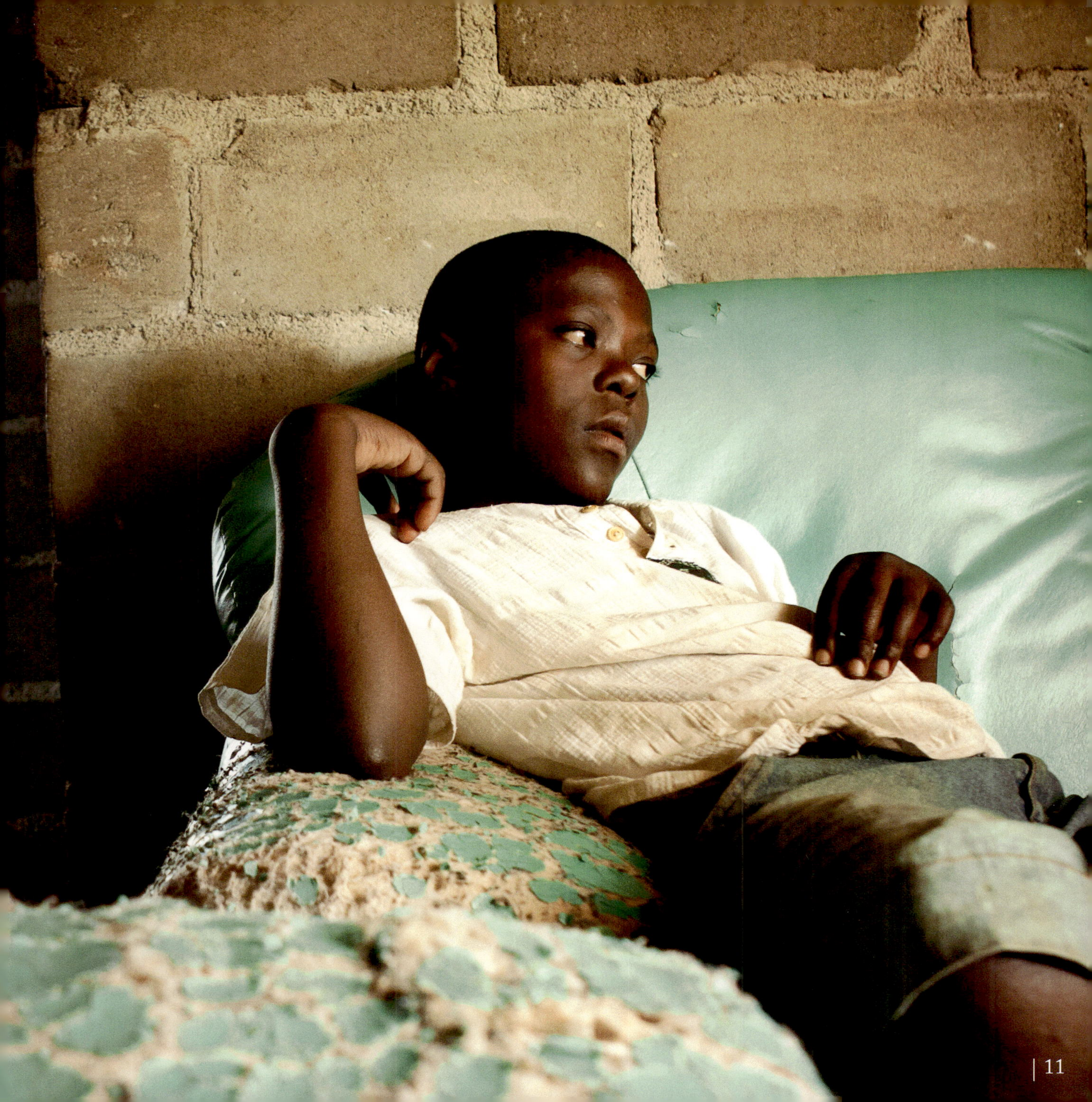

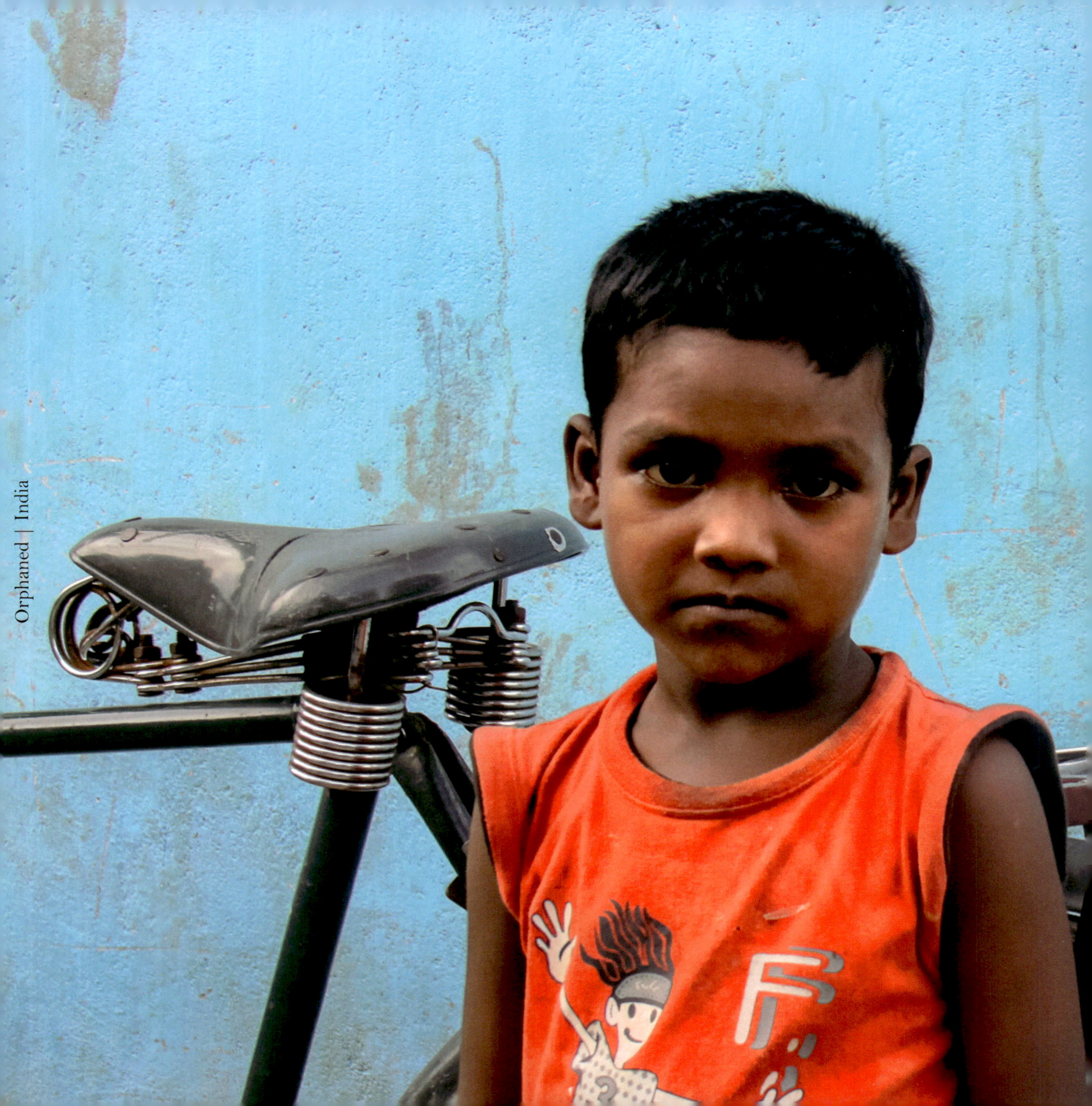

Orphaned | India

Sanjay peers out the top window of the orphanage, waiting for a glimpse of us, anxious to play again as we round the corner of the colorful Indian street. He is living above a pastor's house, in a single room along with ten other orphans. Bunk beds line the room with vibrant blankets and stiff mattresses. With just the clothes on their backs, these orphans live in a minimalist environment, but are provided an education and enough food each day.

Sanjay's family gave him away to the local church because they were unable to properly care for him. Leaving him abandoned, he was placed into this orphanage with others who have lost their parents or were given away as well. Although his basic needs are met, he is still without a father and mother to properly guide him into adulthood. There are times when he sits alone and the moments of his past manifest on his solemn face. He is starved for love – especially from men. Like many of the children in the world, Sanjay longs for someone to love and care for him – he longs to have real parents in his life, who will wait for him with arms wide open.

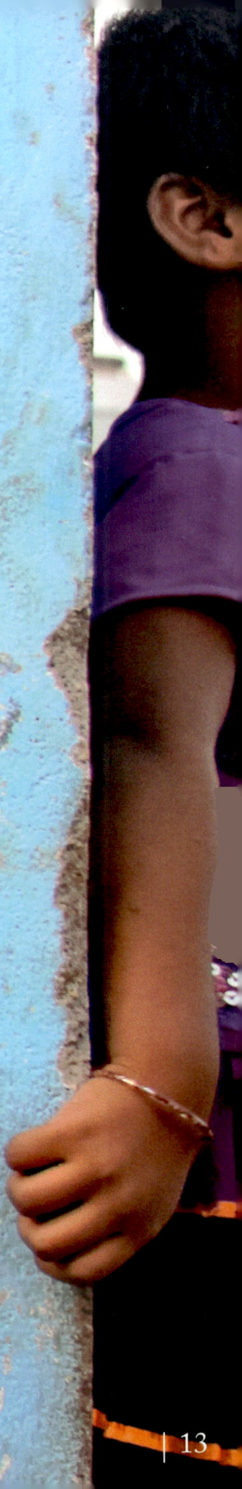

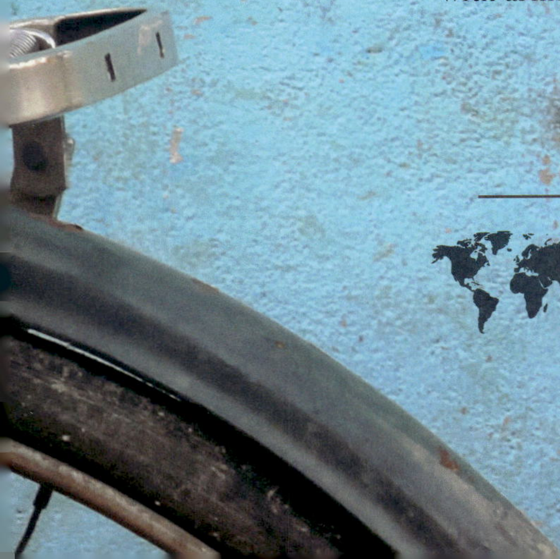

Approximately **130,000 children** [in the American foster care system] are **immediately adoptable**.[2]

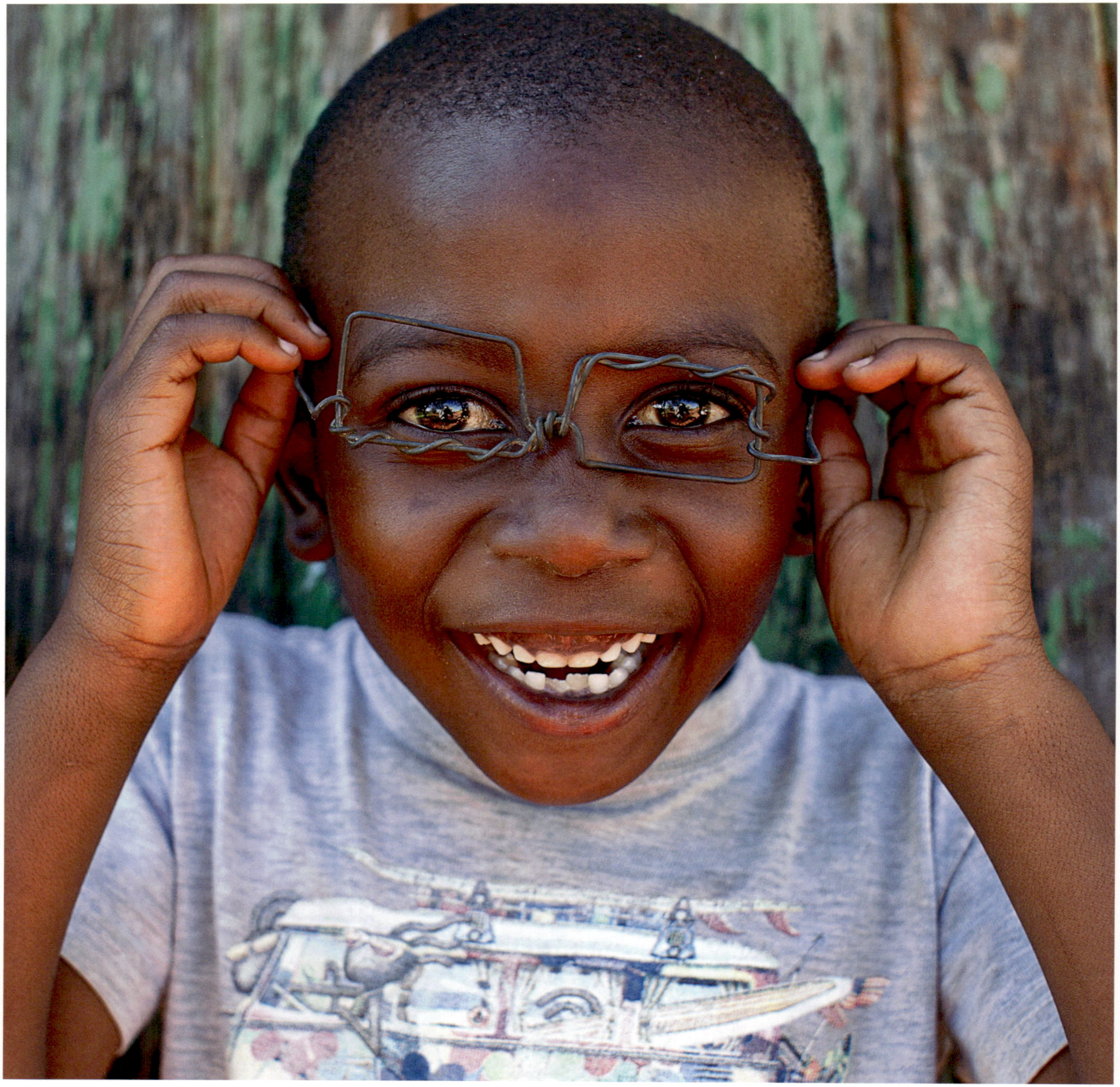

Orphaned | South Africa

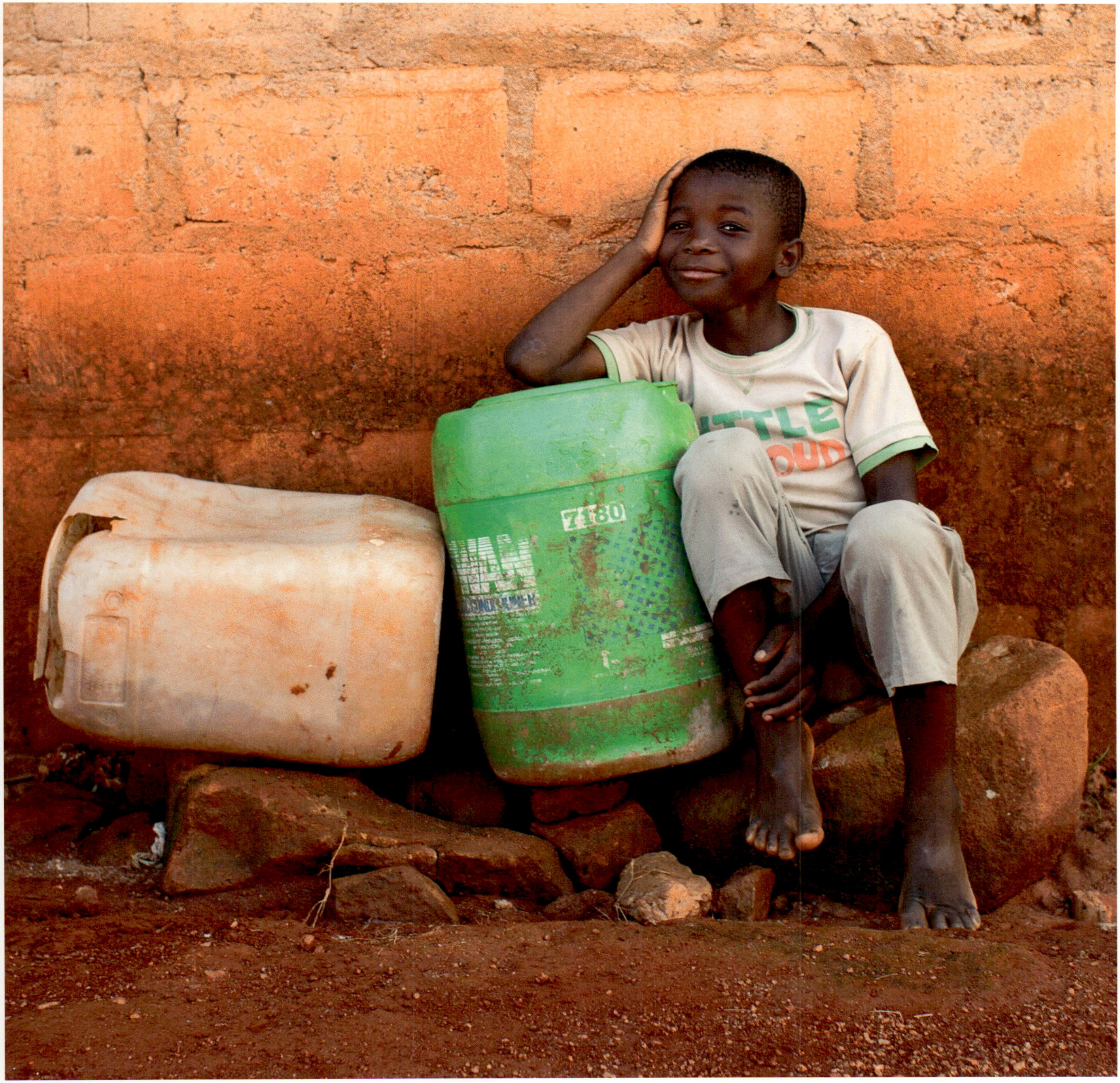
7180

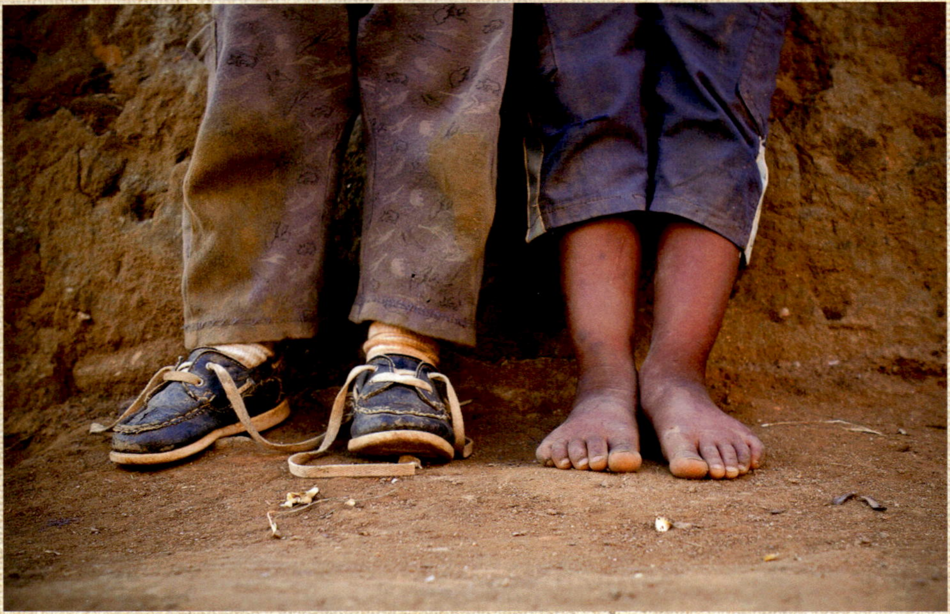

He is obviously sick, with thick green mucus running from his nose. Four-year-old Brother waits in line for one of the few meals he will receive all week. He wears a heavy orange sweater and pants that do not fit, clothing that is inappropriate for the heat of the season. His tiny, bare feet are covered in dirt and it appears he has not been bathed in quite some time. Each week when he receives his plate of food, he eats it with haste, hardly stopping to breathe. He is not simply hungry, but truly starving; not only poor, but orphaned.

Brother is one of approximately 122,000 children living in child-headed homes in South Africa.[3] Faced with circumstances of poverty, disease, death, and abandonment, these children are left to raise themselves. Eight and nine-year-olds must provide for their younger siblings, taking on the role of not only one, but both parents. They do their best to find food, clothing, and shelter; but without the provision and protection of adults they remain some of the most vulnerable and marginalized children in the world.

"The family structure that God designed is falling apart in this community and is single-handedly destroying it."

– John Shaw, Ten Thousand Homes

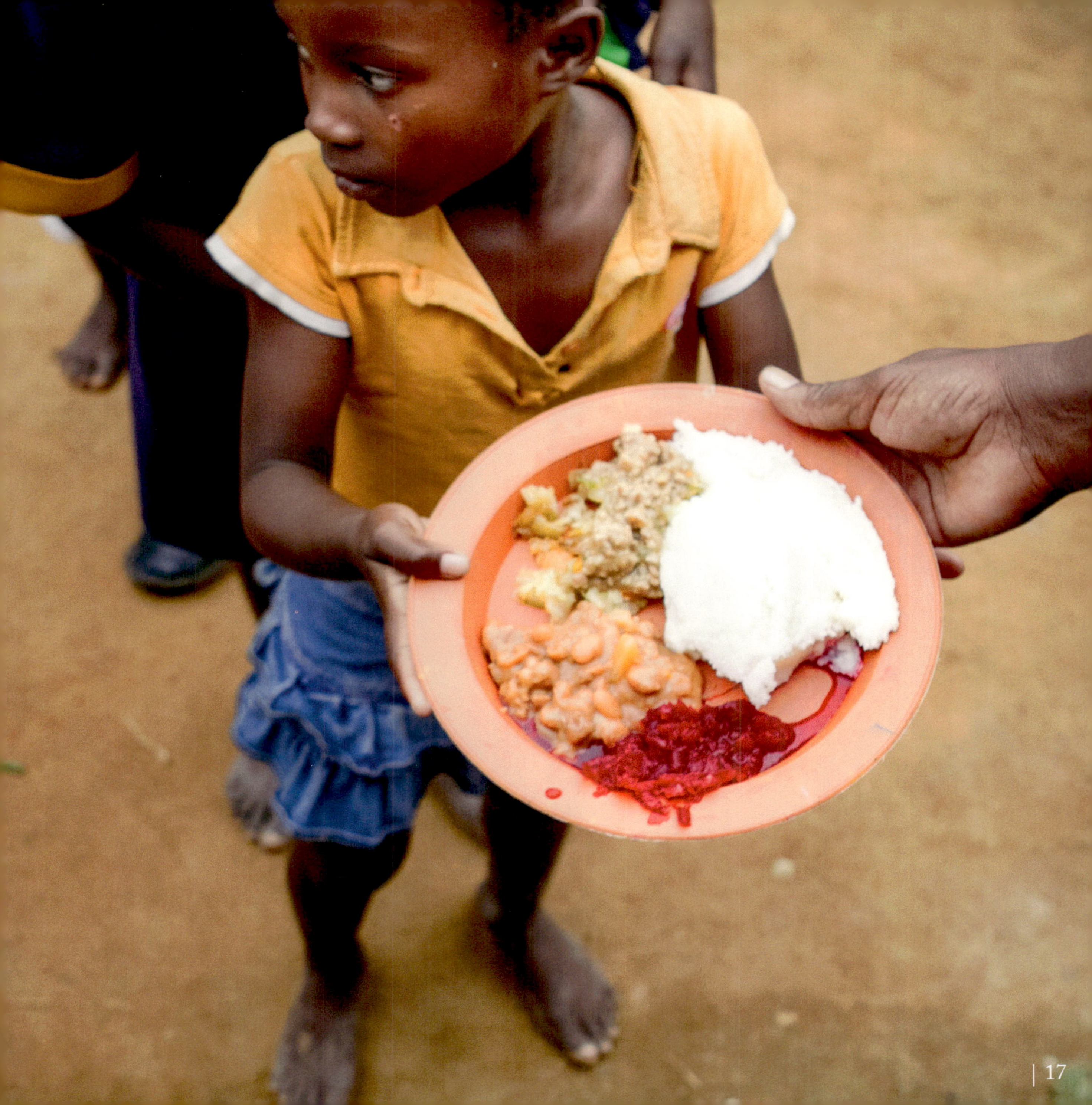

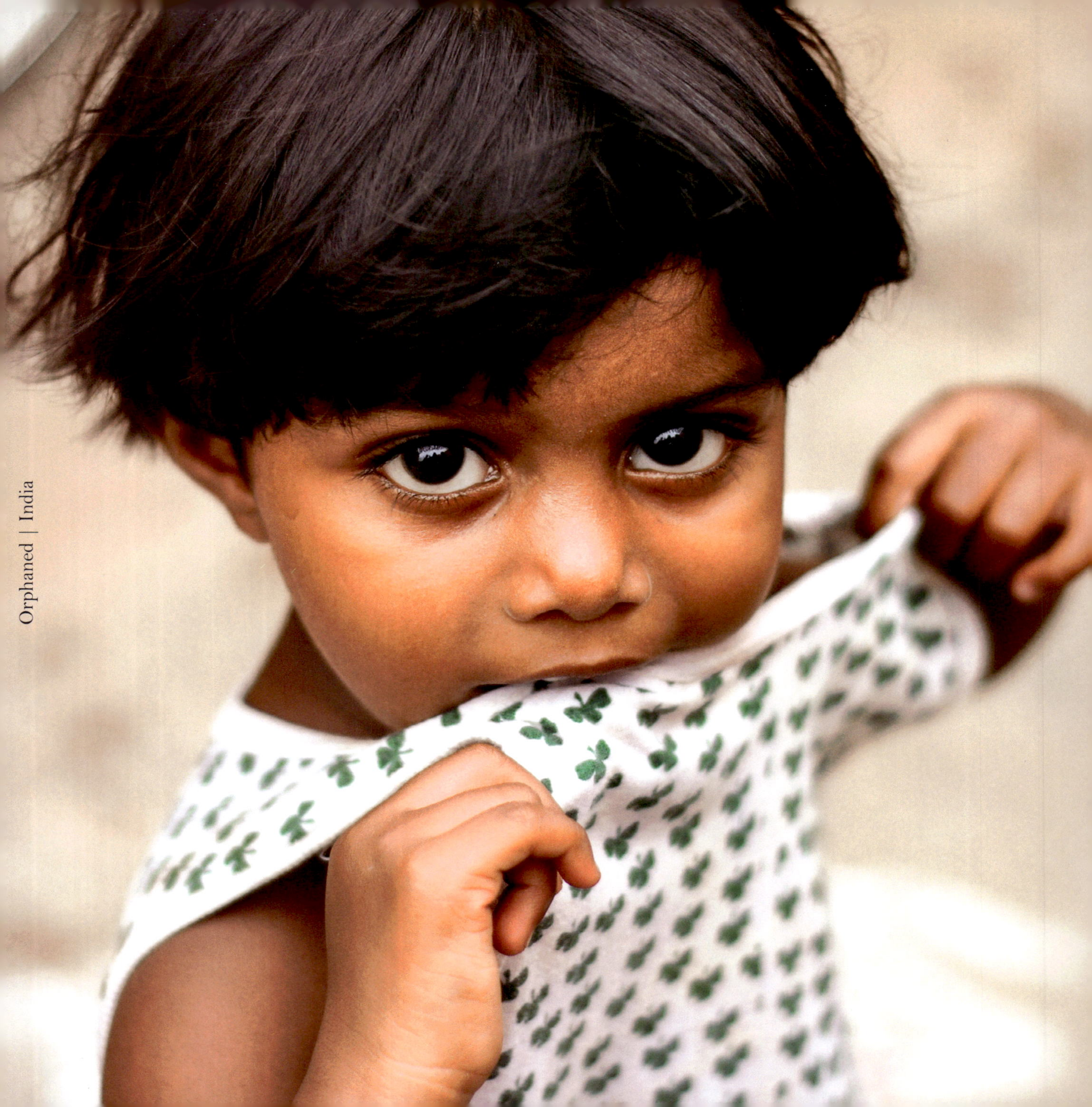

Orphaned | India

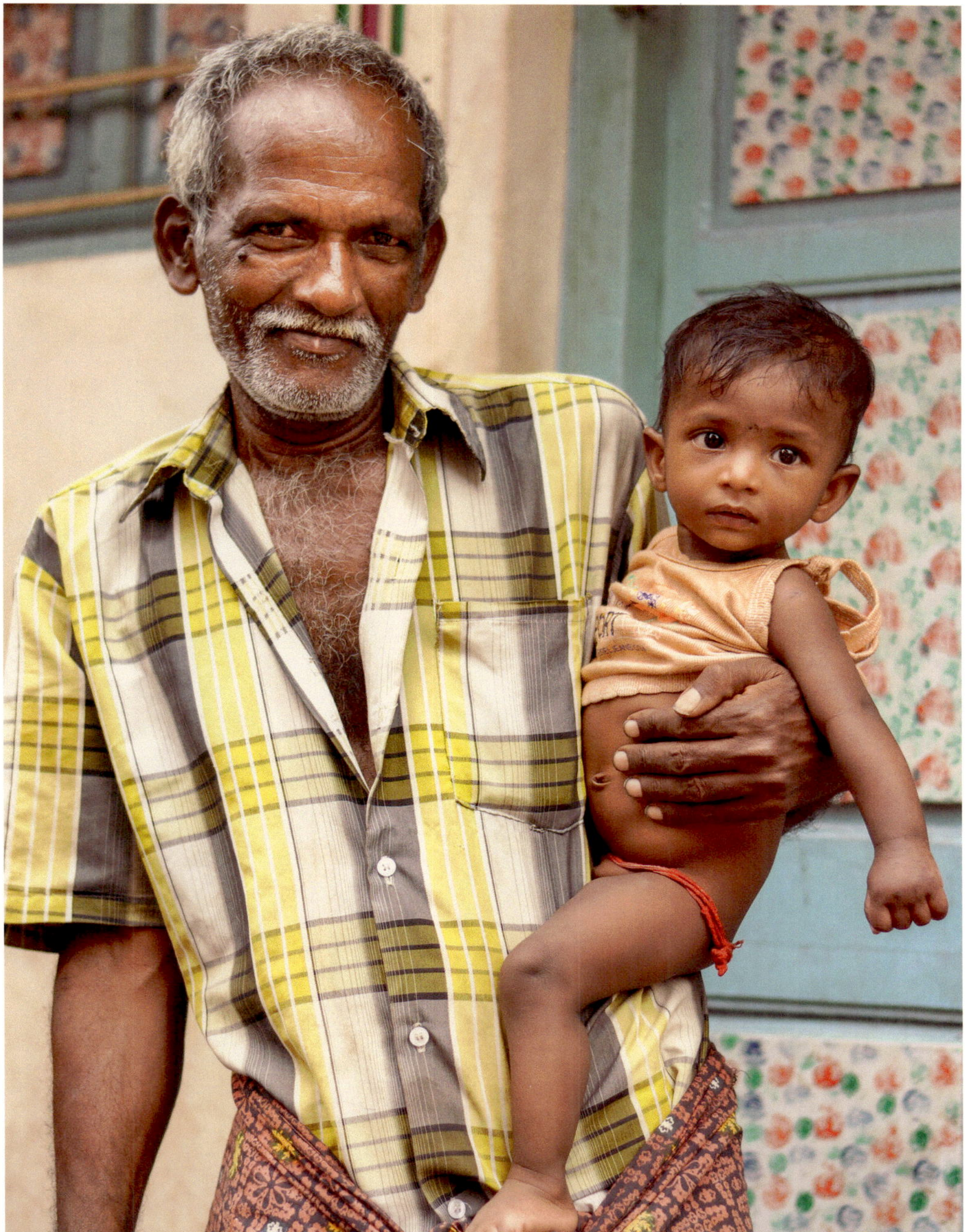

dis·placed

to move or shift from the usual place or position, especially to force to flee a homeland

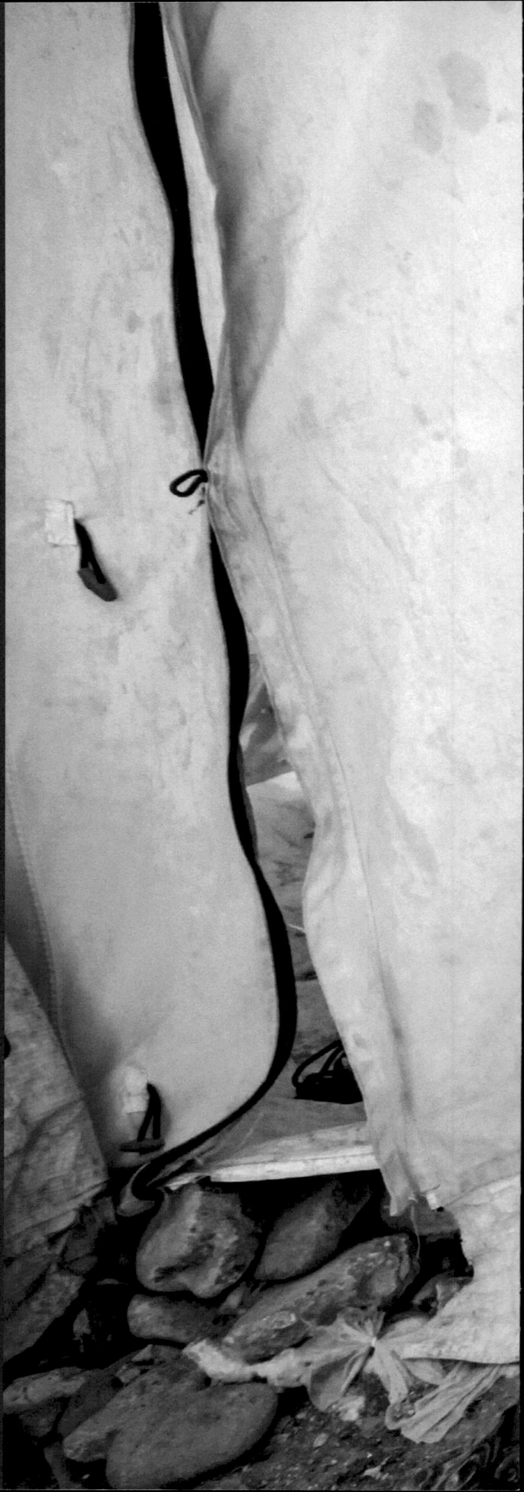

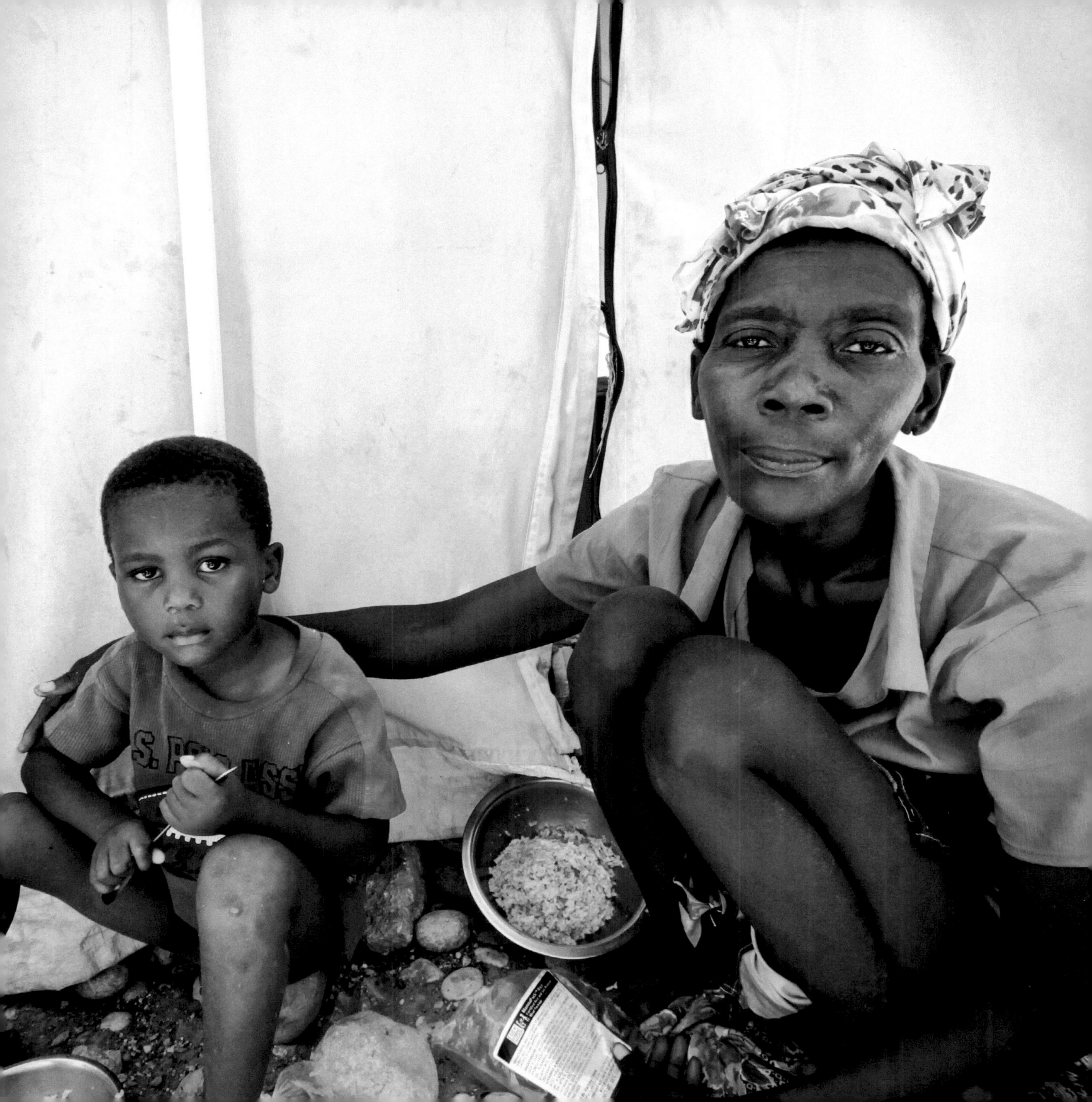

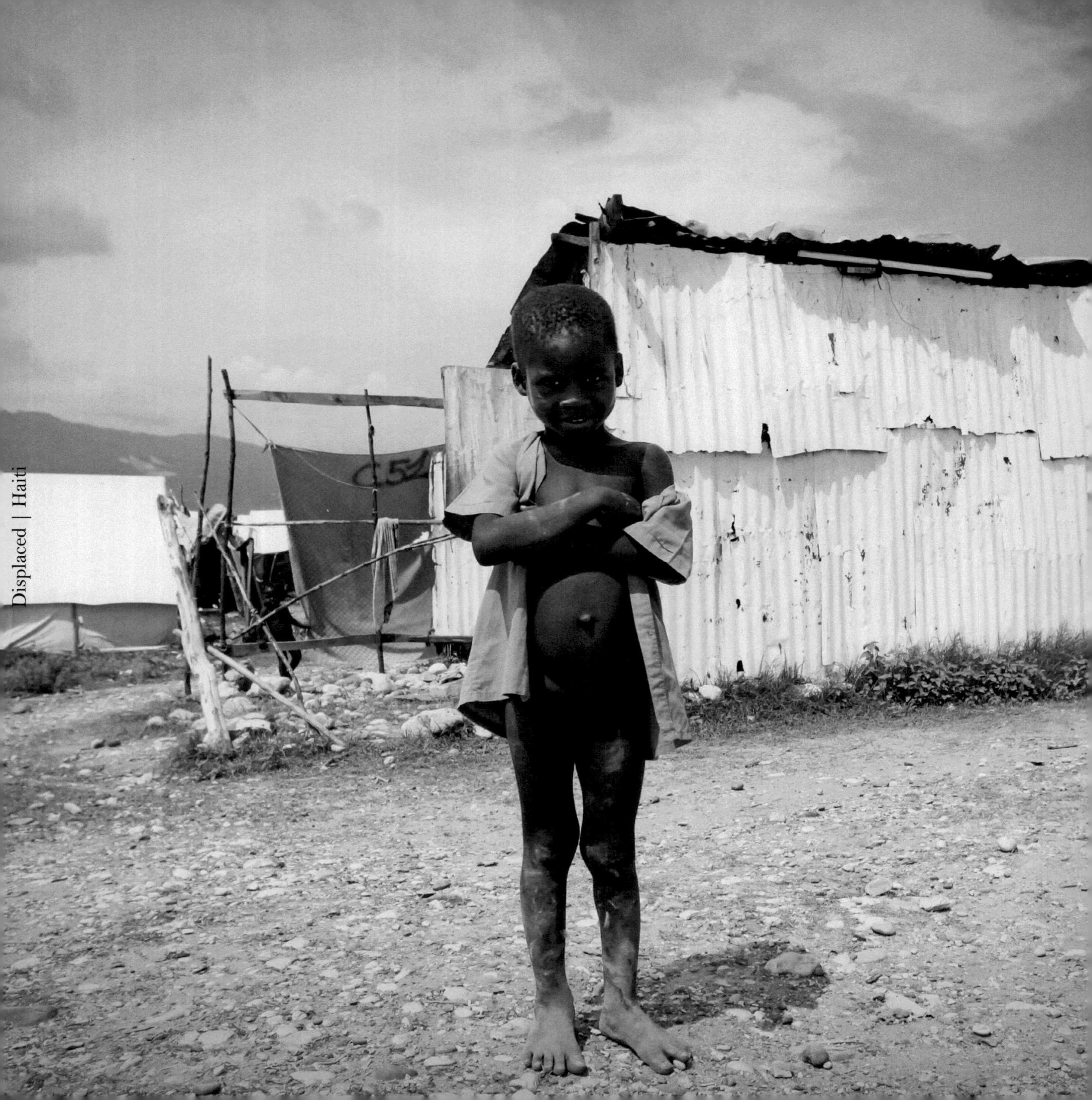

Displaced | Haiti

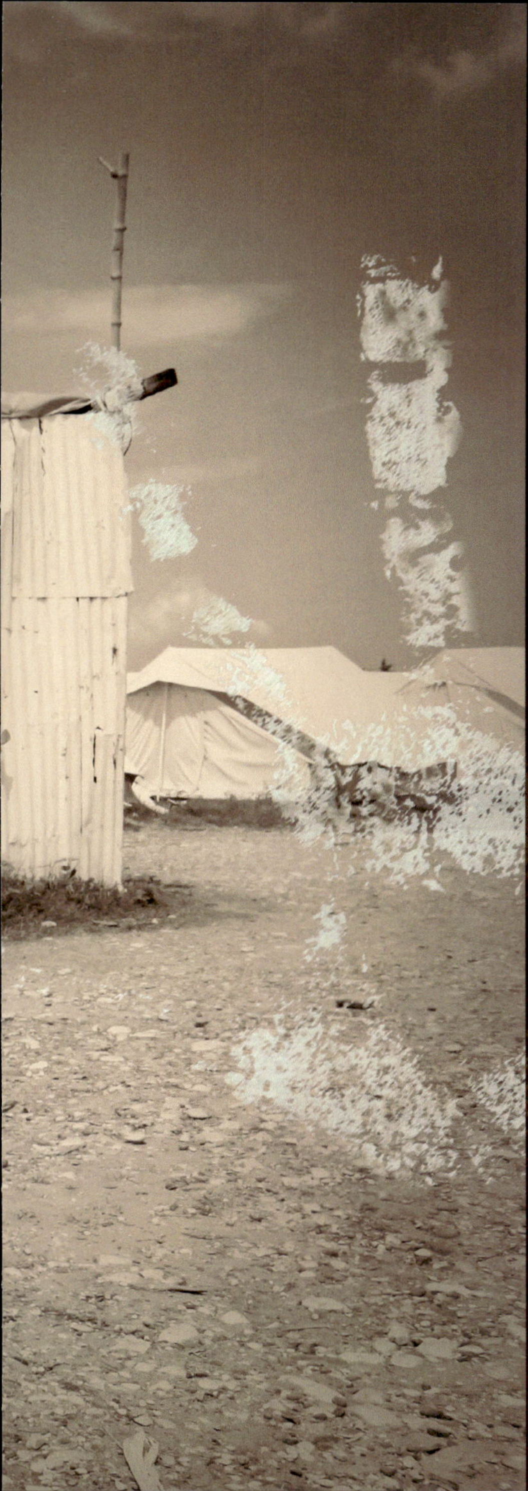

Ansel is naked from the waist down and wears only a tattered, unbuttoned blue shirt that waves in the wind as he runs toward us in the heat of the day in Cite Soleil - one of the largest tent cities in Port-au-Prince, Haiti. He eagerly grabs our hands and leads us deep into the massive tent city to visit his family. Twisting and turning through the maze of tents, shacks, and scraps we arrive and enter his small and decaying home which houses his entire family.

For the first time in our lives, we see what it means to live on less than a dollar a day. The orange hair and ballooned bellies of the children reflect severe malnourishment and the dangerous level of food insecurity, a result of the poverty and violence that surrounds the area. They are vulnerable, hungry, and unclean, surviving the tent city's squalor and unyielding heat. The dehydrating temperatures cause their bodies to pour out pools of sweat while sitting in humid tents that lack any type of air conditioning, a luxury that the industrialized world takes for granted.

Ansel's mother, nearly bursting with another pregnancy, struggles to take care of six children without the help of a father. Preparing their only meal for the day, she bends over a small pot that barely holds enough rice to fully feed two or three bellies. Devastated and displaced, this family and thousands like them rely on meager rations as they attempt to reestablish a sense of home.

There are now **43.3m people forcibly displaced** around the world - including **27.1m internally displaced** people.[4]

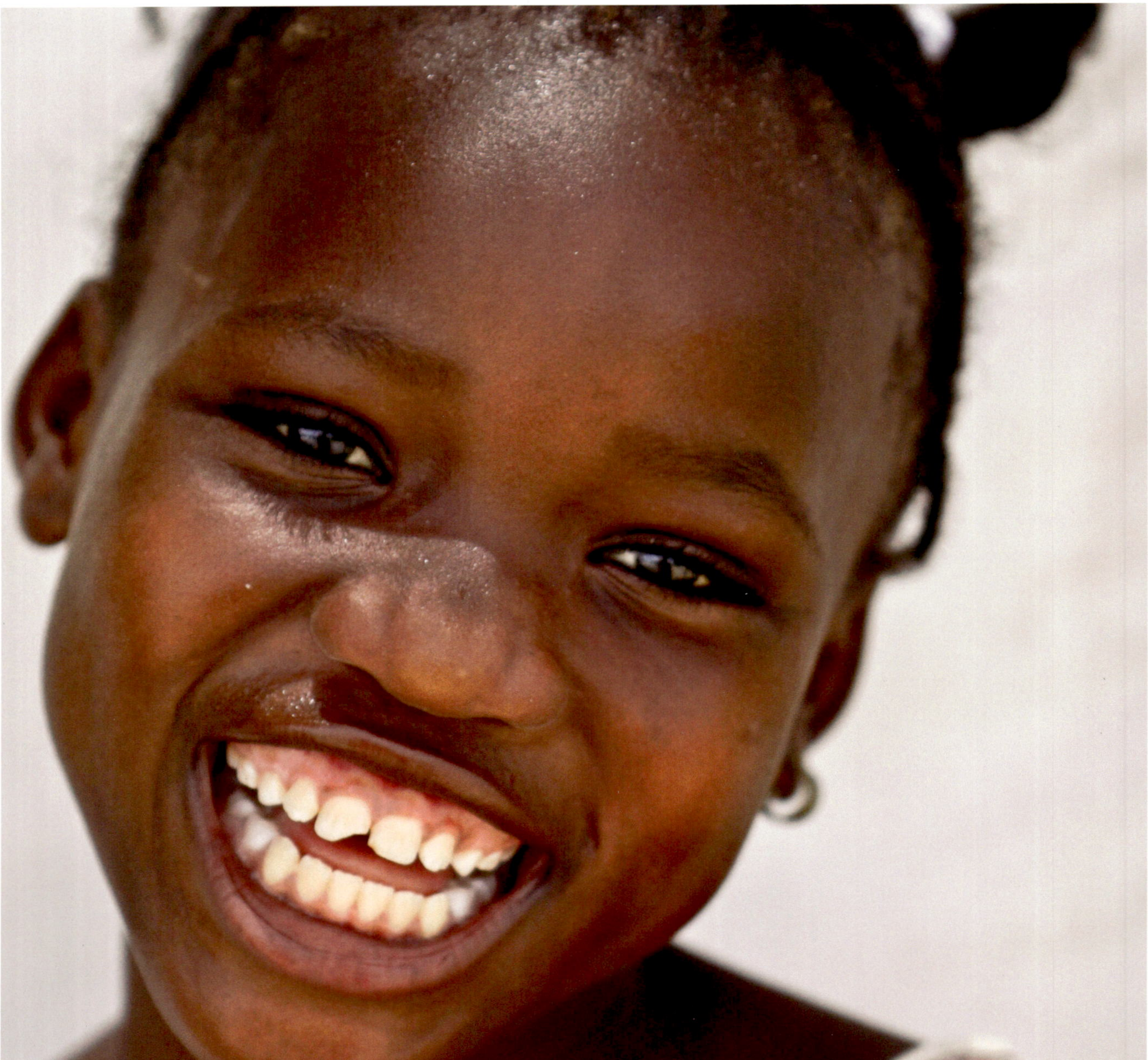

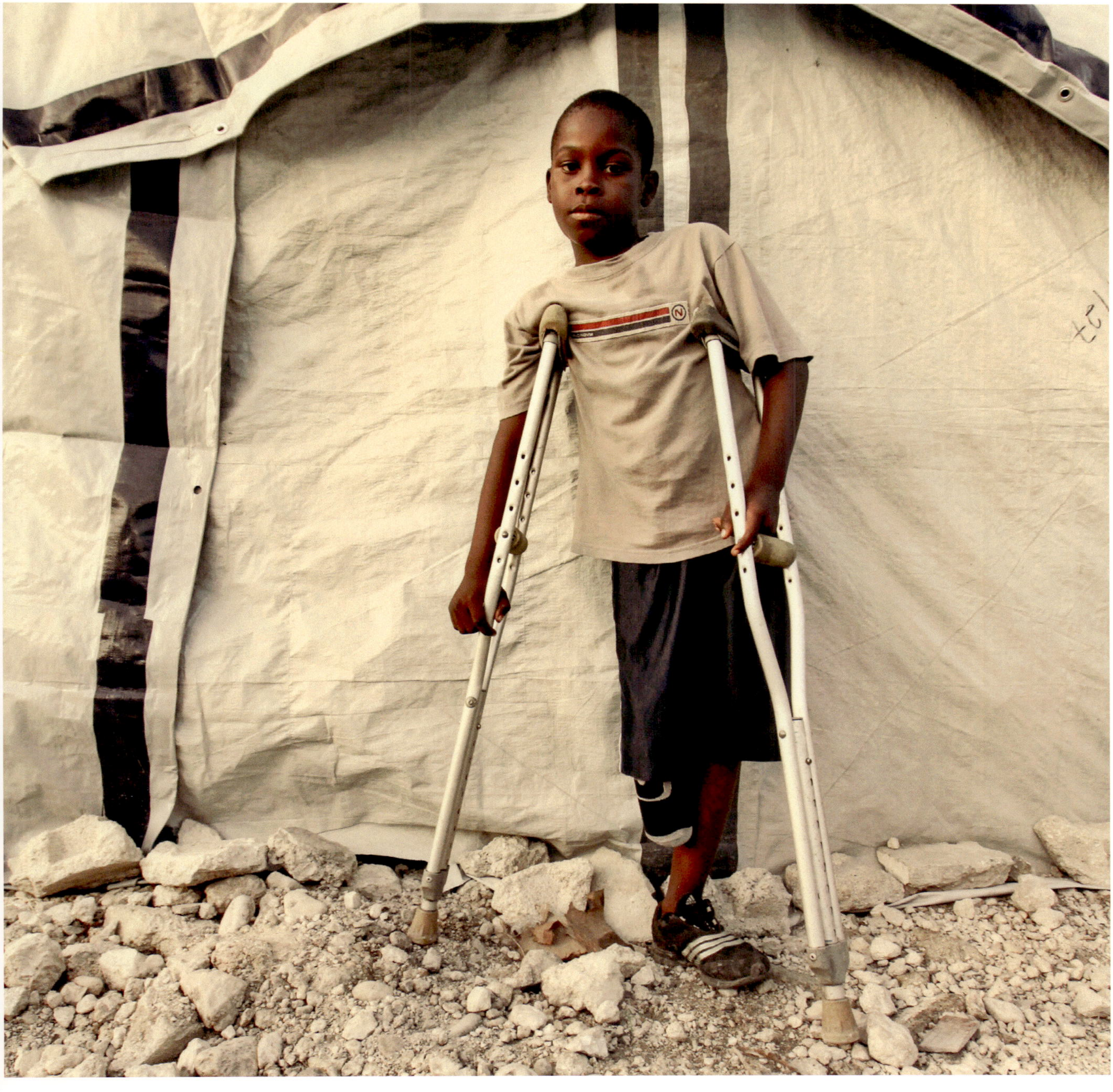

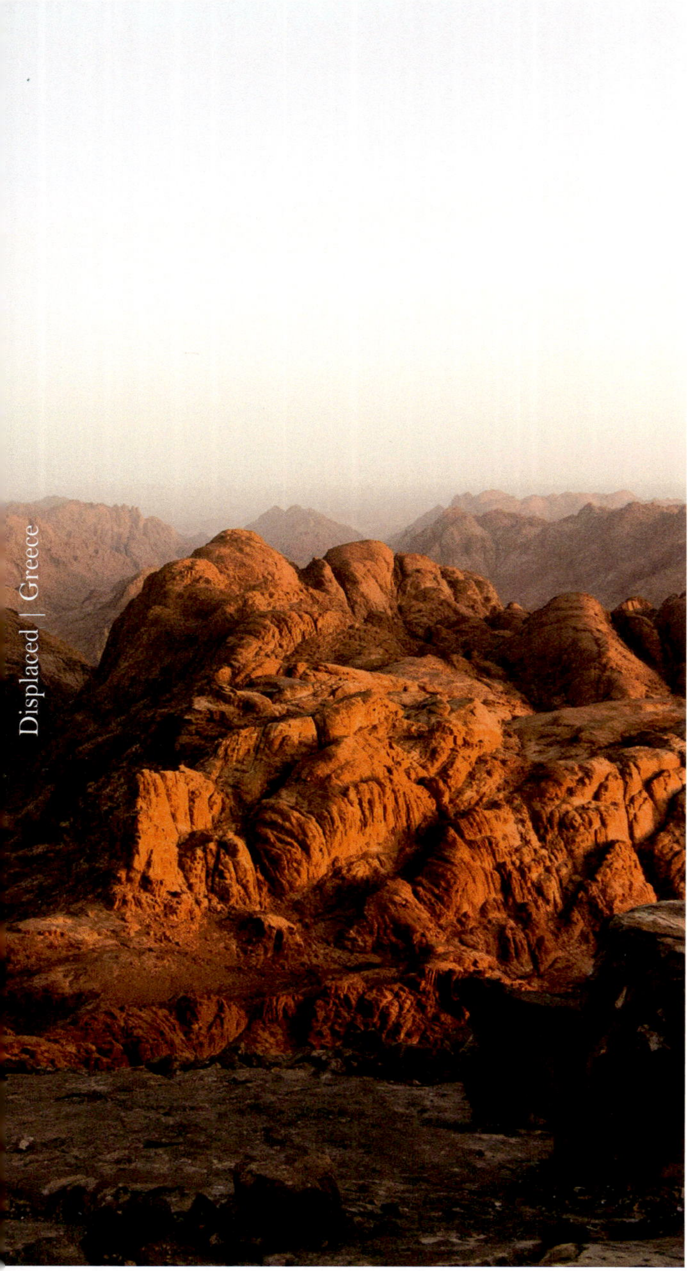

Asaf owned a farm in Kabul, Afghanistan before he became a refugee. One night as his family was sleeping, a man entered their home. He grabbed their oldest daughter, placed a knife at her throat and threatened to kill her if Asaf did not give him money. Asaf handed the small amount of money he possessed to the intruder who then disappeared, leaving his daughter with a small cut on her neck. That is when Asaf knew it was time to leave Kabul, a city where constant kidnappings, murders, and bribes threaten its citizens.

Asaf and his family left Kabul for Herat, the northwestern province of Afghanistan, and set up an auto parts shop there. They lived and prospered in Herat for four years until an arsonist came into the square and set the entire market on fire. Asaf watched in horror as the fire lit up the sky and completely destroyed his shop.

It was time to move again. Asaf decided to leave Afghanistan for Dubai, hoping to find work and a safe place for his family. A formidable city, huge and foreign to them, Dubai turned out to be an extremely difficult place for Asaf to support his wife and four children. After three years of struggle, they decided to move once again, but this time to a European country, with similar hopes of prosperity and safety.

Asaf and his family have been living in Greece for the past two years and every day he scours the streets looking for any type of employment. With no stable work, he earns an insufficient amount to adequately meet their needs. Like many refugees, Asaf strives for a better future for himself and his family. He seeks a home where they are safe, where his children can have an education, and where he is able to provide enough for them to survive.

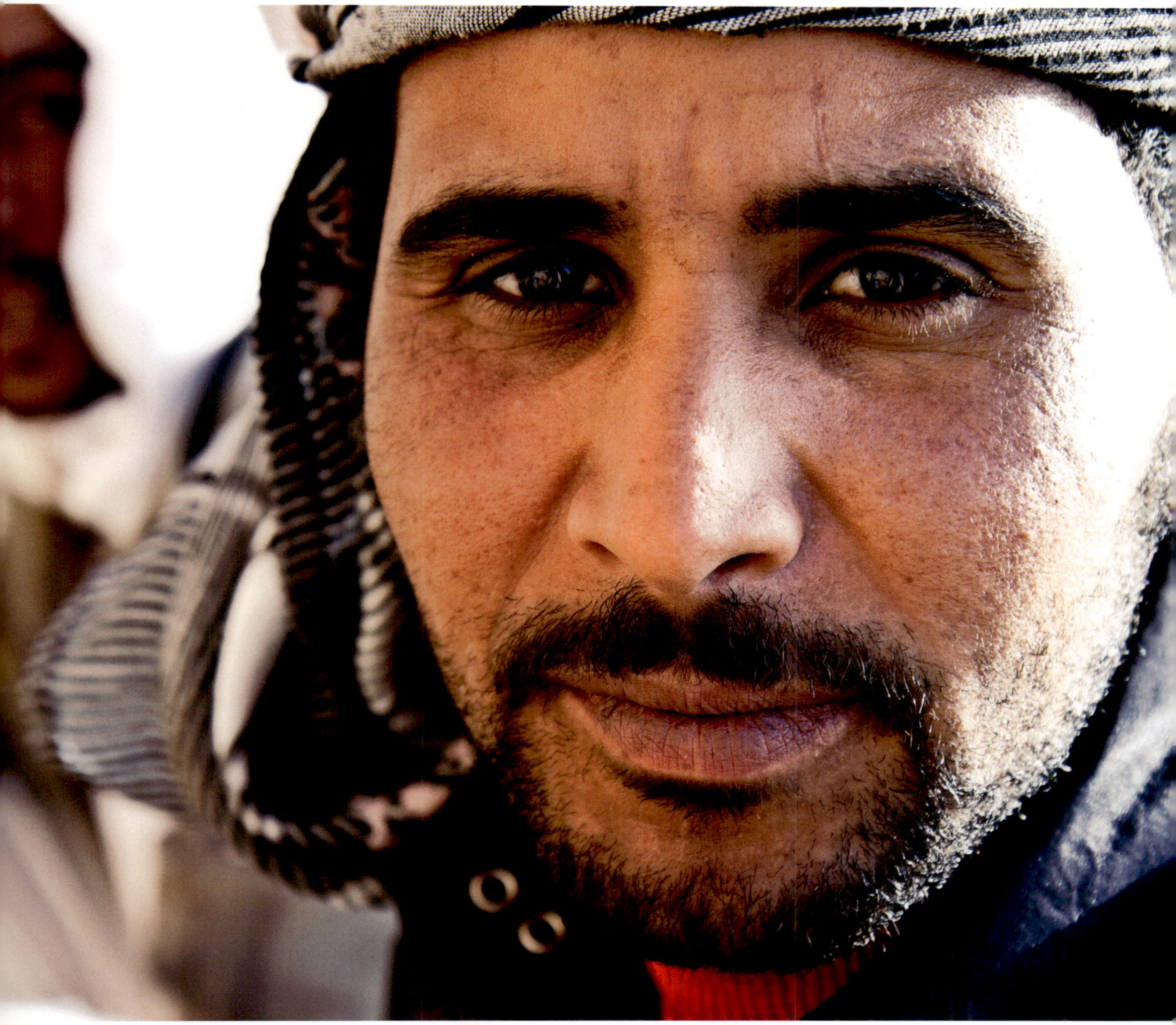

War-Torn

a place or country
severely damaged
by war

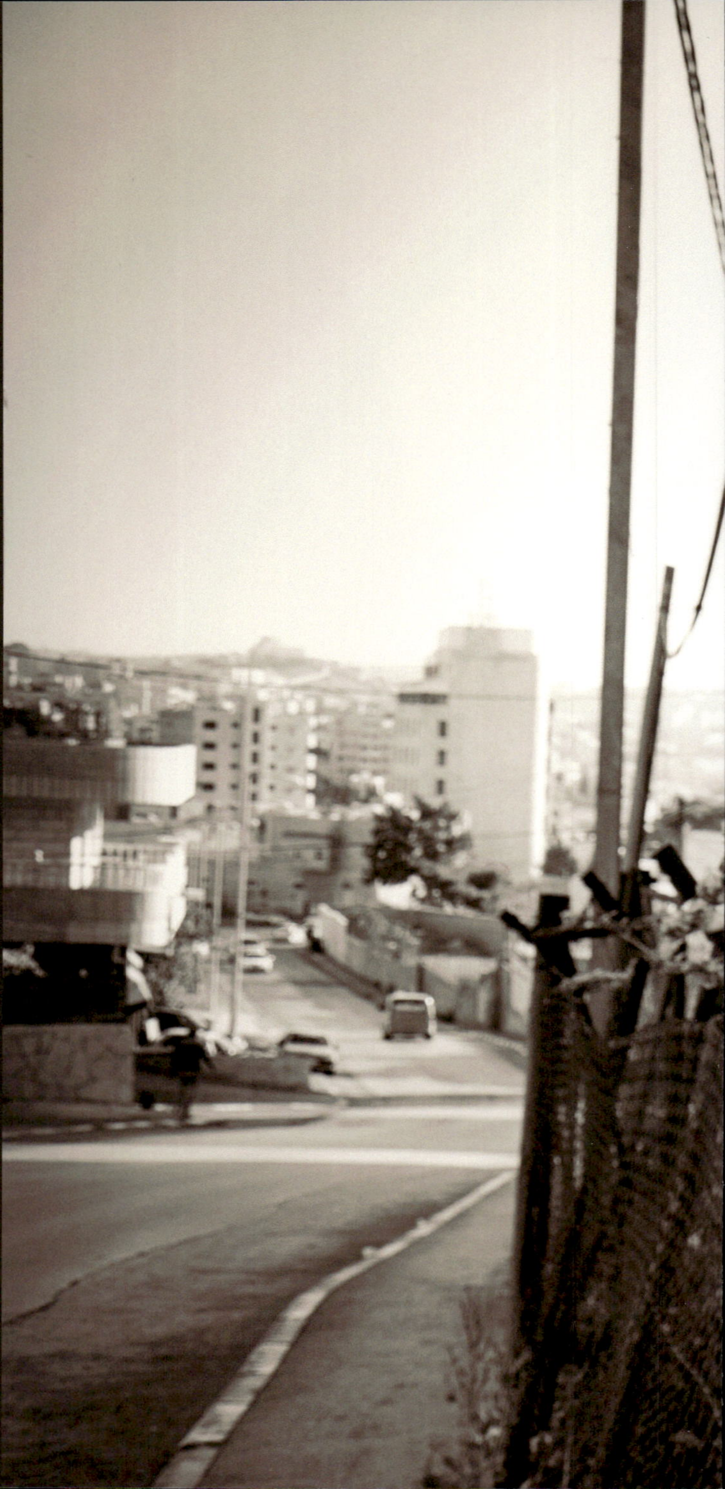

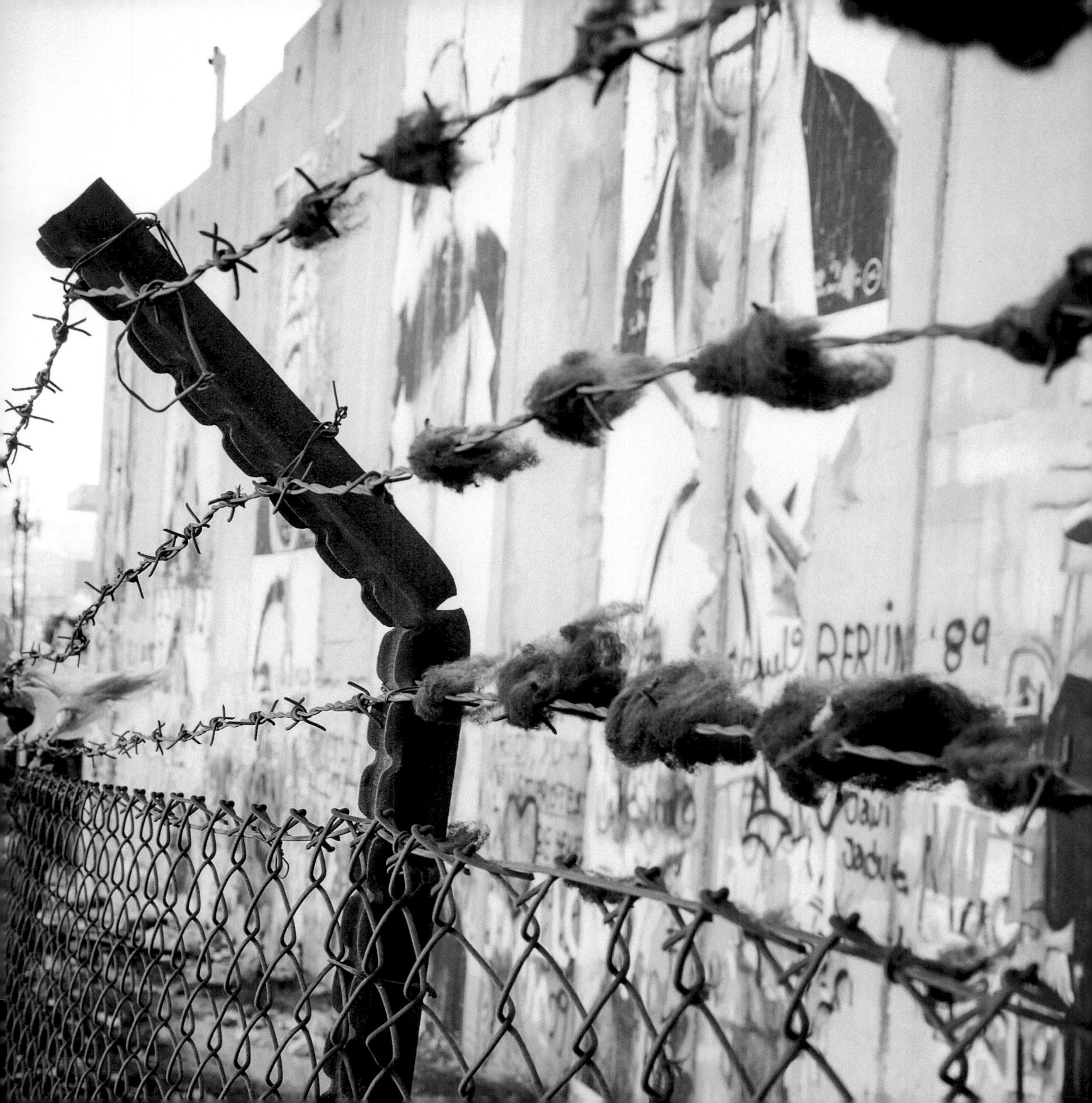
BERLIN '89

Most wars are civil or "intrastate" wars, fueled as much by racial, ethnic, or religious animosities as by ideological fervor. Most victims are civilians, a feature that distinguishes modern conflicts.[5]

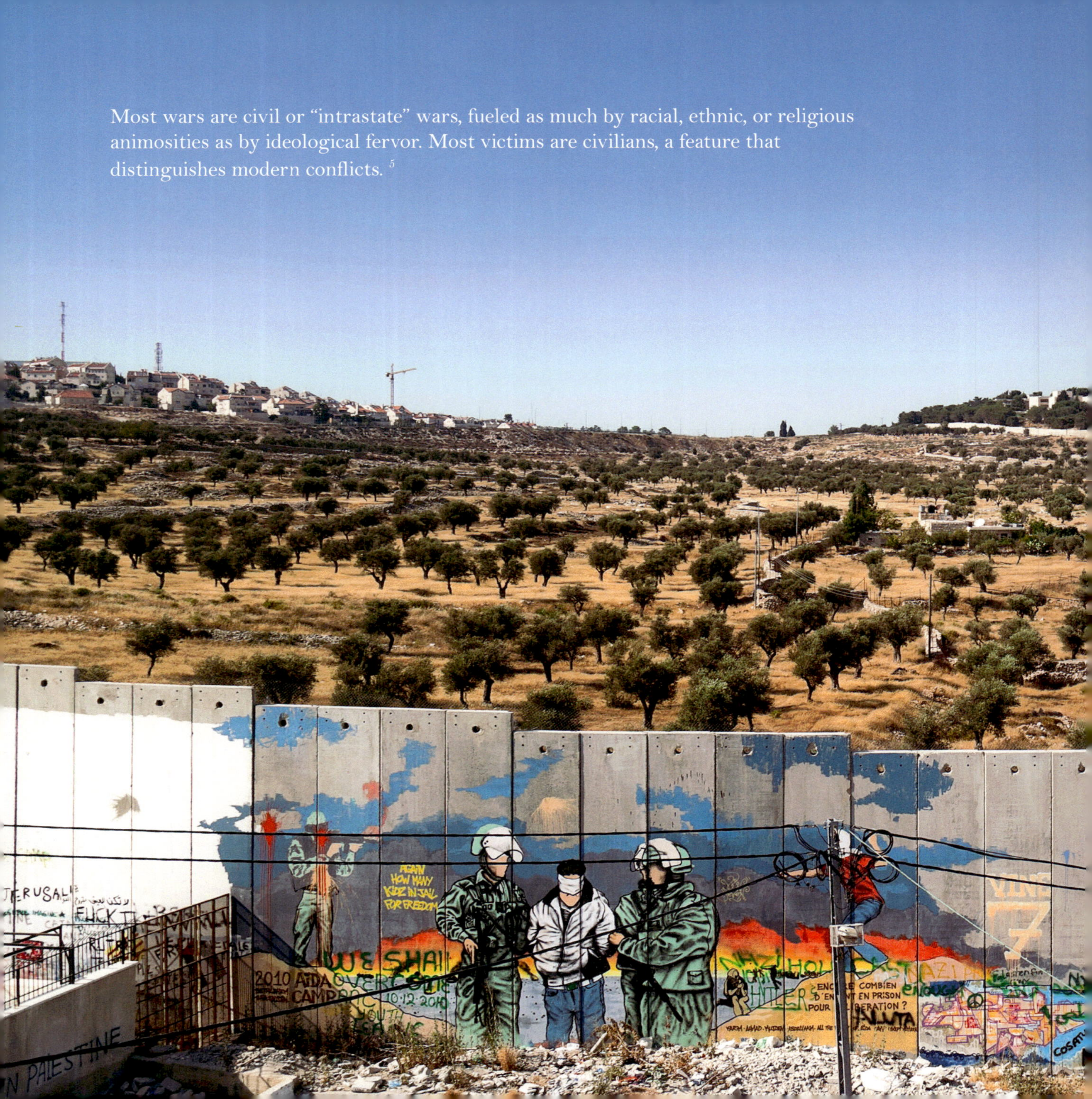

"Ours is a world of nuclear giants and ethical infants. We know more about war than we know about peace, more about killing than we know about living."
- Omar N. Bradley, Senior U.S. Army Commander, WWII

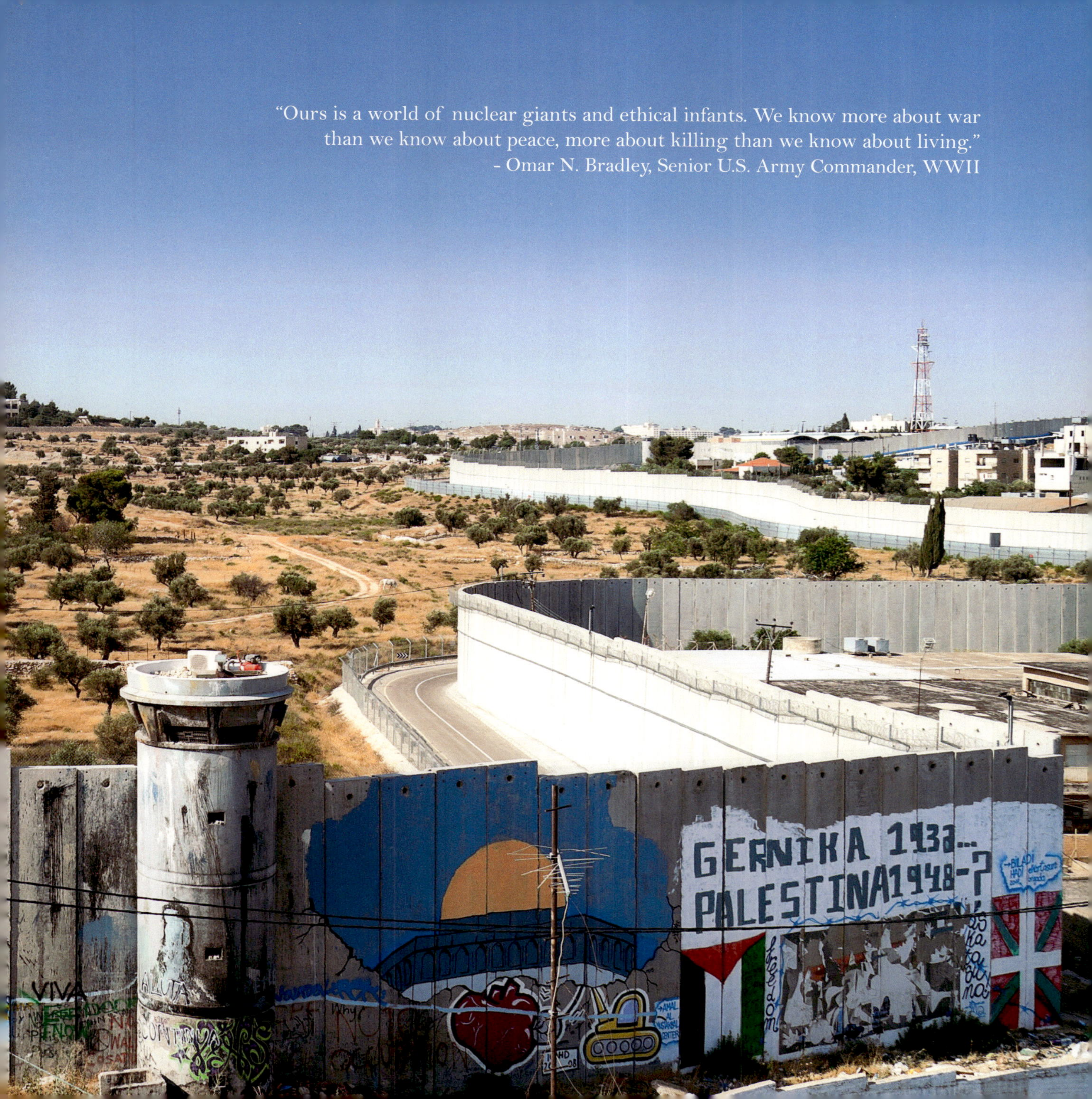

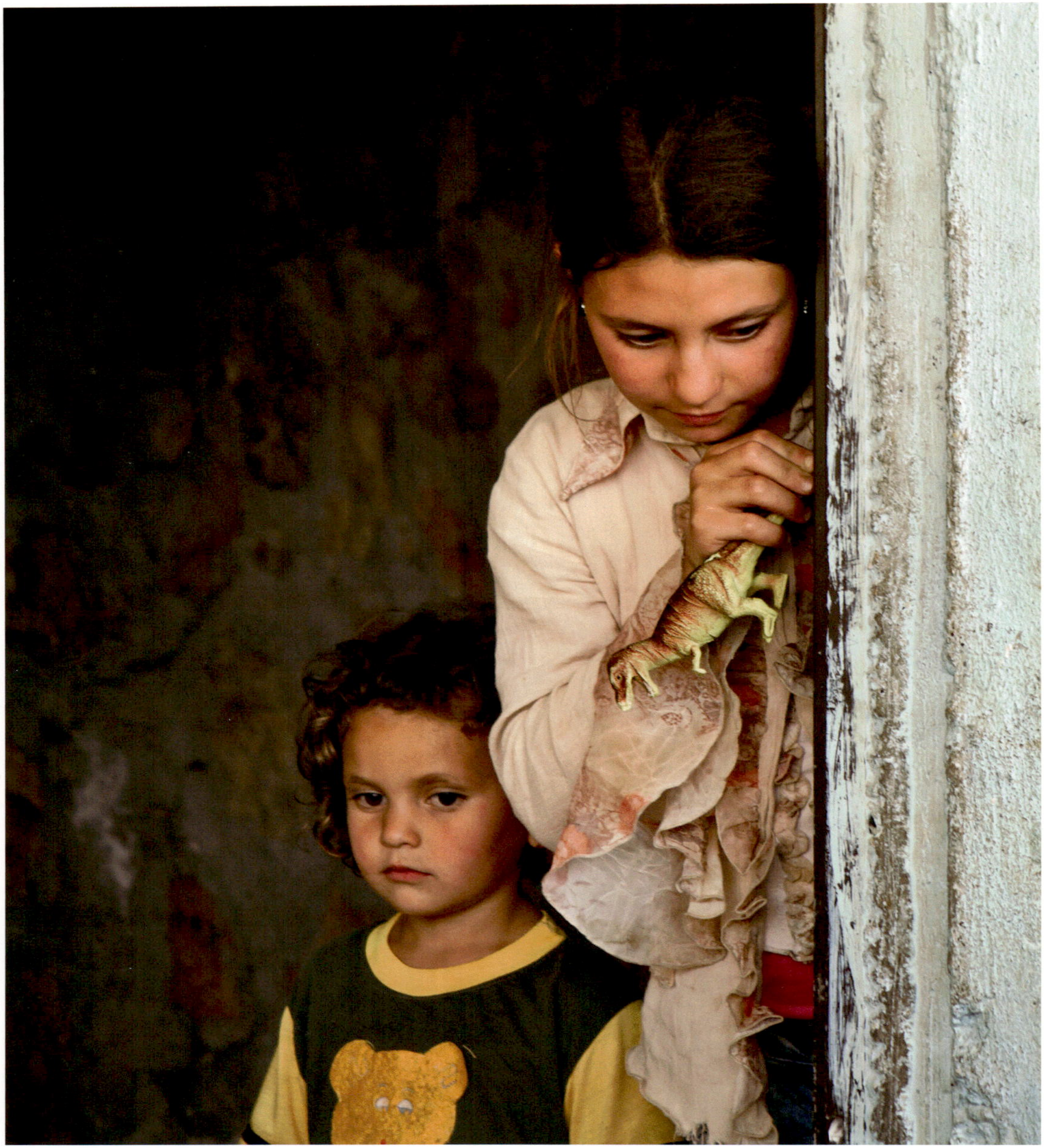

"I don't know what to say. Maybe we don't have the right to live here. Maybe we don't have the right to live at all. I really don't know." - Fatima

The land has been theirs for over a decade, home to this small Palestinian family living just outside Bethlehem. It had taken years to save enough money to build a house, months more for the completion of the construction. Then, in a period of fifteen minutes, everything was destroyed.

Fatima walks over the remains of what, until the night before, had been her home. "Around 6 o'clock, Israeli army jeeps began to show up; a hundred soldiers piled out, then the bulldozer arrived. I was told that I don't have a permit to build, and so the house must be destroyed. I told them I had to take my things, my furniture and clothes outside, but they would not let me. I watched, utterly helpless, as they leveled everything to the ground. We had been living in the house for over eight months and there had been no warning. I asked, 'This is my land, why should I have to have a permit to build on it?' I was not given an answer."

Standing in the rubble, Fatima quietly wipes her eyes and invites us for tea at a neighboring house. Her strength is astounding as she gazes up at the maze of barbed wire that creates a fence just off the edge of her property. Behind it loom white high-rise houses, a clear sign of an Israeli settlement. Living in its shadow, this is not the first time this family had faced opposition.

"This is our reality. They can come and destroy our house, the concrete, the walls, but they cannot destroy our home. We still have our family."

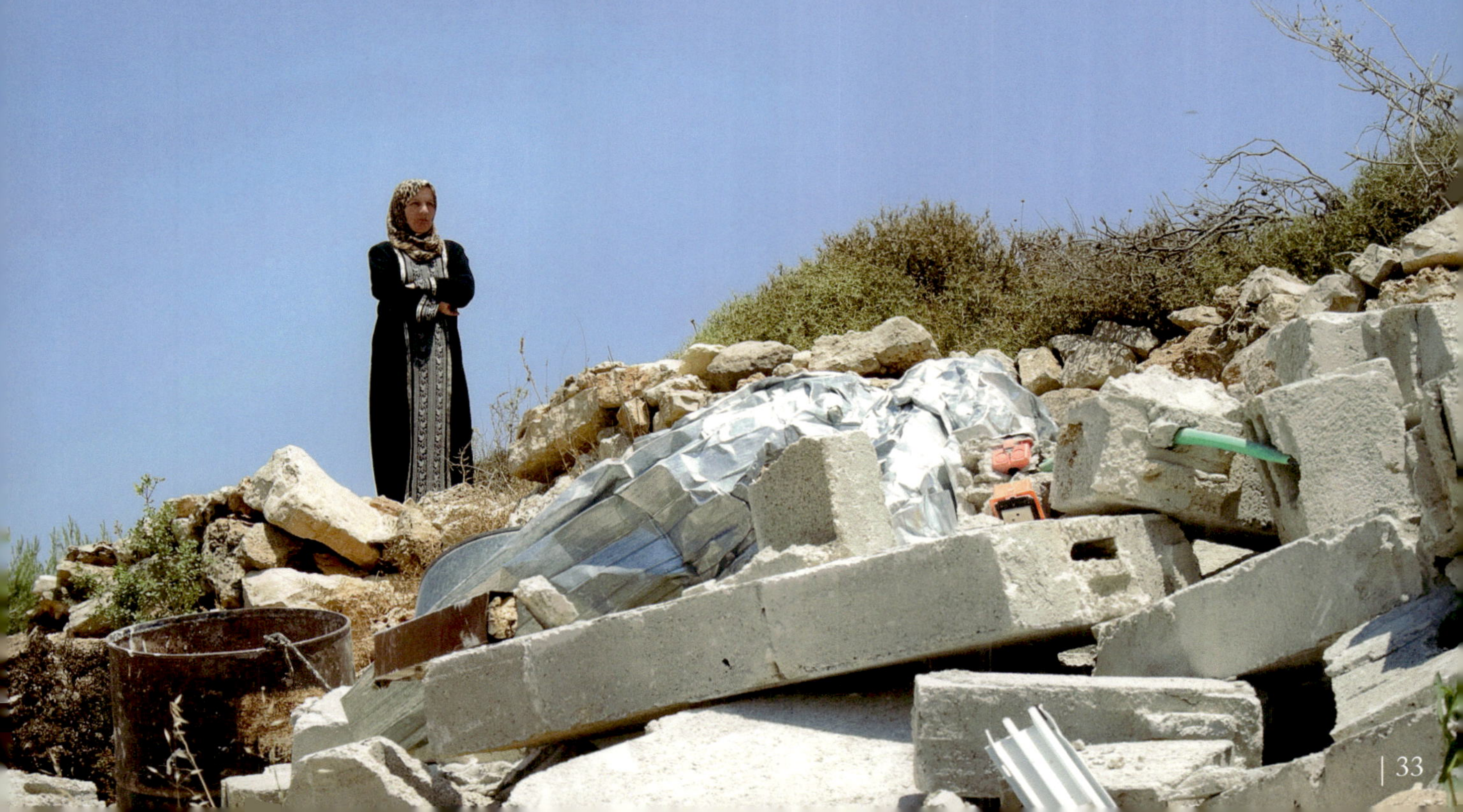

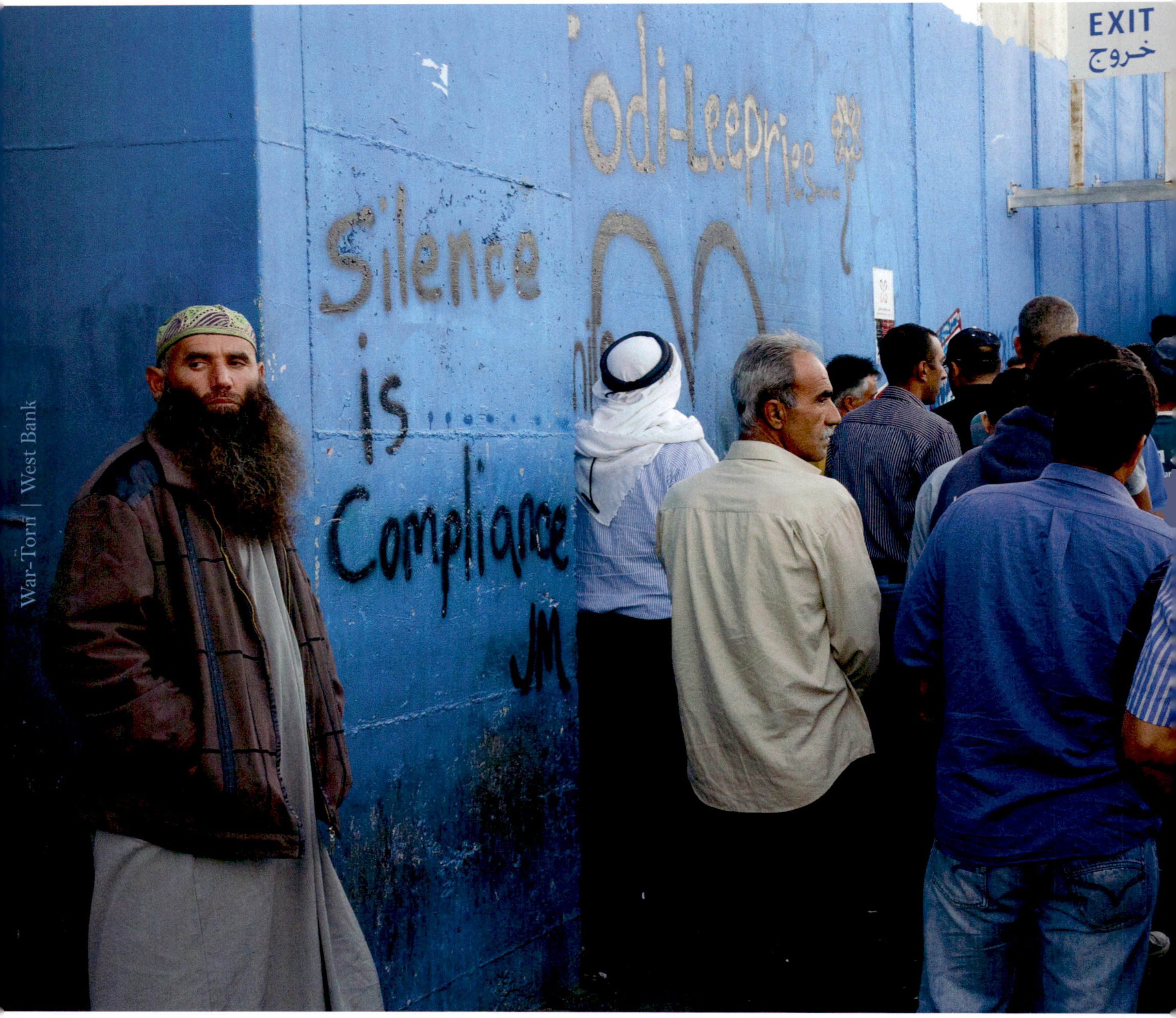

War-Torn | West Bank

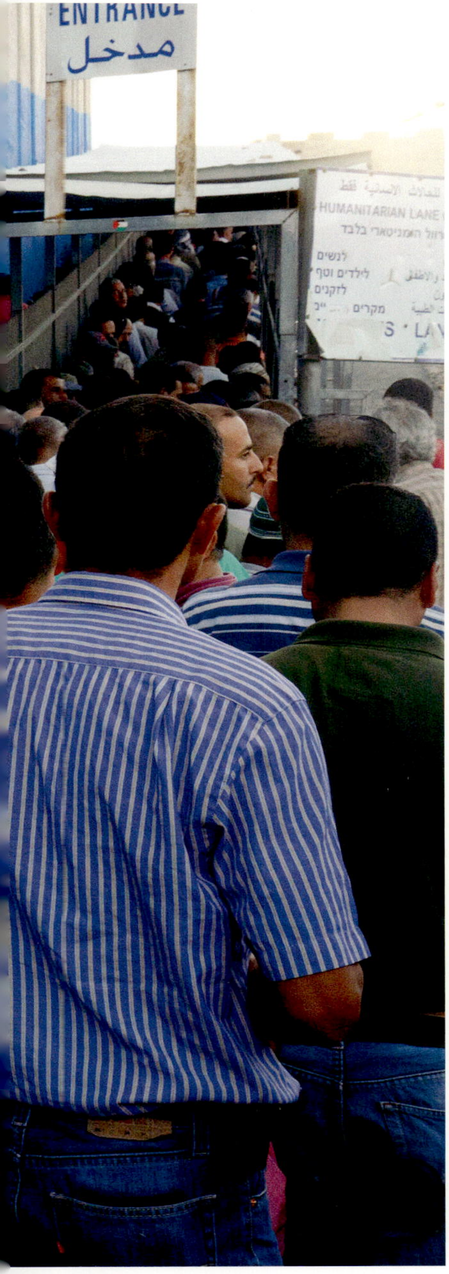
ENTRANCE
مدخل
HUMANITARIAN LANE
לנשים
לילדים וטף
לזקנים
מקרים

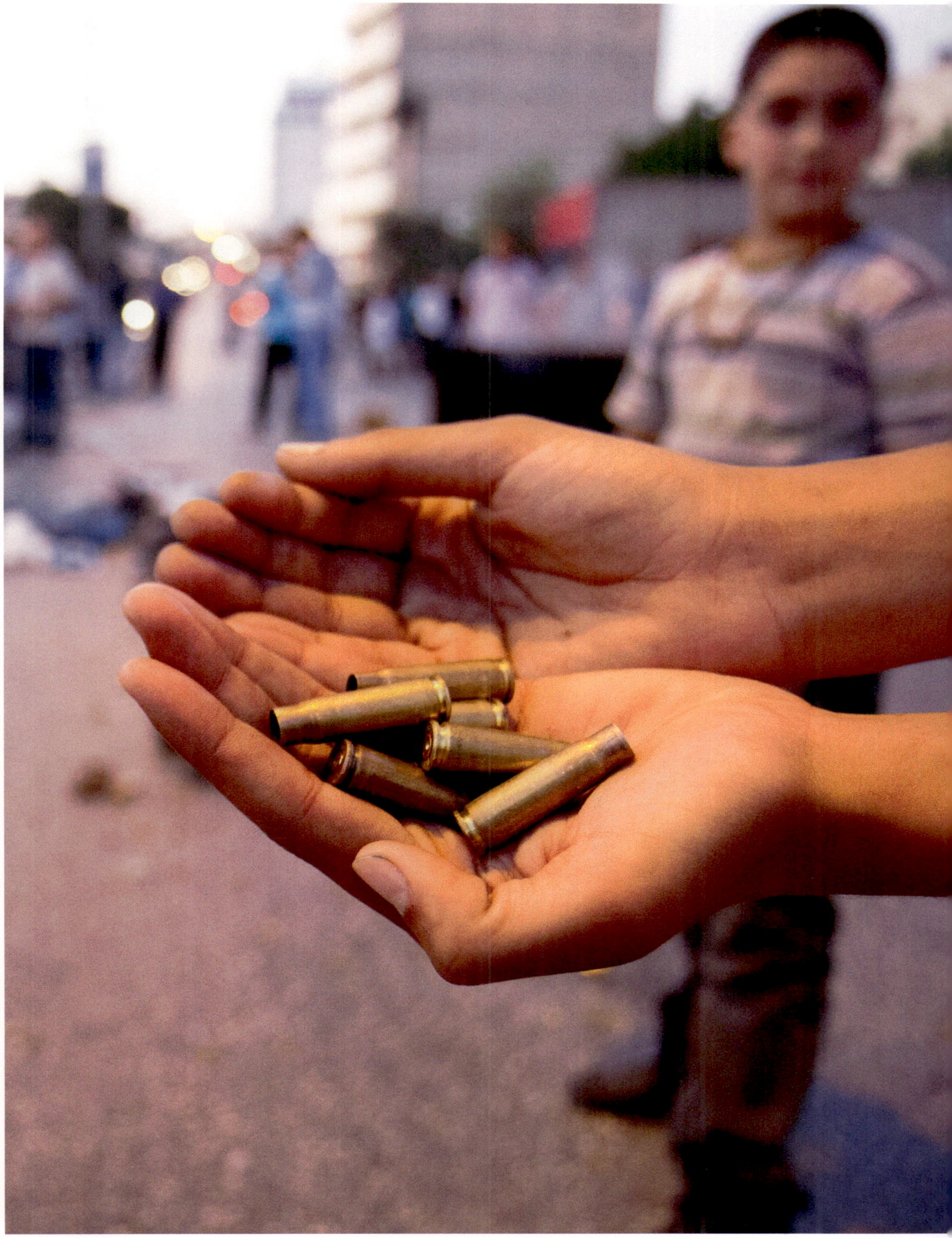

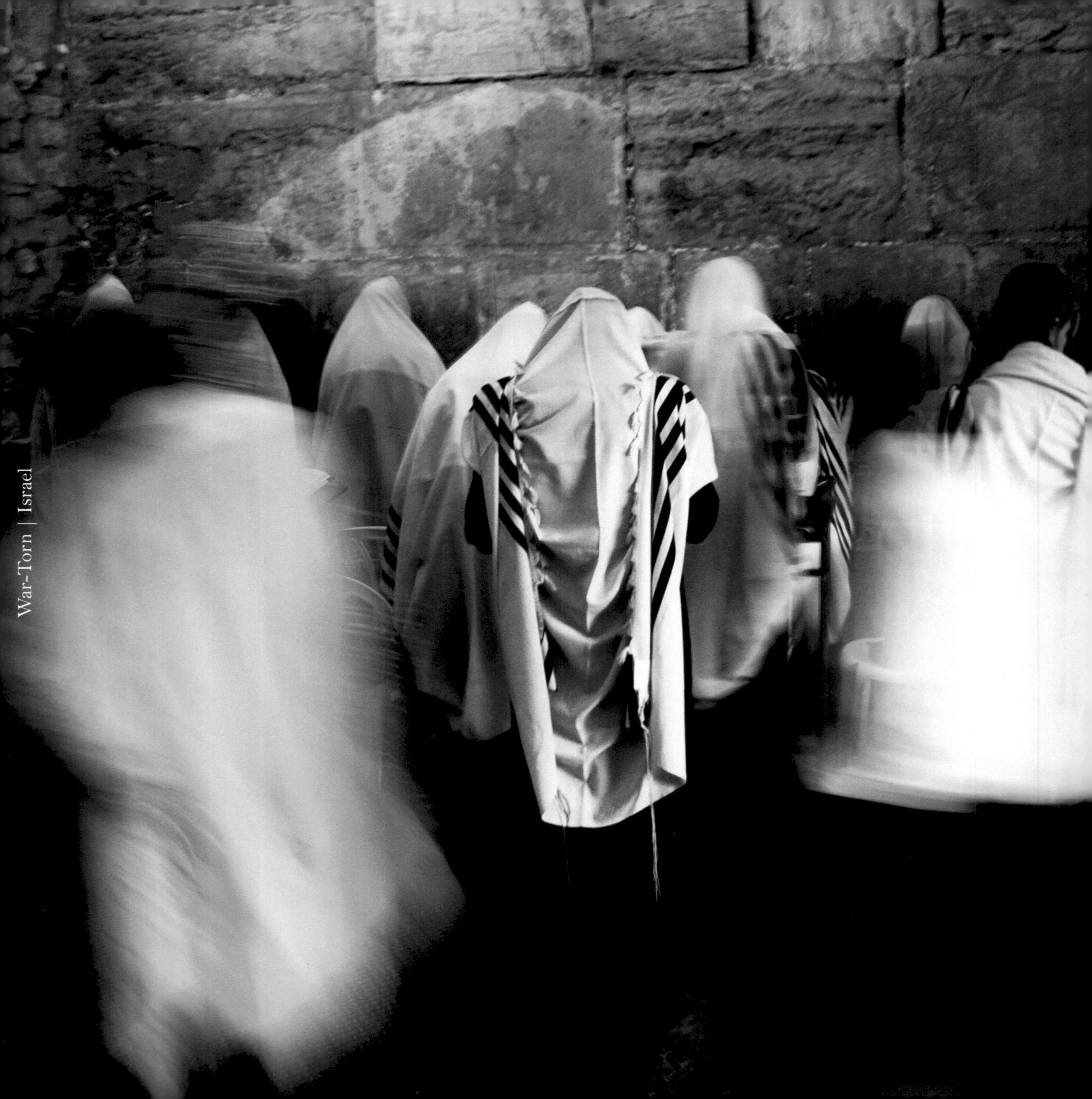

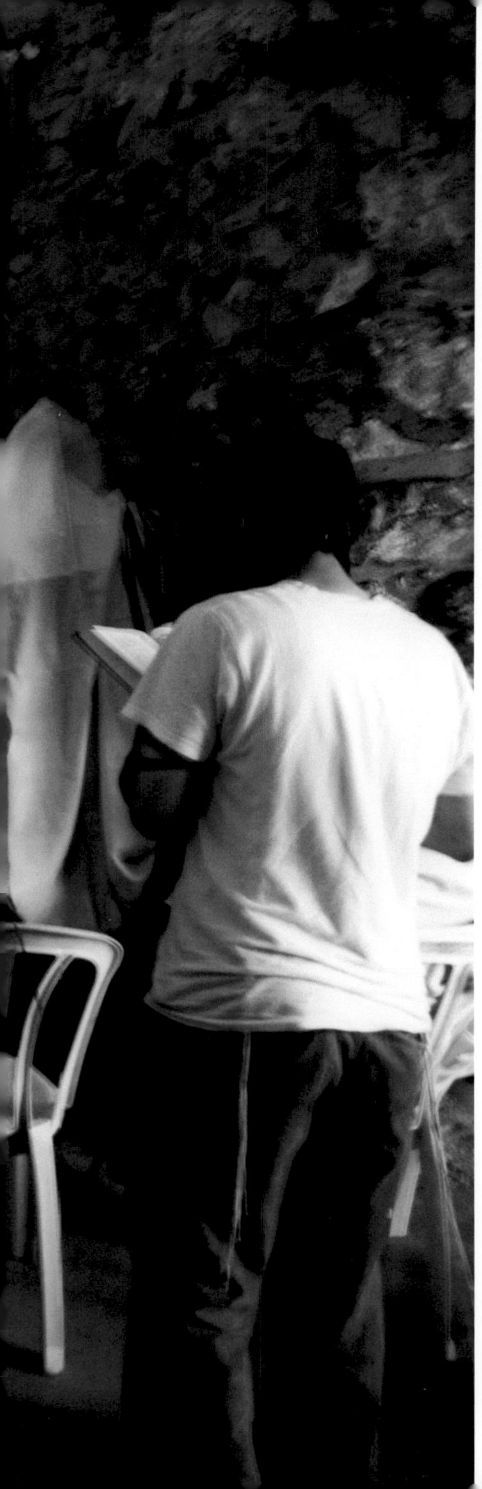

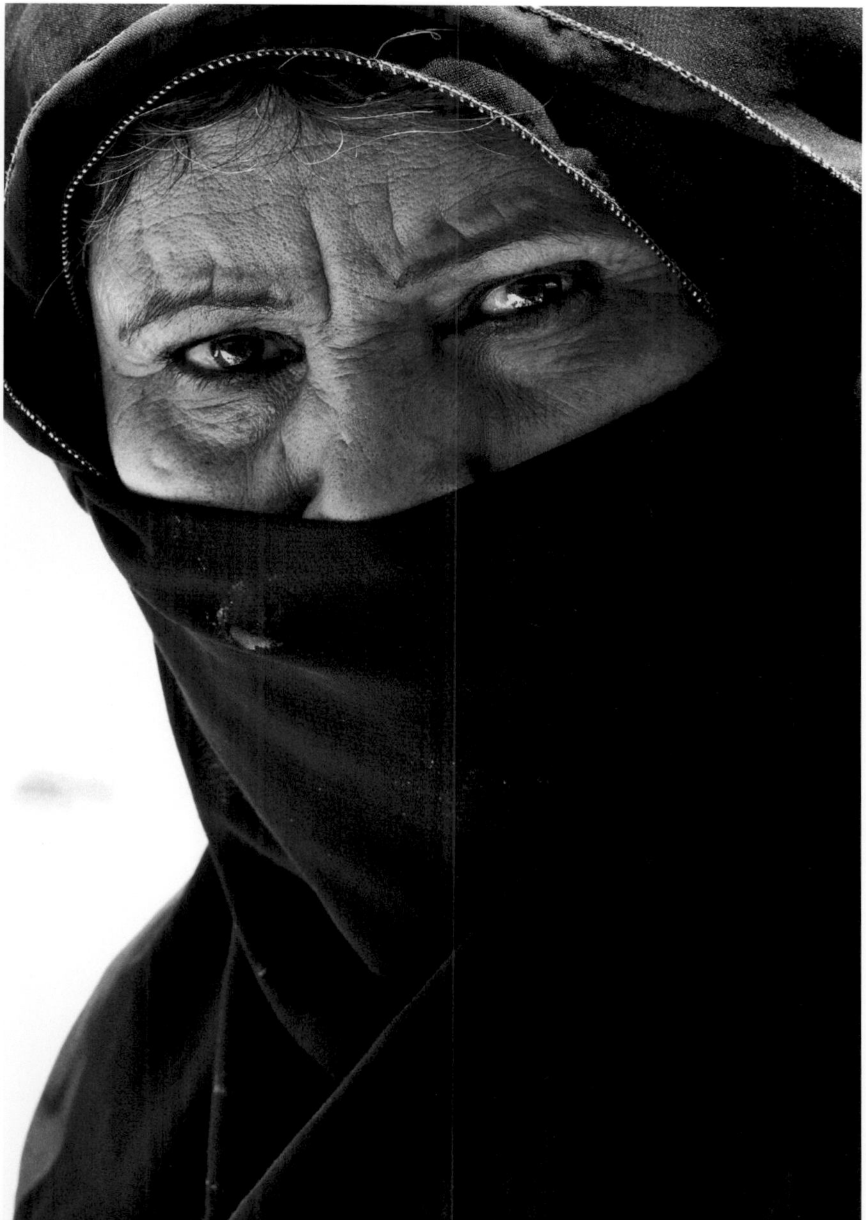

"You know, when you see your son lying there with no way to help him you can justify things like hate, bitterness, and judgment. I could blame the Arabs, but does either side really know what they are doing?"

Early in the spring of 1998, a nineteen-year-old Israeli soldier was driving back to his military outpost. He came upon a group of rioting students from a Hamas university who stood waiting, cameras ready, for the sole purpose of killing an Israeli soldier. They stopped his car, pulled him out, and beat him within an inch of his life. They kicked, they punched, they pulled at his eyes and hair, they spat on his bleeding face, and then left him for dead. Fourteen years later he remains in a state of deep depression and paranoia - a result of the hatred that continues to split Israel and Palestine.

His mother sits, deep lines carved into her weary face. She glances out the window, gazing at the ancient city that is Jerusalem, her home. When asked, "As a mother how do you forgive these men that sought to kill your own son?" Leah states, "When you forgive someone, you don't require justice, you don't require payback, you don't demand anything. You release them, and so you release yourself. Then, and only then, can you move on."

Leah was given the chance to testify against one of the men involved in her son's beating. As she stood in court looking this man in the eyes, wanting to feel hatred, wanting to see him thrown in prison, she experienced the power of complete forgiveness. She looked at her son, a silent shell slumped over in his chair, then to the man responsible. Suddenly the scene changed in her mind and only two very young, very confused men remained. Hard pasts, hard futures, and both prisoners - prisoners to the history, beliefs, and politics of their nations.

"We've got victim, hate, victim, hate. There has to be a coming together. There has to be a defusing of what people perceive to be the enemy. Both sides just want a place to call home, a place of safety and retreat; a place that is their own."

- Leah

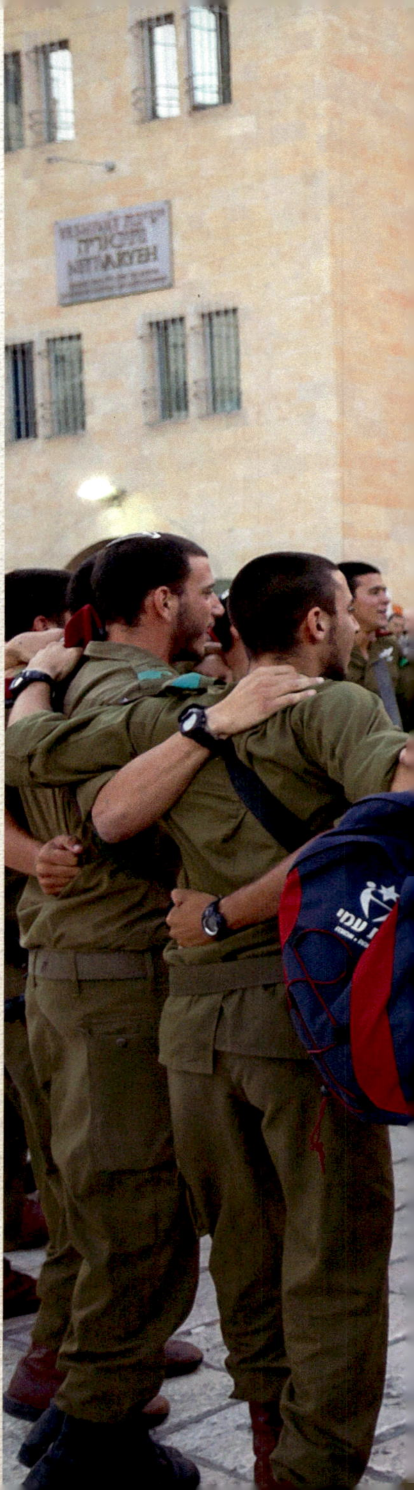

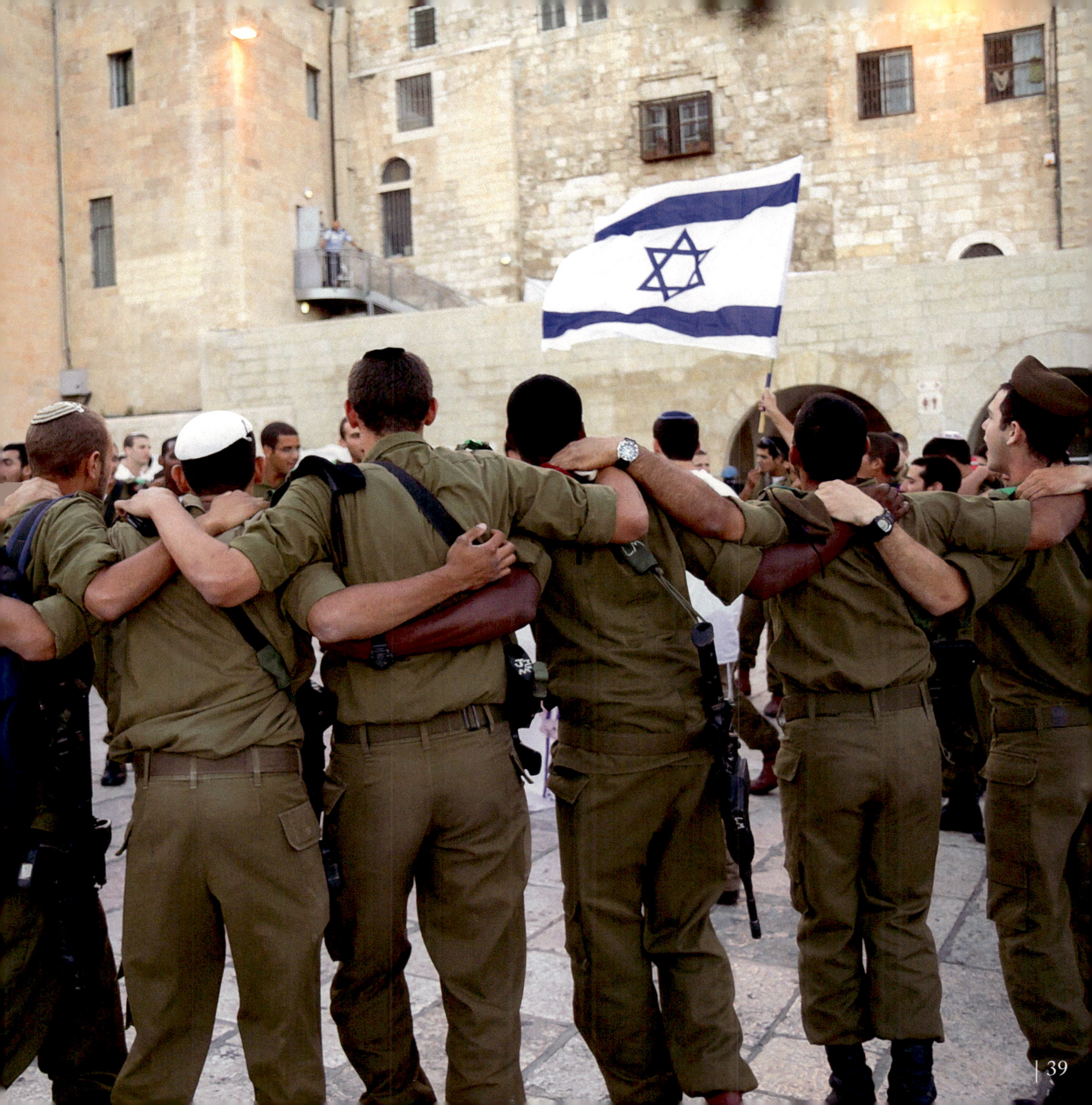

I·so·lat·ed

separated from others;
solitary or singular

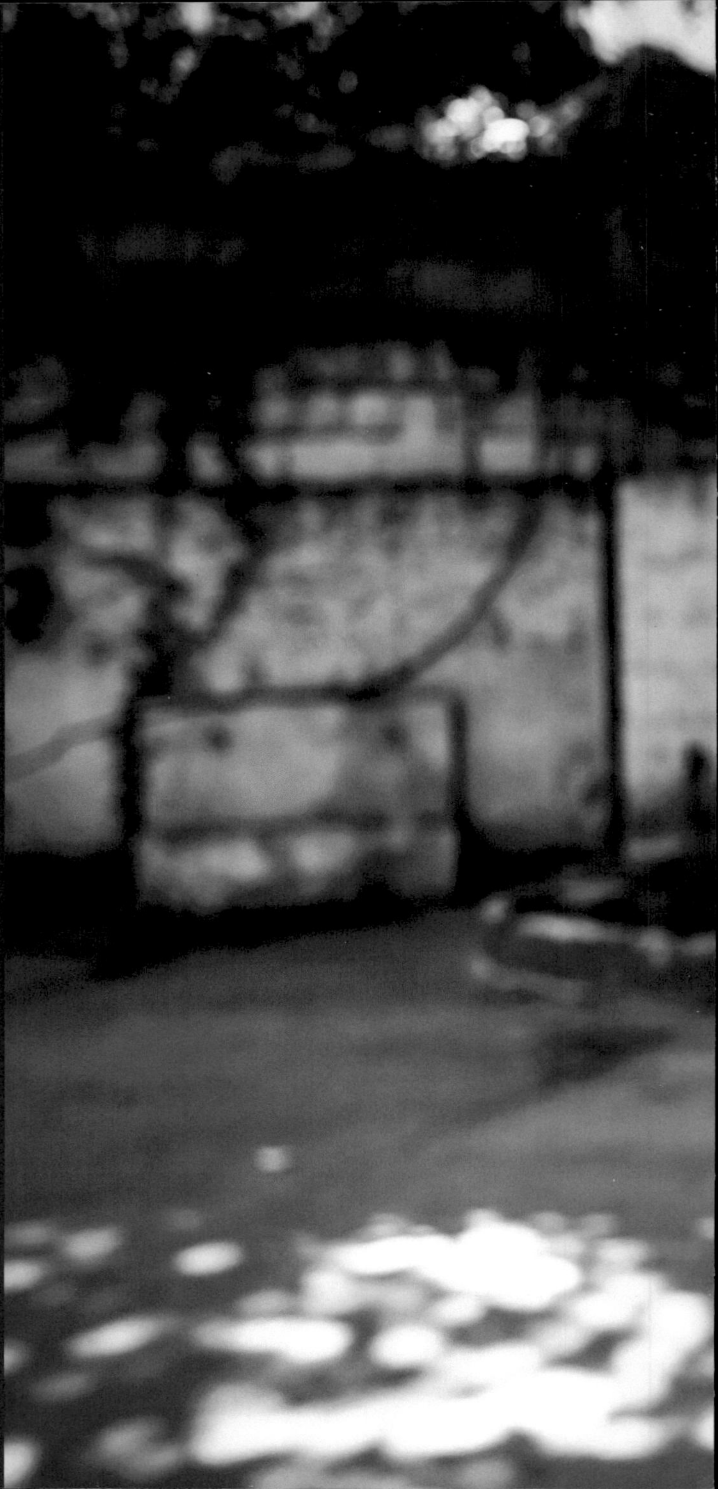

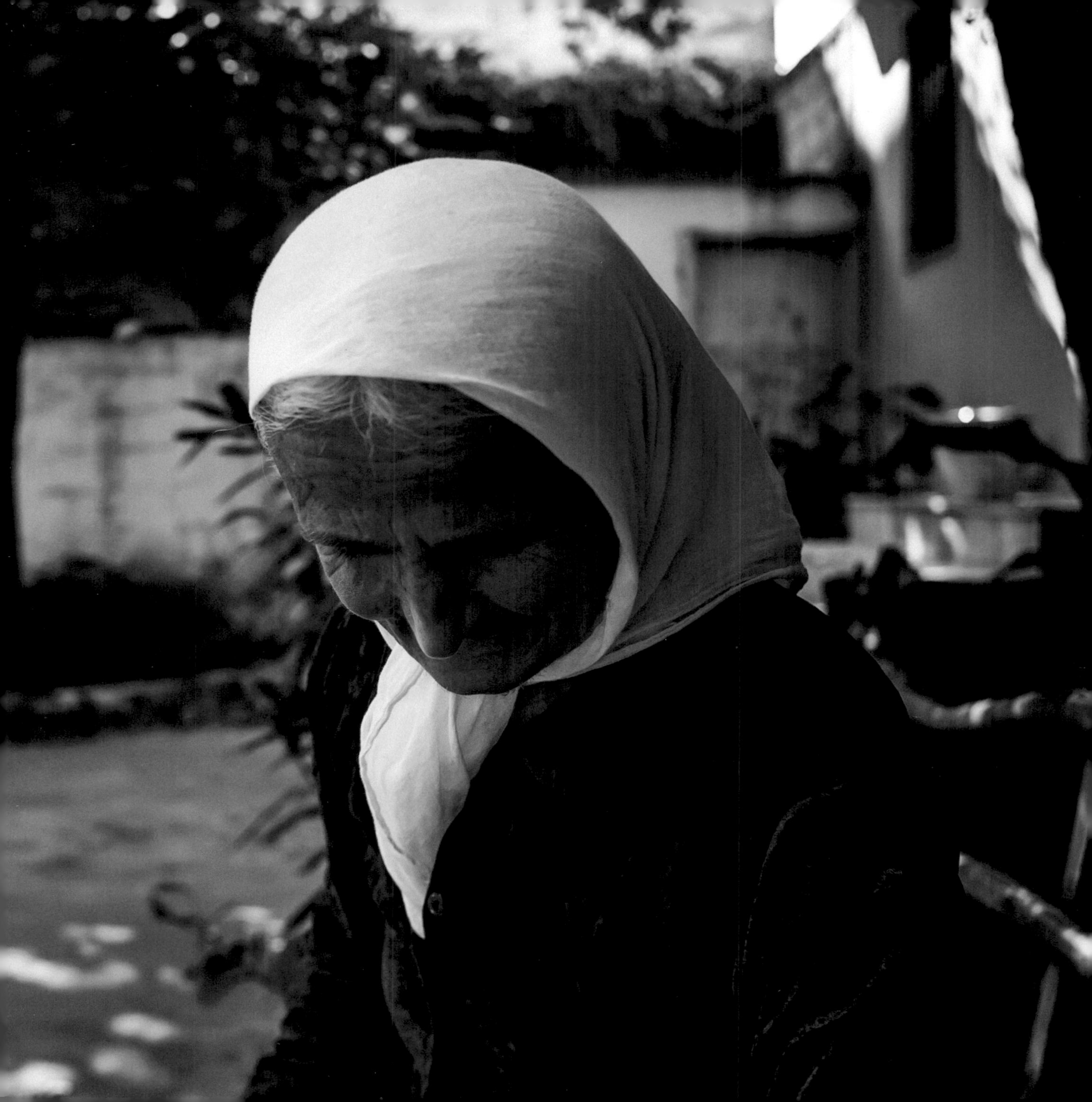

In the barren expanse of land far outside of town, rows of stark, uniform buildings run parallel to one another. Each room we pass houses another patient with a similar story of loss, despair, and abandonment. Peering out from the doorways of their small cement rooms, the residents wait in hopeful anticipation that today might be the day someone comes to visit them. But the stigma towards leprosy runs deep in India and those that contract the disease are hastily deserted in colonies of isolation, never to see their parents, spouses, or children again.

Imani sits on the floor in the doorway like the others, with only a sheet around his waist, his body a frame of bones delicately draped with a thin layer of skin. No longer able to digest food and immobilized by his disease, he tells us of how he contracted leprosy by an unknown means in his early forties. Once a goldsmith, the crippling effects of his disease began to interfere with his work. When his family learned of his diagnosis, they brought him to the colony and never returned to visit him. It has been thirty-five years. With no income or support and little access to medical care, Imani and many others like him are left in a waiting game to die.

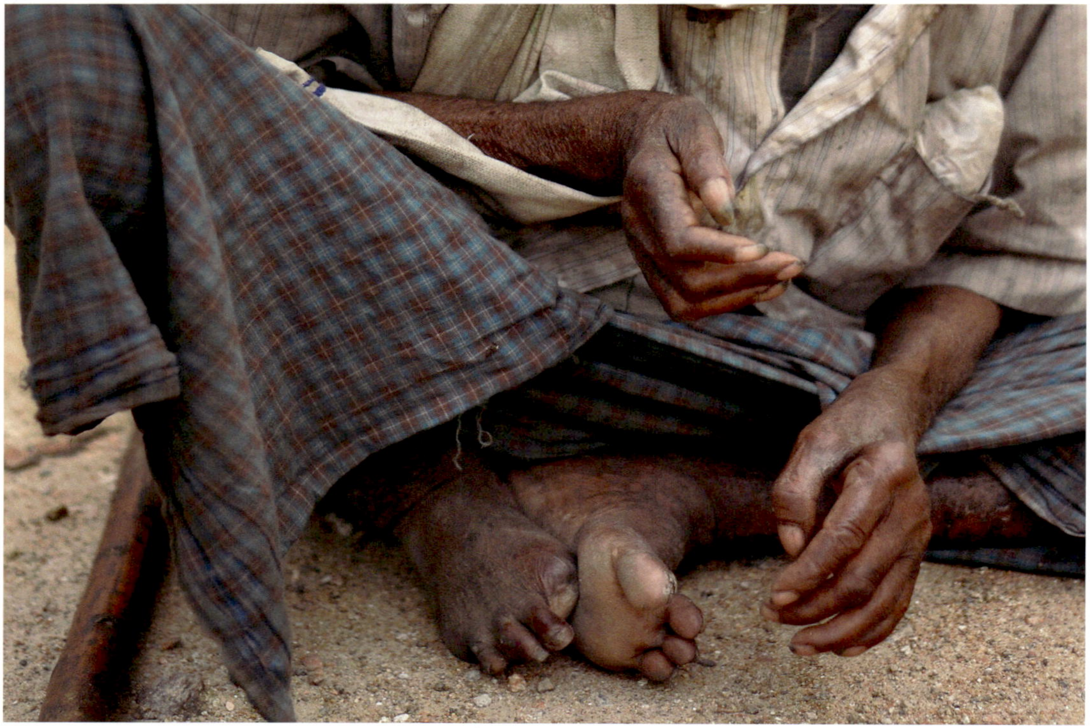

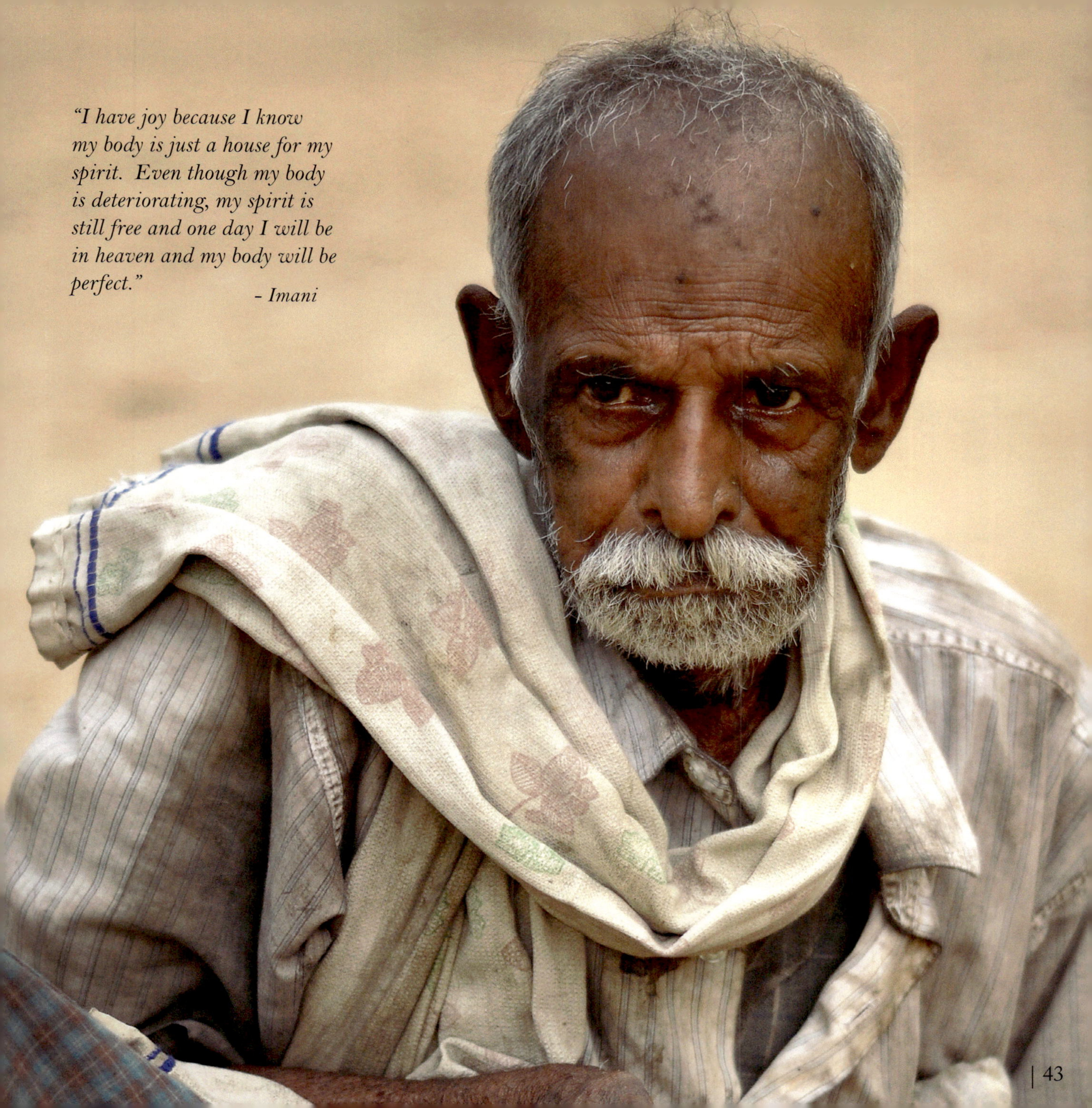

"I have joy because I know my body is just a house for my spirit. Even though my body is deteriorating, my spirit is still free and one day I will be in heaven and my body will be perfect."

- Imani

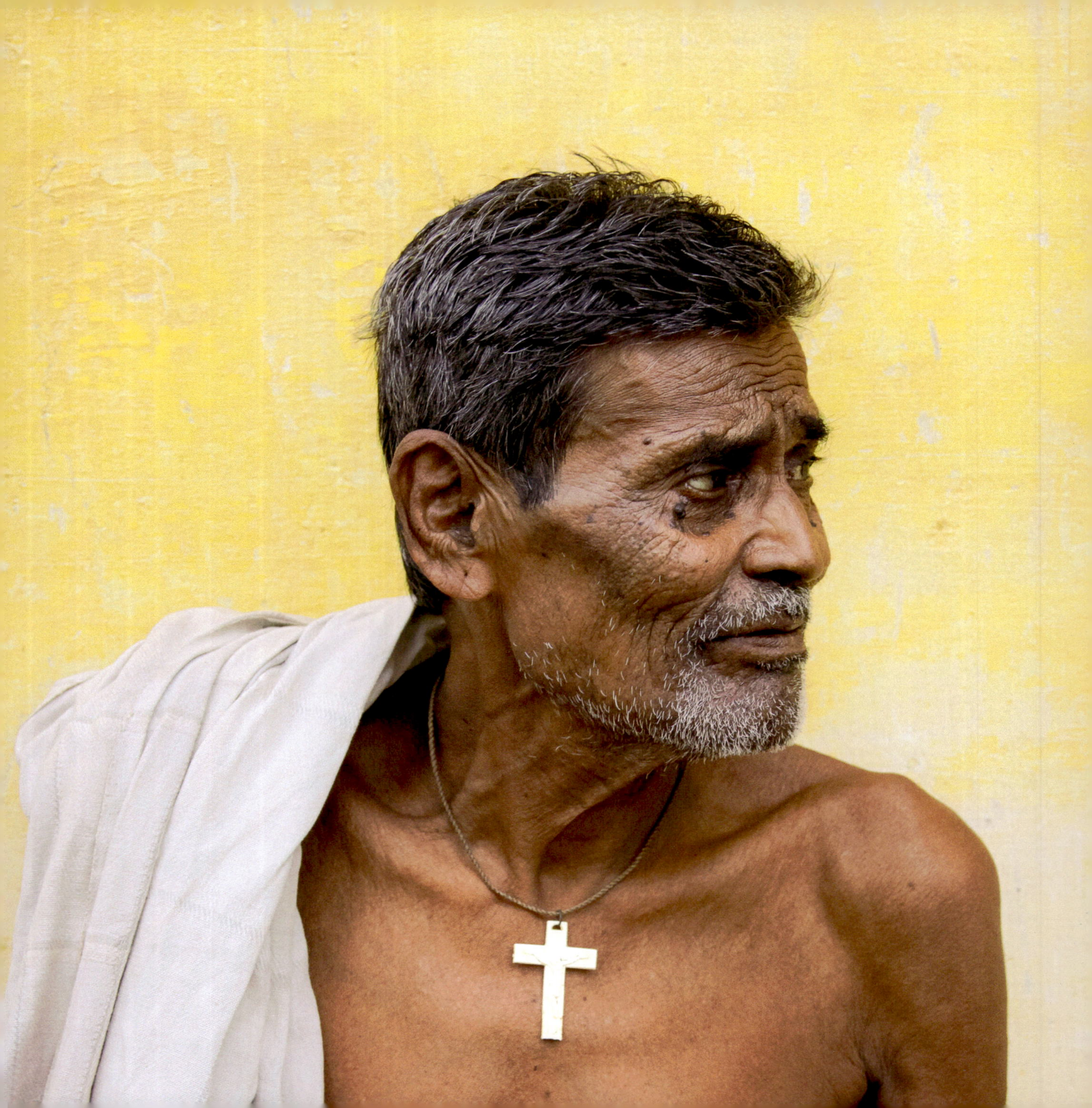

"I have come to realize more and more that the greatest disease and the greatest suffering is to be unwanted, unloved, uncared for, to be shunned by everybody, to be just nobody."

- Mother Teresa

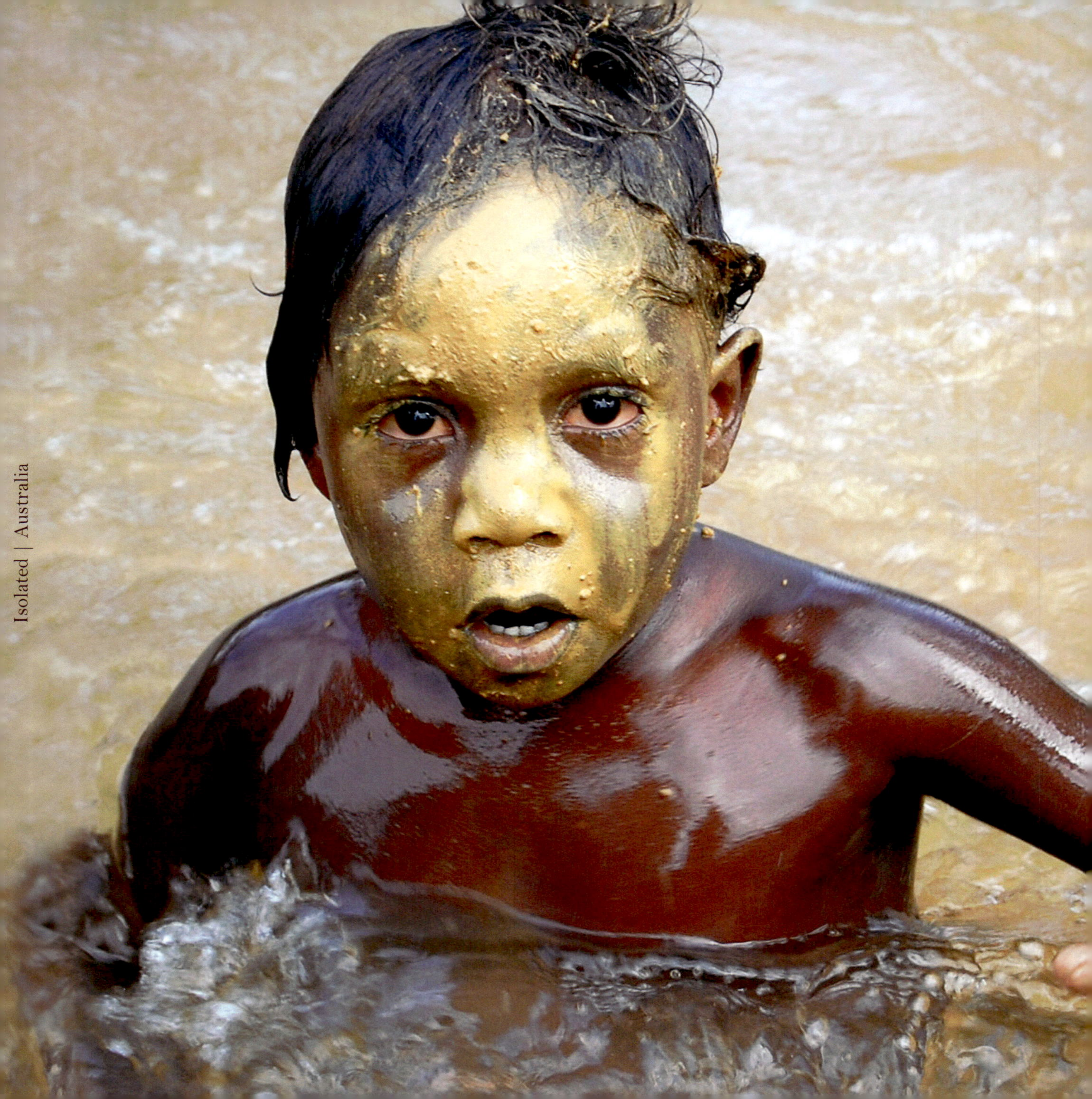

Isolated | Australia

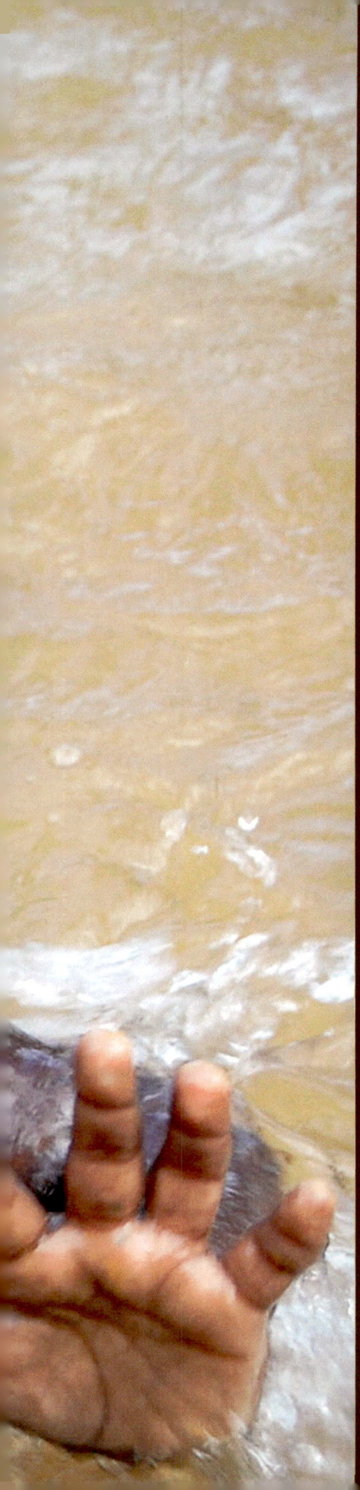

The road turns to dirt, a bellowing cloud of bright orange dust behind us. Deep in the Northern Territory of Australia, there is nothing to be seen but the barren land. Known for its vast vacancy and scarce population, the outback is defined by isolation.

Miles from any sign of civilization, the tiny town stands alone on the horizon. An Aboriginal community of about 160 inhabitants, Belyuan is made up of rundown houses and makeshift shacks. As we draw closer, a group of children run toward our jeep, jumping on the back with squeals of joy. As we step to the ground a small girl immediately raises her arms, begging to be held. She is covered in dirt, hair matted to her head in clumps. There are no other signs of life in the village, only a strange sense of solitude haunting the empty streets.

Alone on the outskirts of society, many Aboriginal communities like Belyuan are caught up in a cycle that reoccurs with each generation. Their poverty results in a lack of education, lending itself to a high rate of unemployment. Alone and desolate, the adult population often turns to alcohol to cope. Children are left neglected and the isolation of the community breeds isolation within the family. As this young girl clings to us, desperate for outside contact, her vacant eyes tell the story of a people secluded and segregated.

Young [Australian] Aborigines are **four times more likely to commit suicide** than their non-indigenous counterparts. [6]

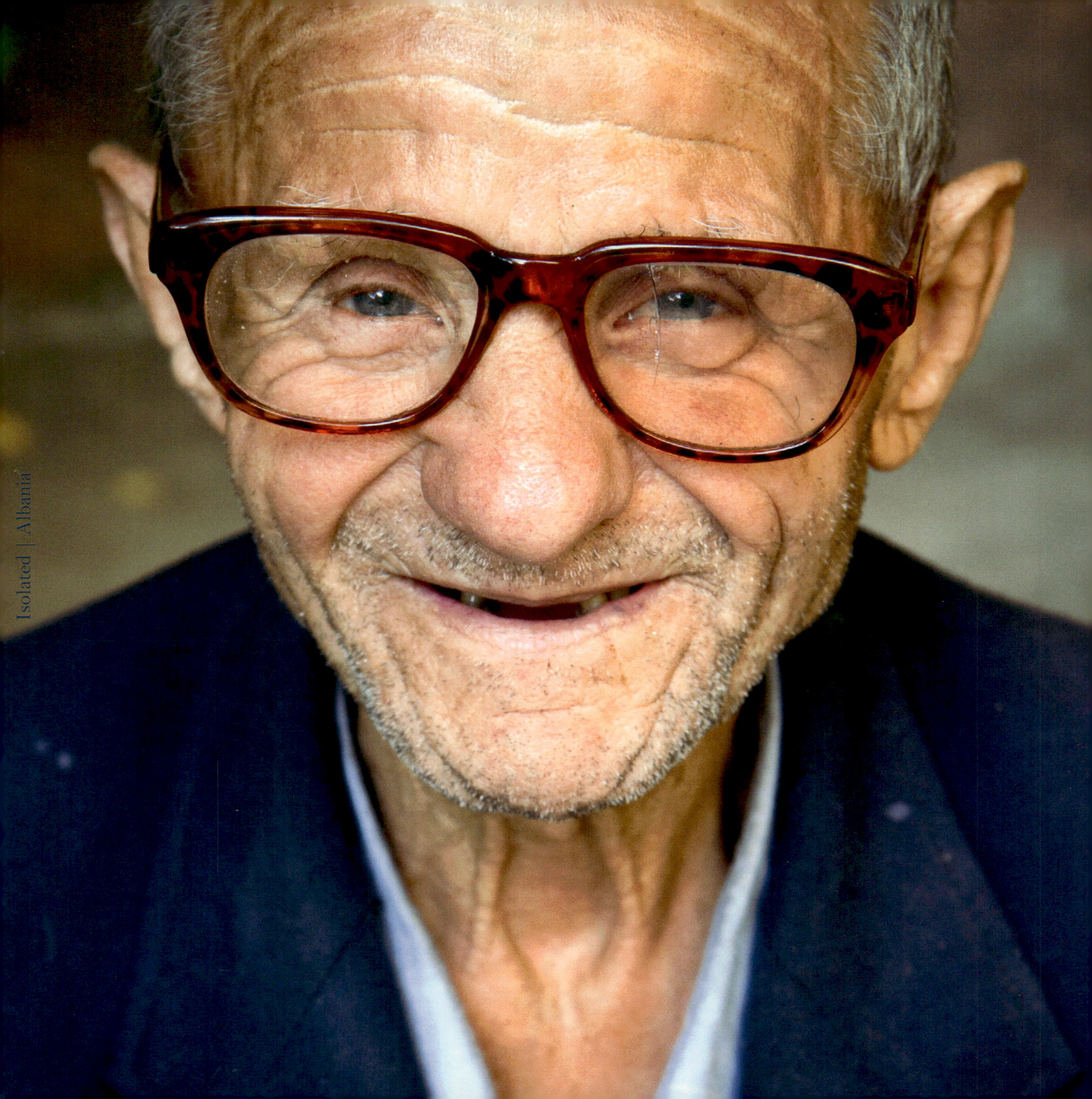

The room is divided like a high school cafeteria, cliques huddling together and humming with life and energy. Everyone in the room is over the age of seventy; an array of white hair, crooked teeth, and heavily engraved faces. So many stories and experiences represented with each wrinkled smile. Safet was a journalist, Adnan a teacher, Triphon a soldier; and now here they sit, Albania's forgotten generation. Cast aside during the rise out of communism, they look back on those years now with angst, knowing the change was for the better, all the while struggling to survive.

"During the days of communism we had jobs, we had a home, we had food on our table. Now we have nothing." - *Hassan*

It is overwhelming to look around the room, thinking of the lives lived: the struggles, the achievements, the joy, the pain. These worn faces have been through World Wars, years of communism, even the death and rebirth of their nation. Now they are here, eating at a soup kitchen. For many, with no home and no family to care for them, this is their only meal for the day. How many stories are going untold? How many lives are ending unnoticed?

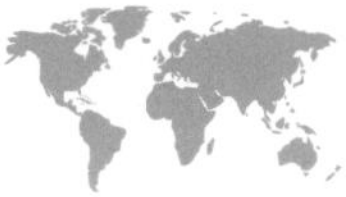

Every year an estimated **2.1 million** older Americans are victims of physical, psychological, or other forms of **abuse and neglect**.[7]

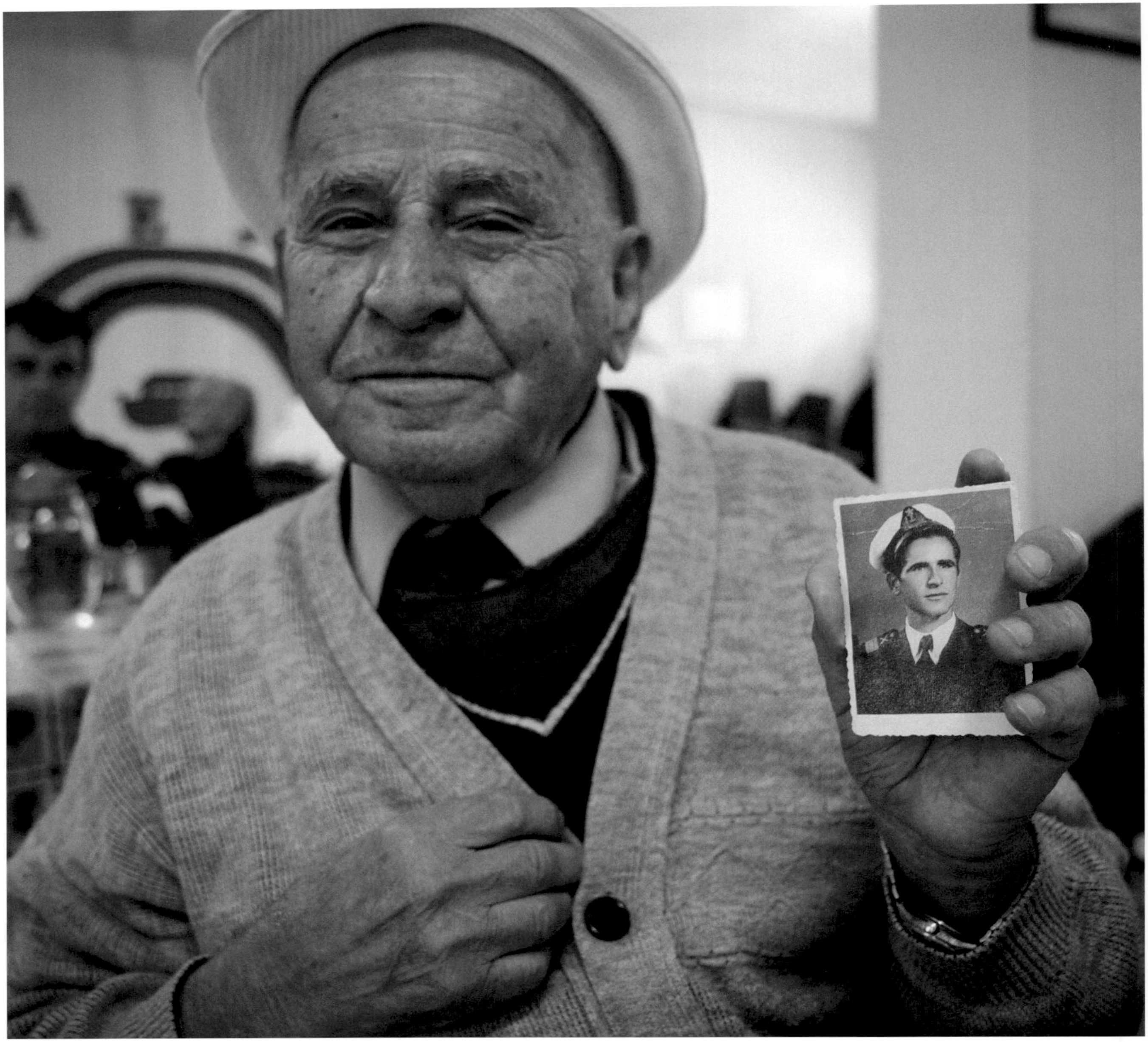

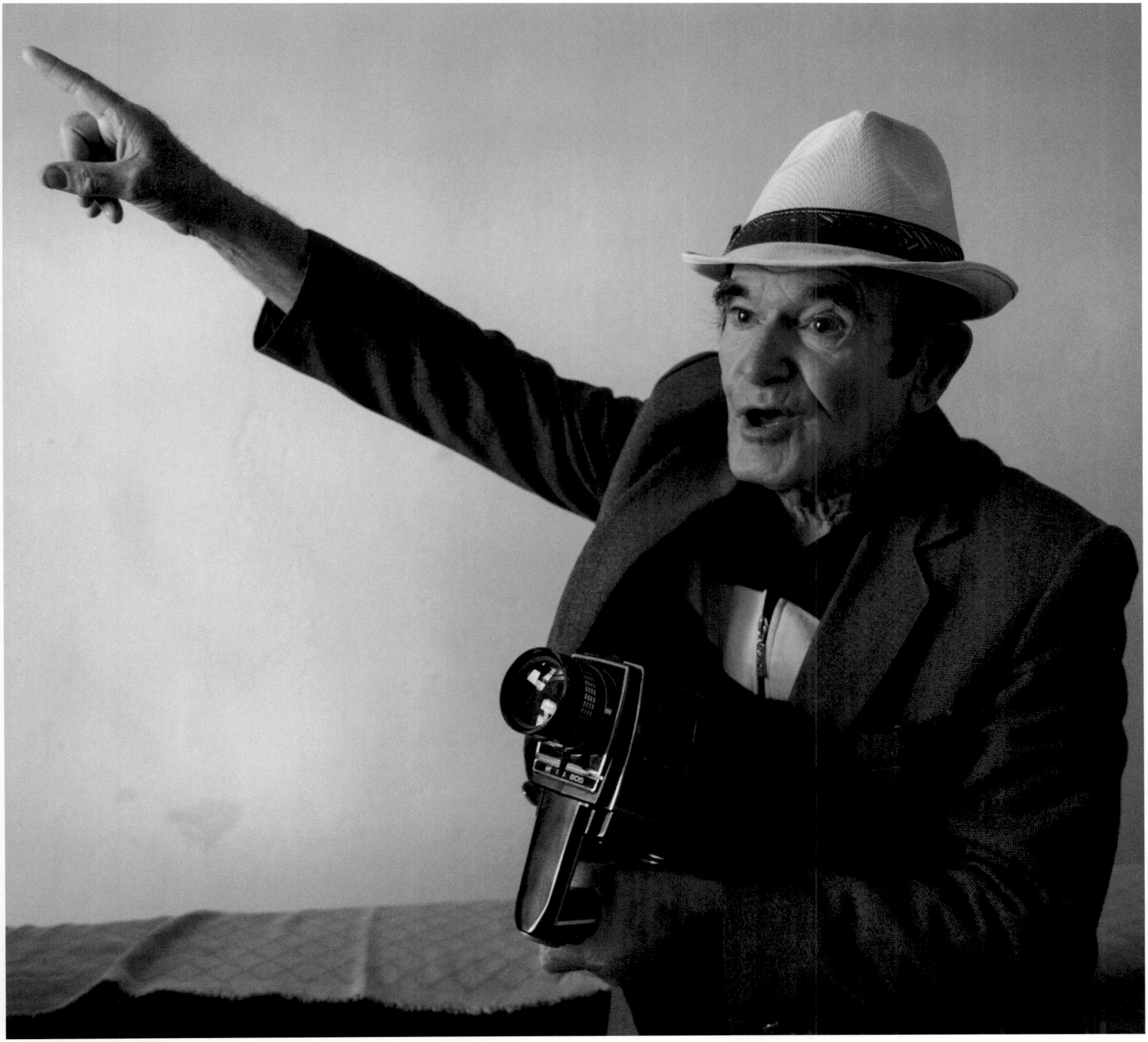

Home·less

a person who lacks a
fixed, regular or adequate
nighttime residence

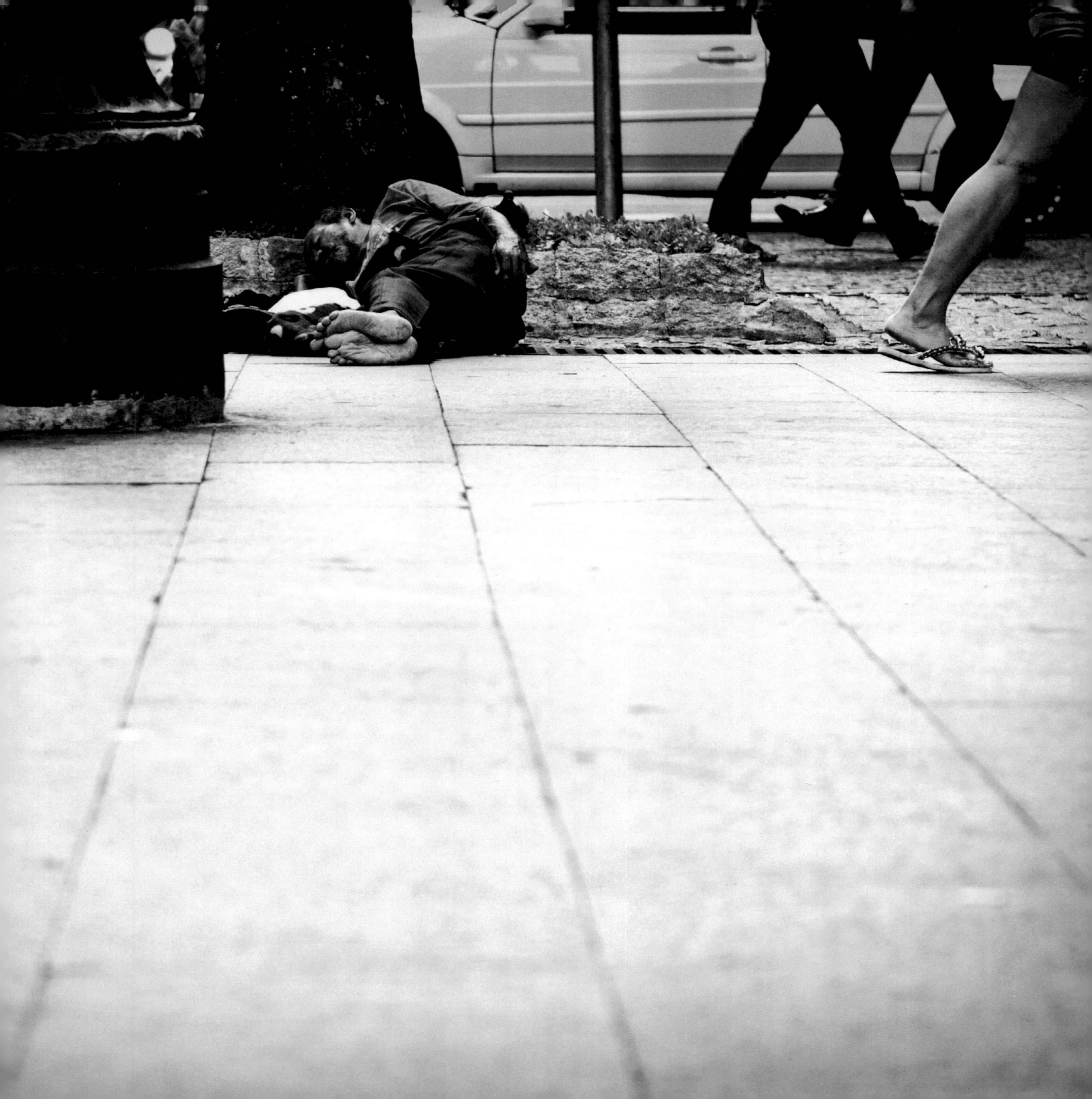

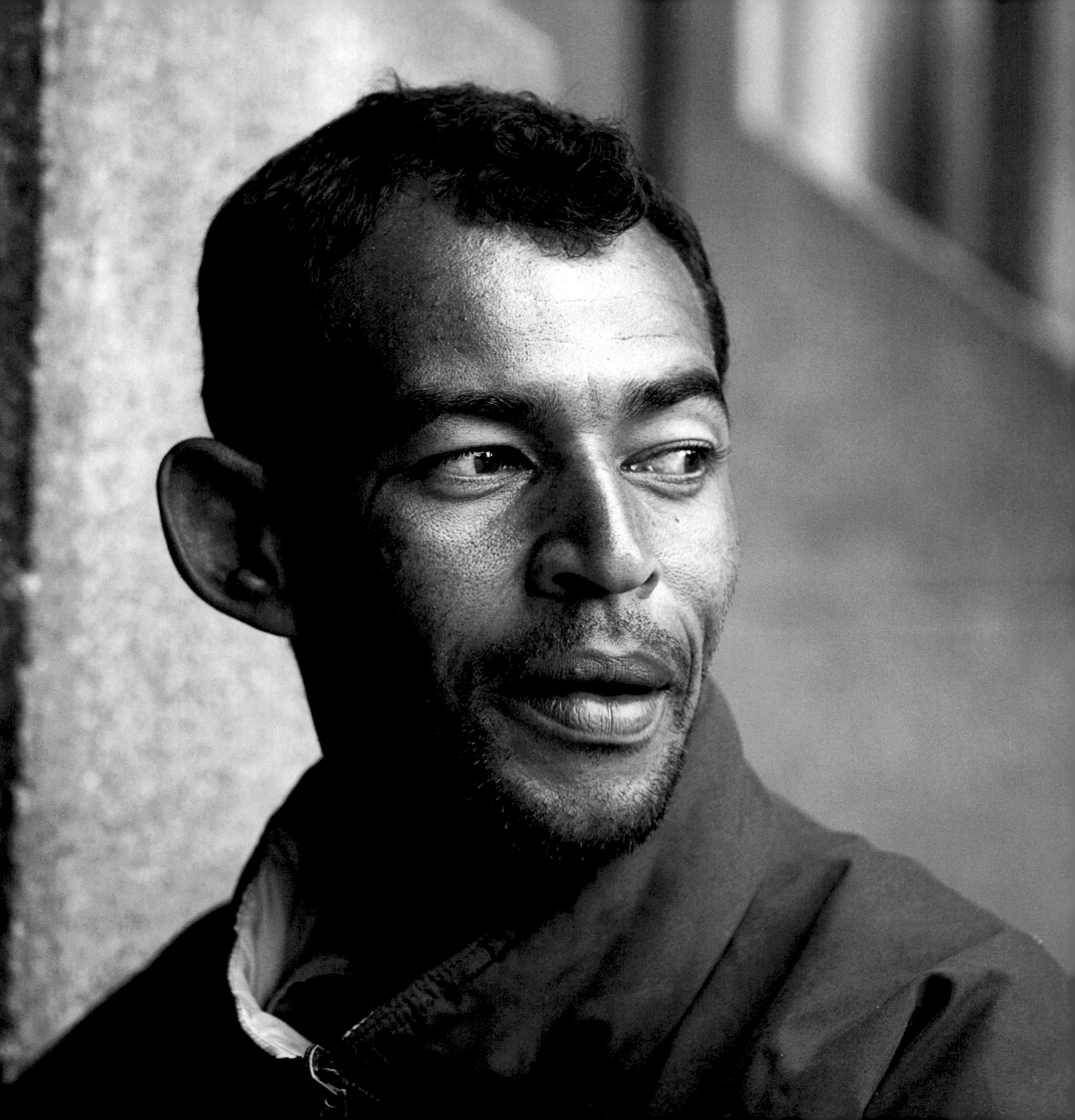

Homeless | Brazil

Jose sits in front of the towering doors of Catedral da Sé, invisible to most of the hundreds of visitors who walk past him each day. Only a few pause to give him a coin or two. Like many homeless people, he wears his weariness on his face. Small scars and lines construct his worn visage, a tired countenance that details years of hardship.

Originally from the northeast of Brazil, José was a child when his family visited São Paulo for vacation. Both parents died in a tragic car accident during the trip and he quickly became a street kid; a young boy left alone in one of the largest cities in the world.

"You learn honesty on the streets," José states as he leans forward from his perch in the cobbled square. "In 1998 a truck filled with donated food came to the square to feed the homeless. When I walked up to the truck I could smell the arsenic and tried to urge the people not to eat the contaminated food." Despite José's earnest warnings those who were starving and desperate continued to devour the poisoned food. Many unsuspecting homeless, who believed they were partaking in an act of compassion, died. The insidious murder of innocent people was used as a solution to rid the area of the homeless. José shrugs his shoulders and simply states,

"It's easier to say I'll kill you, than I love you."

An estimated **100 million people** are **homeless** worldwide.[8]

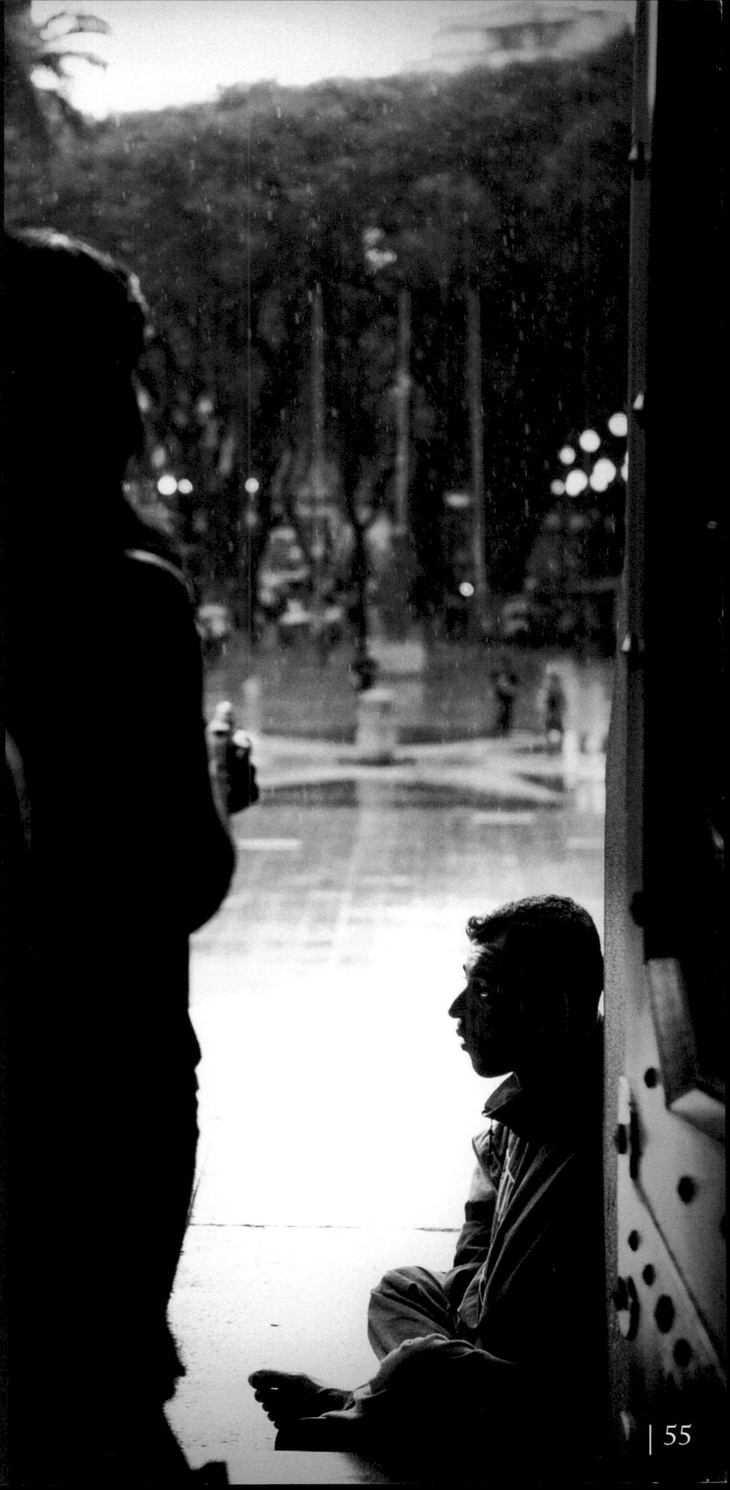

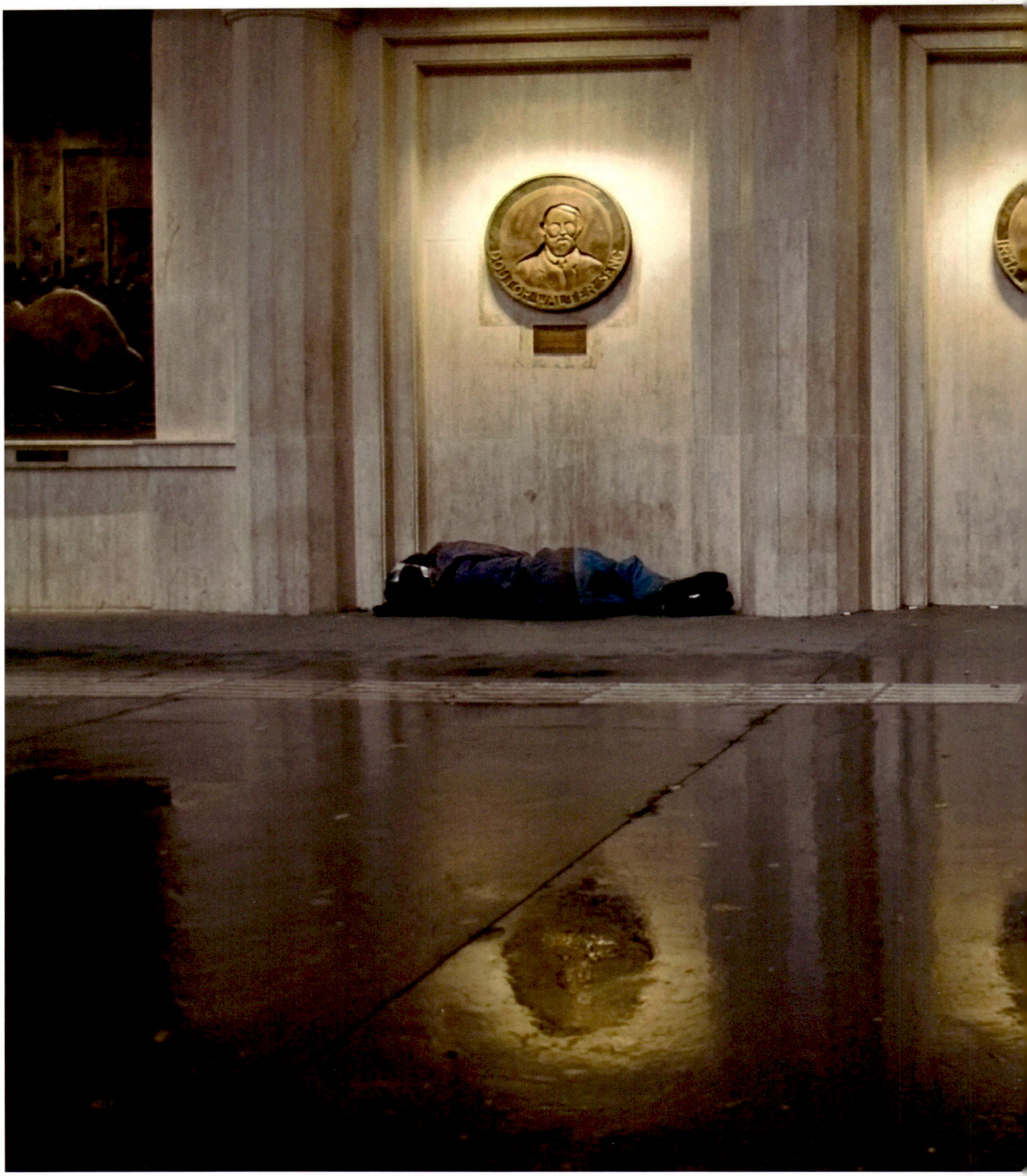

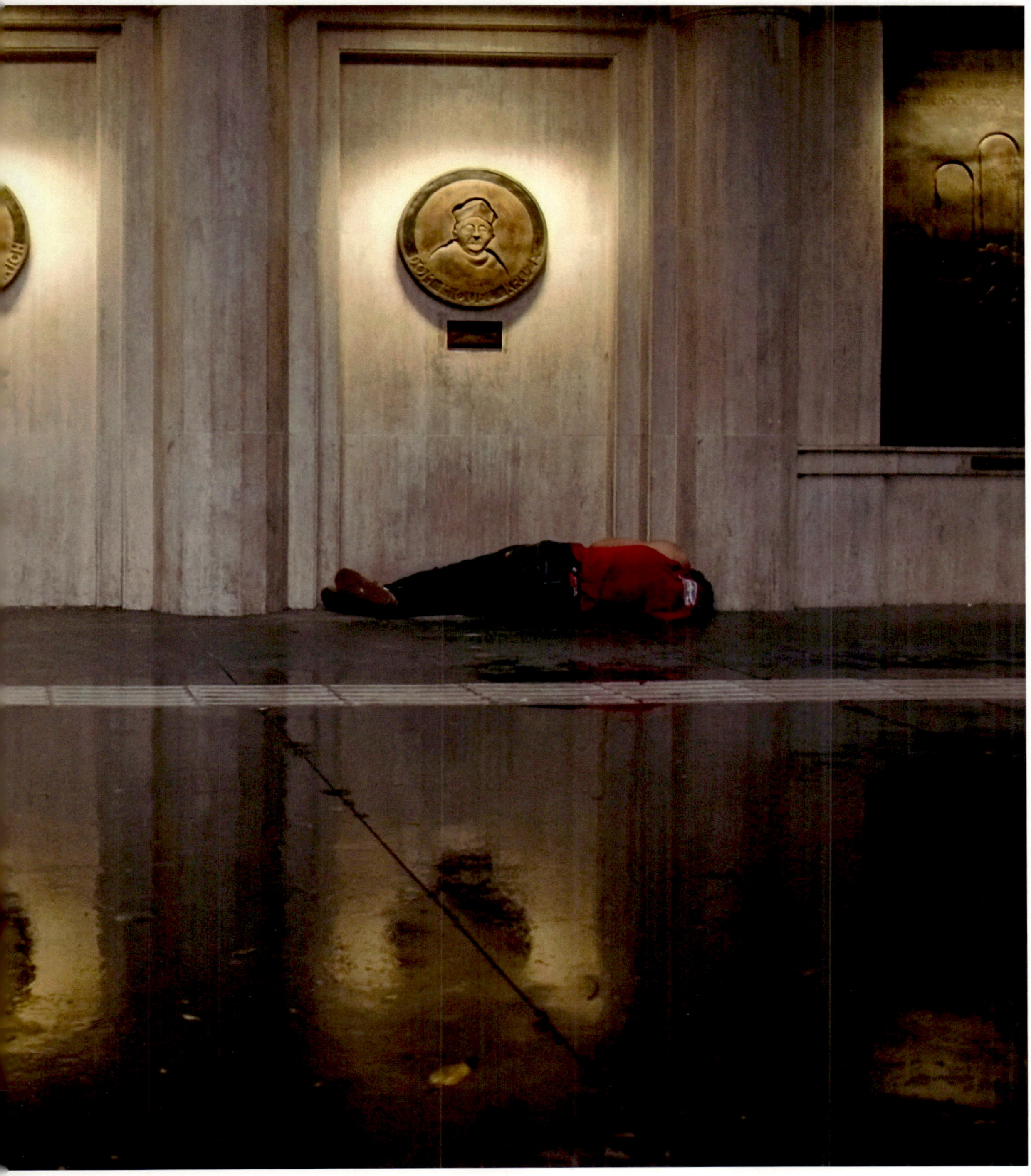

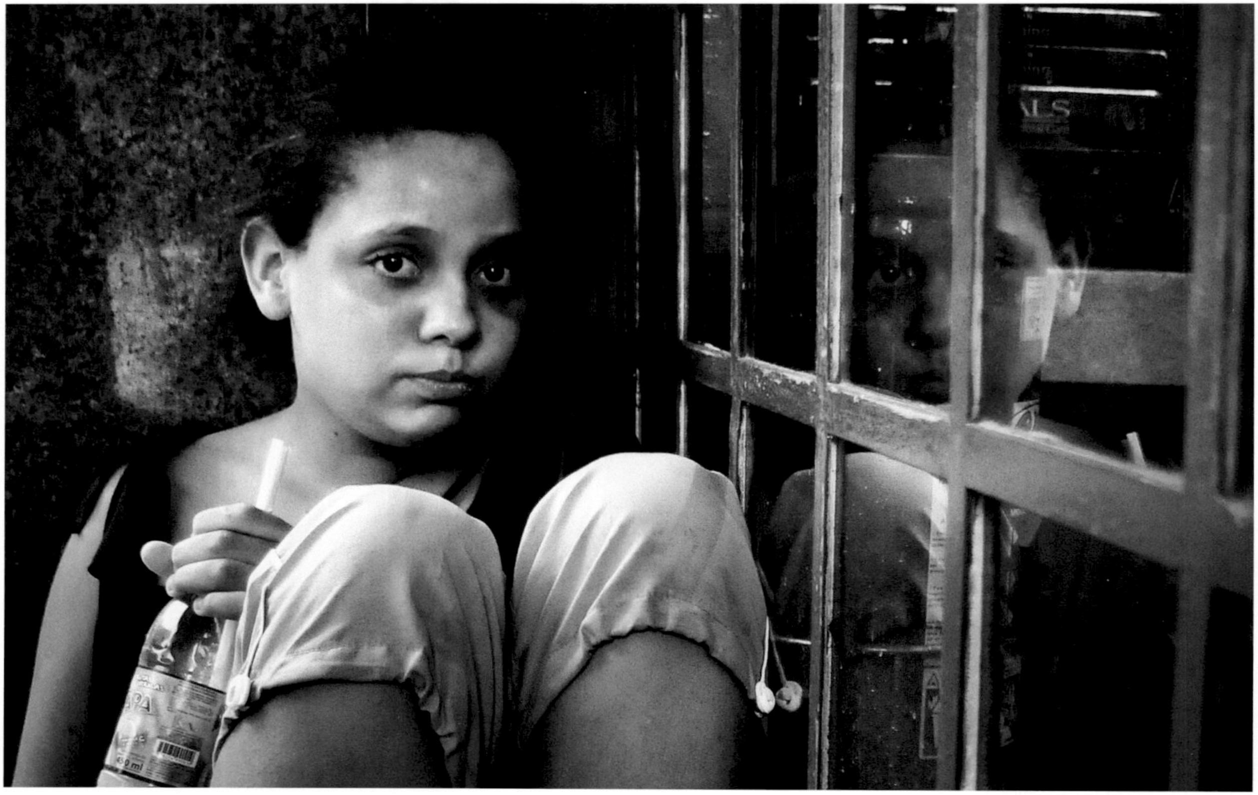

Her face is round and soft, the suggestion of childhood in her cheeks. The left side of her body is painted purple and blue, the memoirs of undeserved violence. In the chaos of the hospital waiting room she looks up, lips twitching in an attempted smile before she lays her weary head on her shoulder - safe at last.

Her name is Jagatha, and she is a twelve-year-old resident of the streets of São Paulo, Brazil. Driven out of her home by an abusive father, she sought refuge with the thousands of other homeless children in the city. She soon became easy prey to drugs and prostitution. One night, while sleeping in a park, an intoxicated man approached Jagatha and began savagely beating her. Cuts, bruises, and cracked ribs - these will heal, but what about a cracked spirit? There is no easy road to recovery, no simple way to change a mind so tainted by its harsh realities.

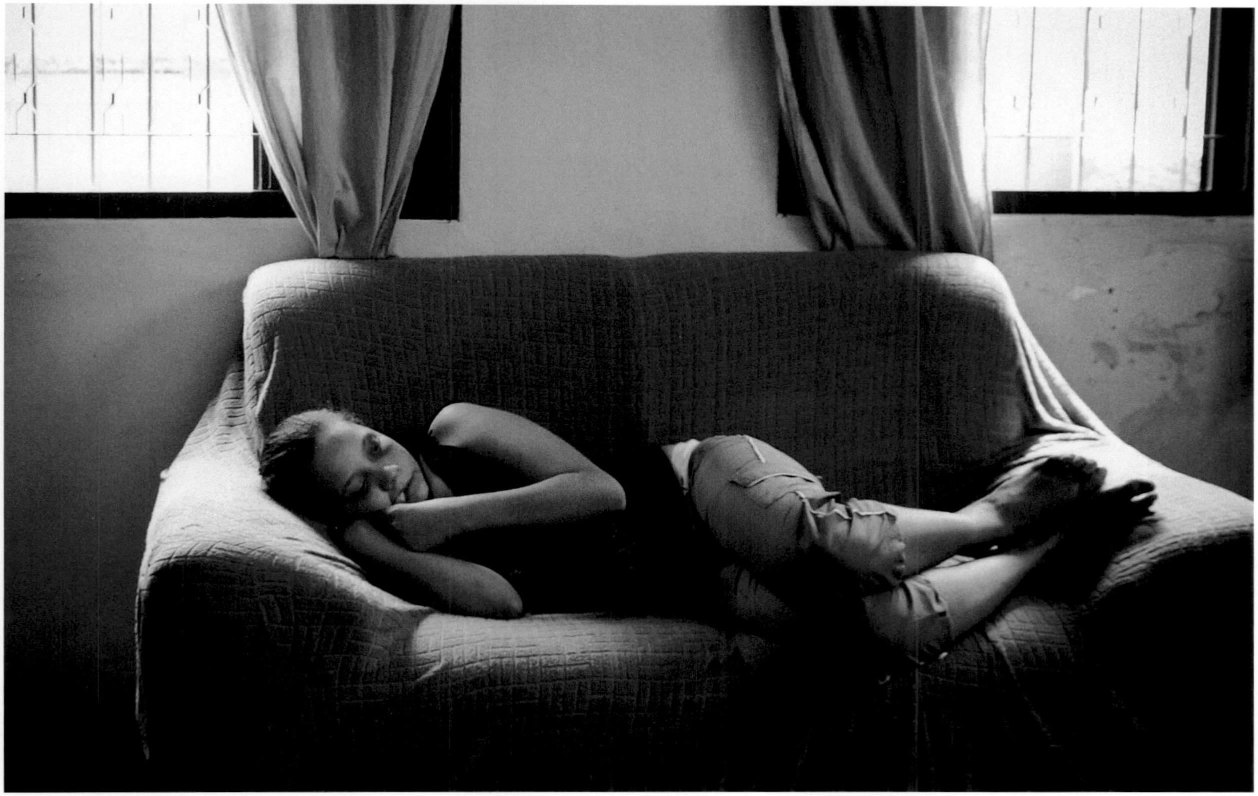

Her face is round and soft, childhood returning with the flush of her cheeks. The bruising surrounding her brow is fading, but it is clear the pain goes much deeper than broken skin. In the safety of Casa Taiguara, a shelter for street children, she struggles to find her place. She sits for hours, arms drawn around her chest, lost in a world of memories.

Her name is Jagatha, and she is no longer a resident of the streets of São Paulo. She has a house to live in, a bed to sleep in, but what of a home? How does one begin to restore their view on something that has only harmed them? For years, Jagatha has separated herself from emotion and relied on her instincts for survival, to suddenly be in a home is shockingly unfamiliar. This shift in reality is what has children like Jagatha walking out of shelters and back onto the streets. Back to drugs, gangs, or pimps - the basic need to belong to someone or something.

Ru·ins

the remains of
something destroyed,
disintegrated or decayed

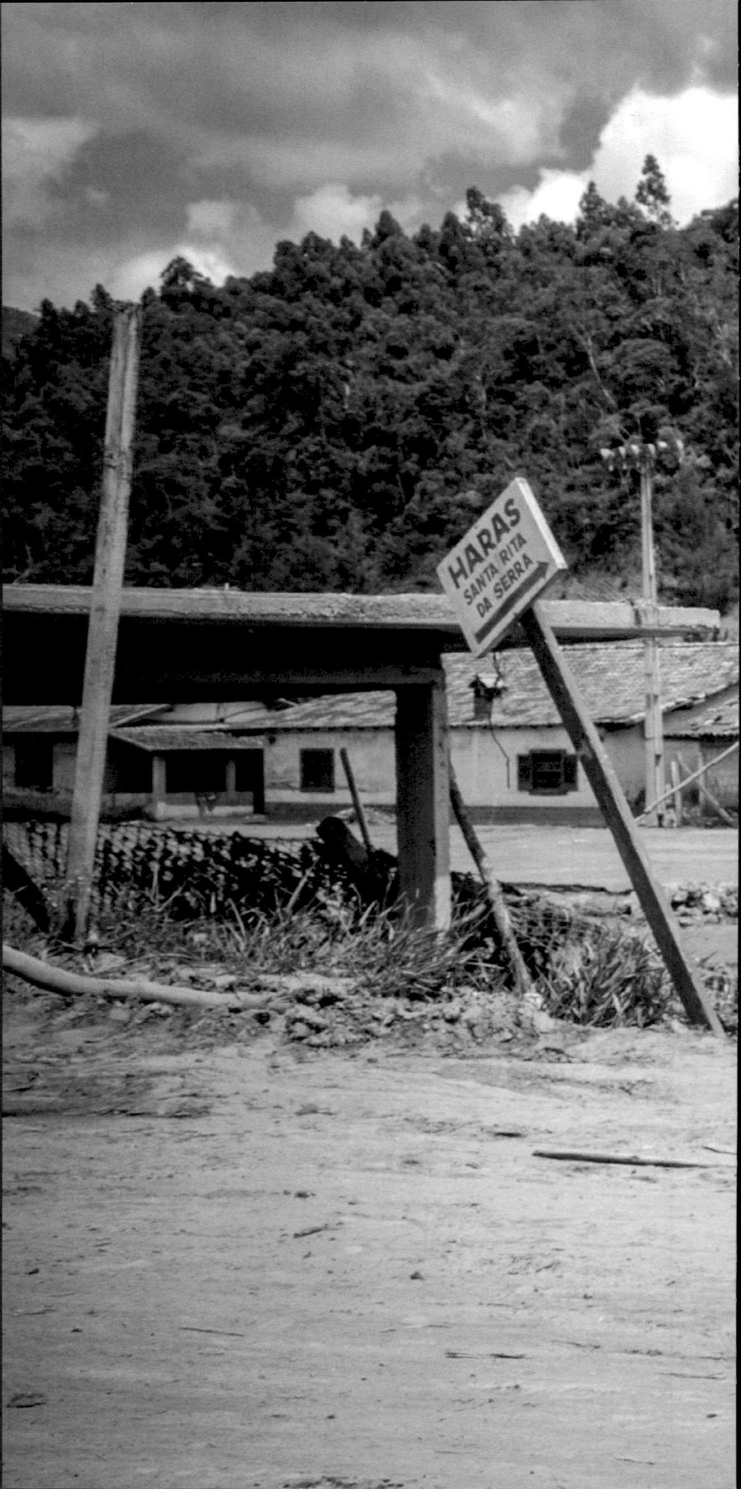

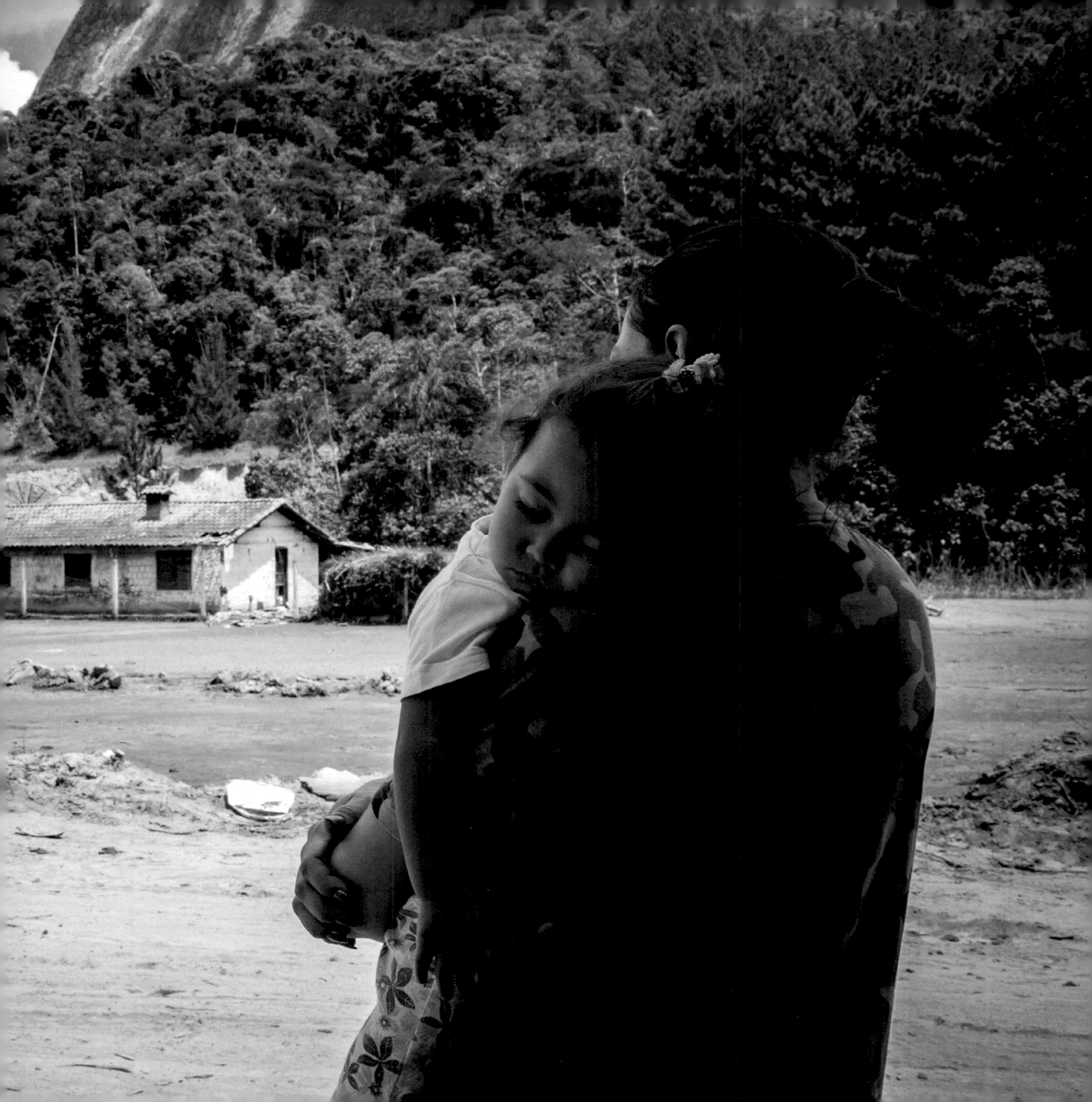

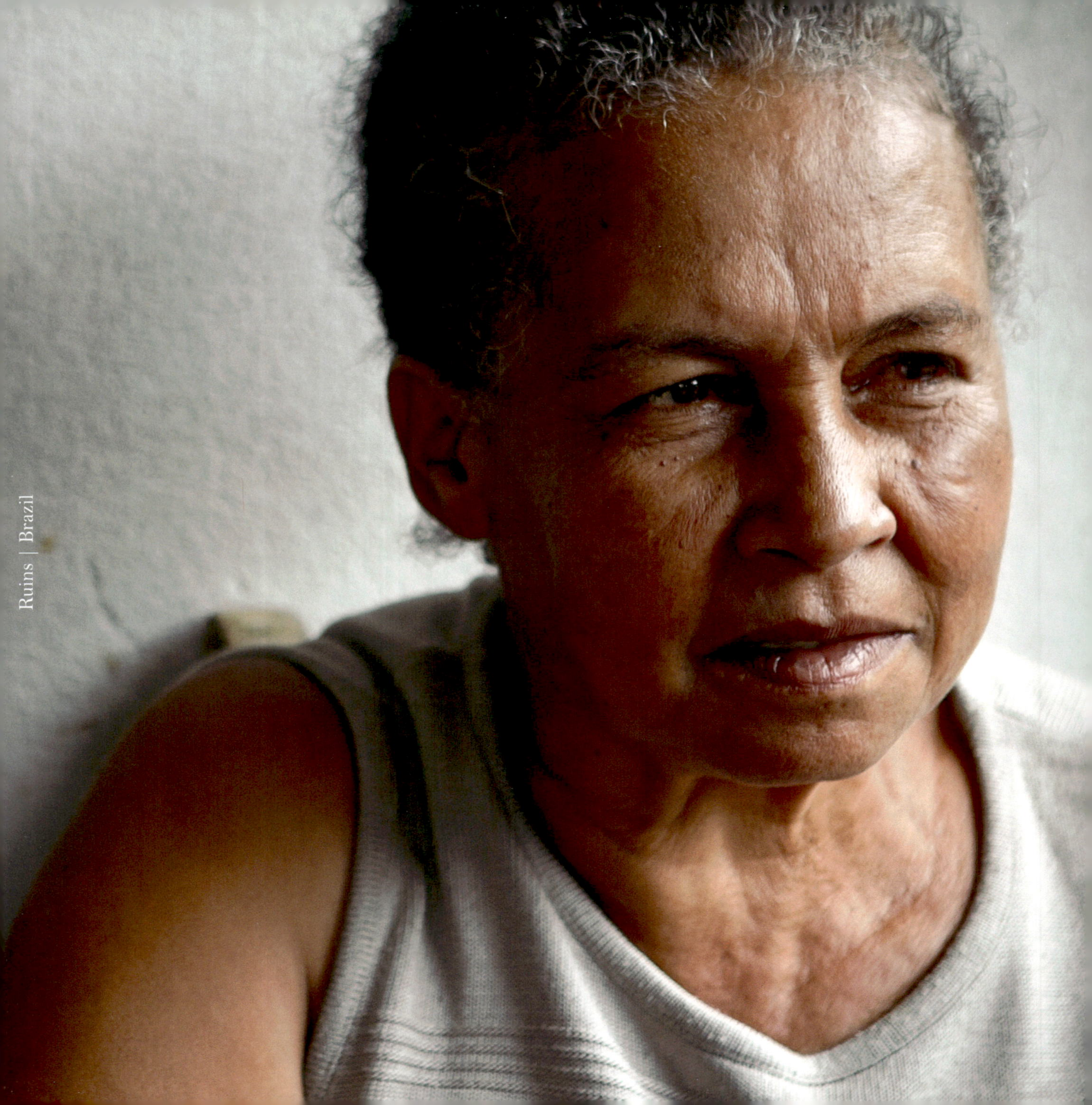

"I was sleeping. We woke up to a noise that sounded like a fleet of helicopters circling above us. The house shook. I got out of bed and got lost in the kitchen, looking for a match. I managed to turn on the lamp and I went out onto the porch. I yelled and yelled, but nobody heard me." - Dona Gege

On the morning of January 12, 2011, numerous small mountain towns in the state of Rio de Janeiro waited for the sun to rise on the aftermath of the massive flood that ripped through their communities the night before. Entire homes were swept away or buried in the rubble, roads broke open, cement bridges collapsed, and thousands of people died or went missing in what has been considered the greatest natural catastrophe in Brazil's history.

With faulty reports and inaccurate death tolls reaching the media, these small farming towns remained in dire need long after donations stopped arriving. Families were torn apart, crops were destroyed, and people were left homeless and helpless, at the mercy of the world. Unfulfilled promises by the government to bring relief and aid have stunted the survivors' ability to rebuild what was lost.

Dona Gege sits on her porch, overlooking the ruins. A fifty-five-year-old resident of Vieira, Brazil, her voice is thick with grief as she says, "We had heard there were many survivors in another hospital, so we had hope that they were still alive. But we are left missing them." Her ex-husband's house, located at the base of the mountain where the flood first hit, was completely buried in rubble, not a trace of the house could be seen. In addition, her brother's house where eight of her relatives lived, situated no more than fifty feet from her own, had been completely washed away in the night with only the foundation remaining. She lost nine family members that night. As she speaks of her pain she says quietly,

"It feels like my heart doesn't beat anymore, it just gets beaten."

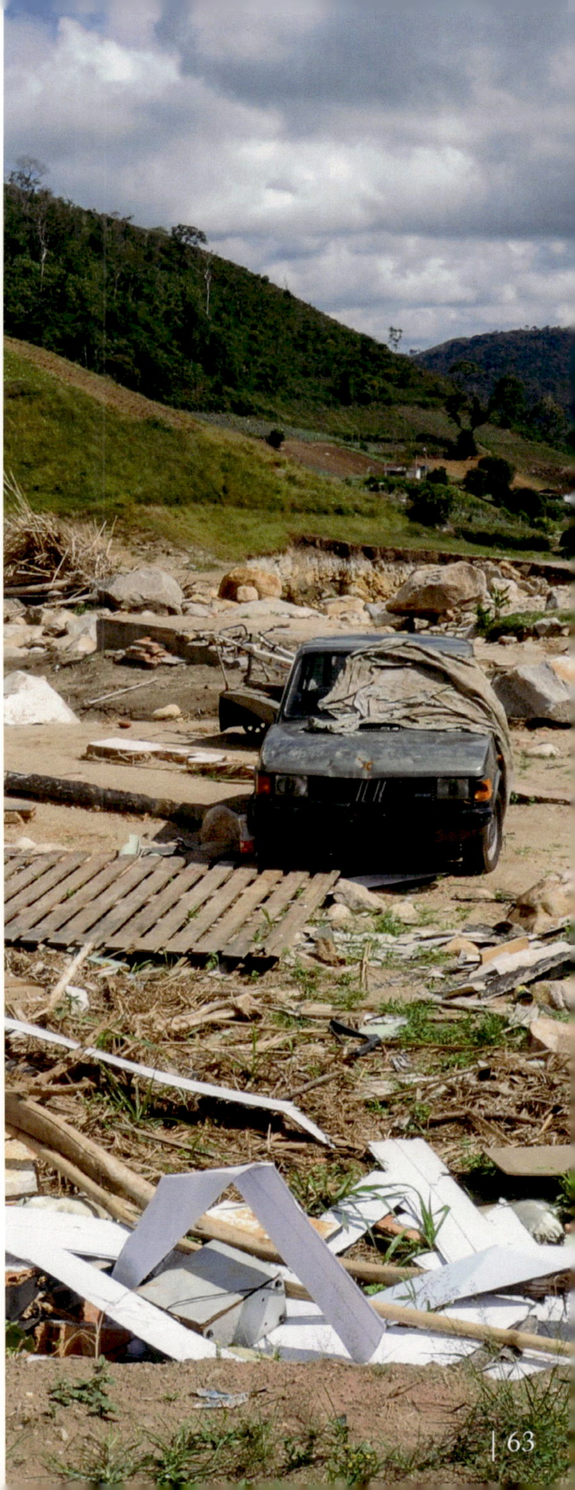

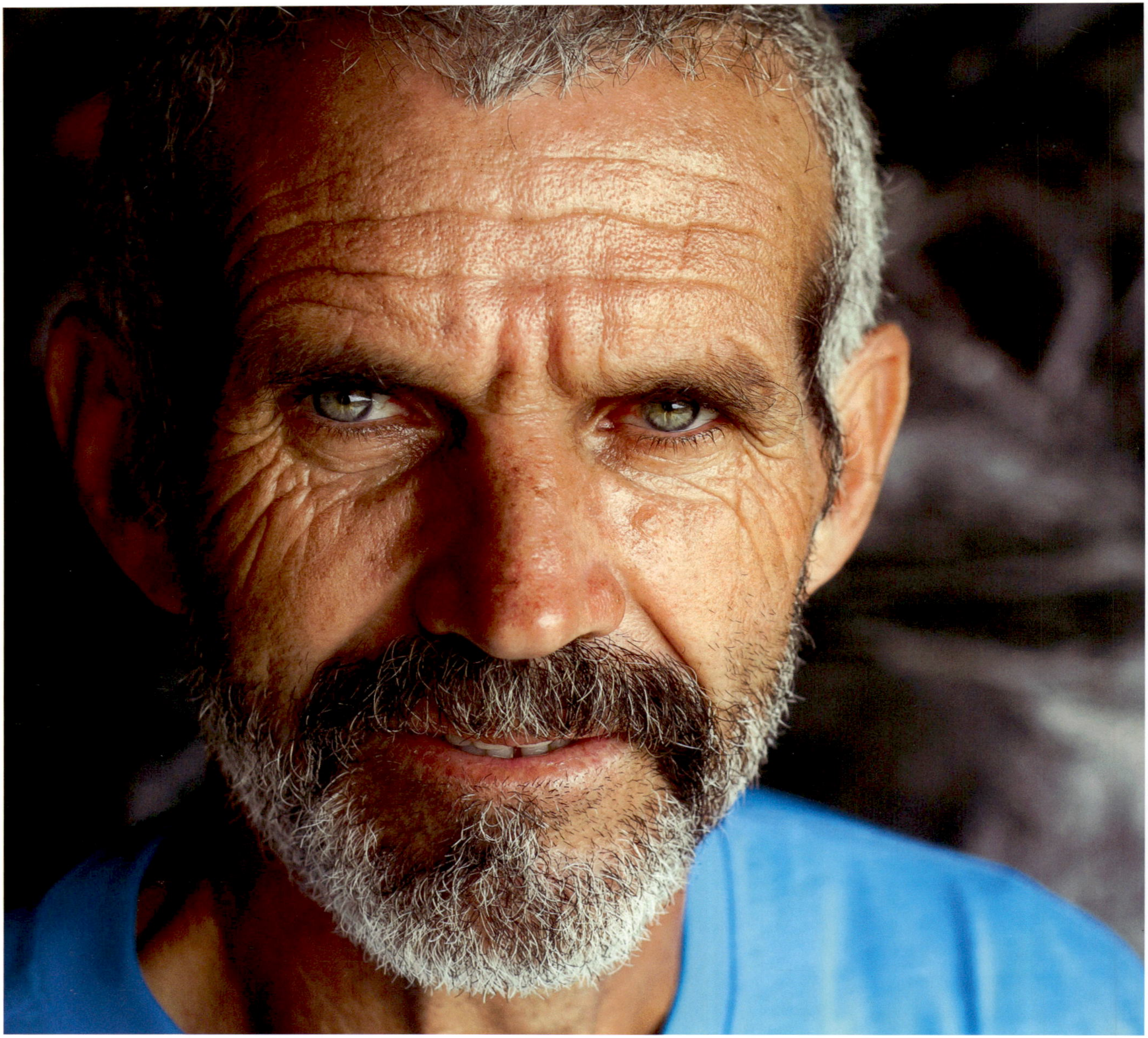

Ruins | Brazil

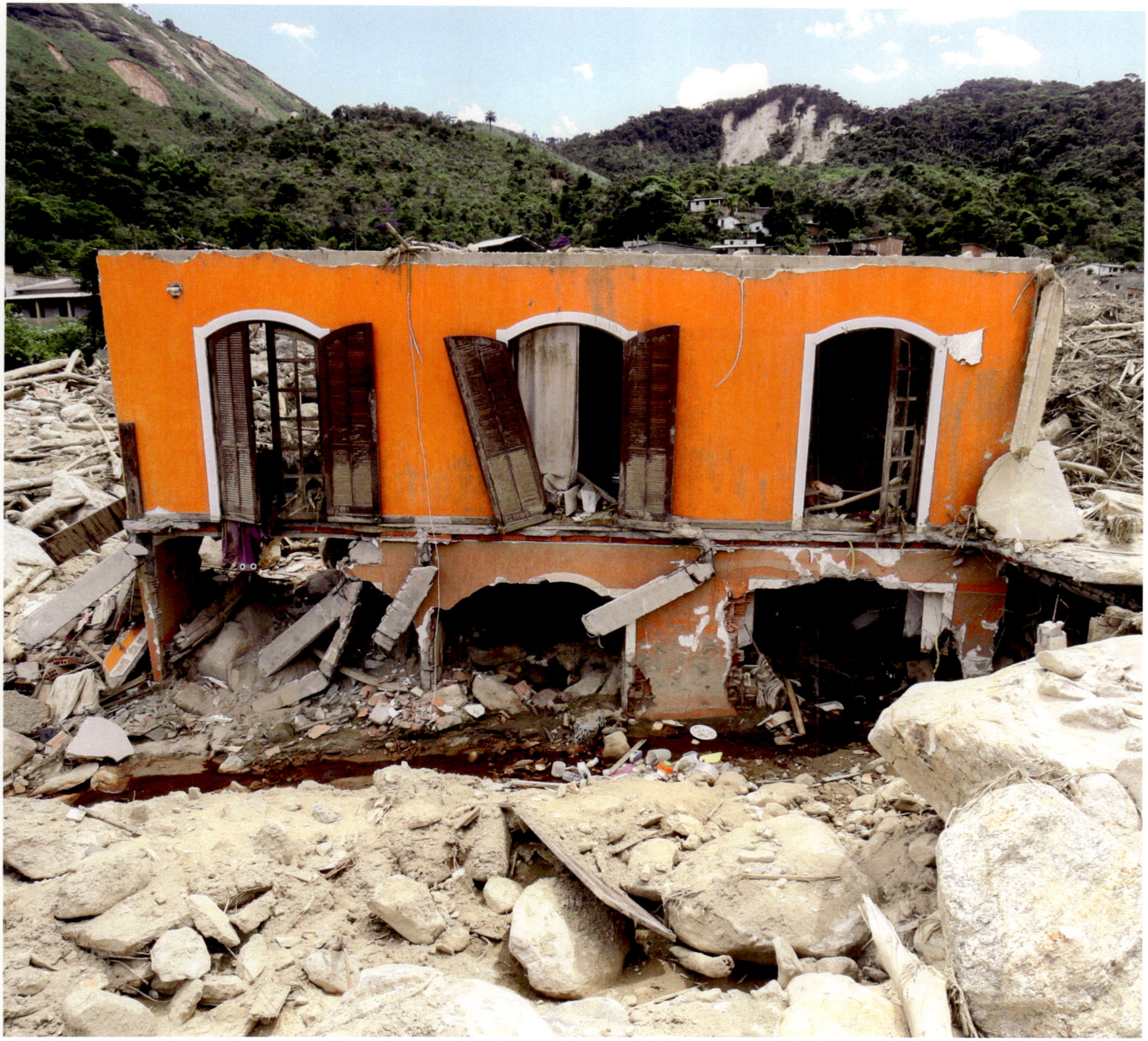

In the last two years the world has experienced earthquakes, floods, typhoons, heat waves, droughts, tornados, and landslides that have killed well over a quarter of a million people. In 2010 alone, "more people were killed worldwide by natural disasters than have been killed in terrorist attacks in the past 40 years combined." [9] A brief look at the world's most devastating natural disasters of 2010 and 2011:

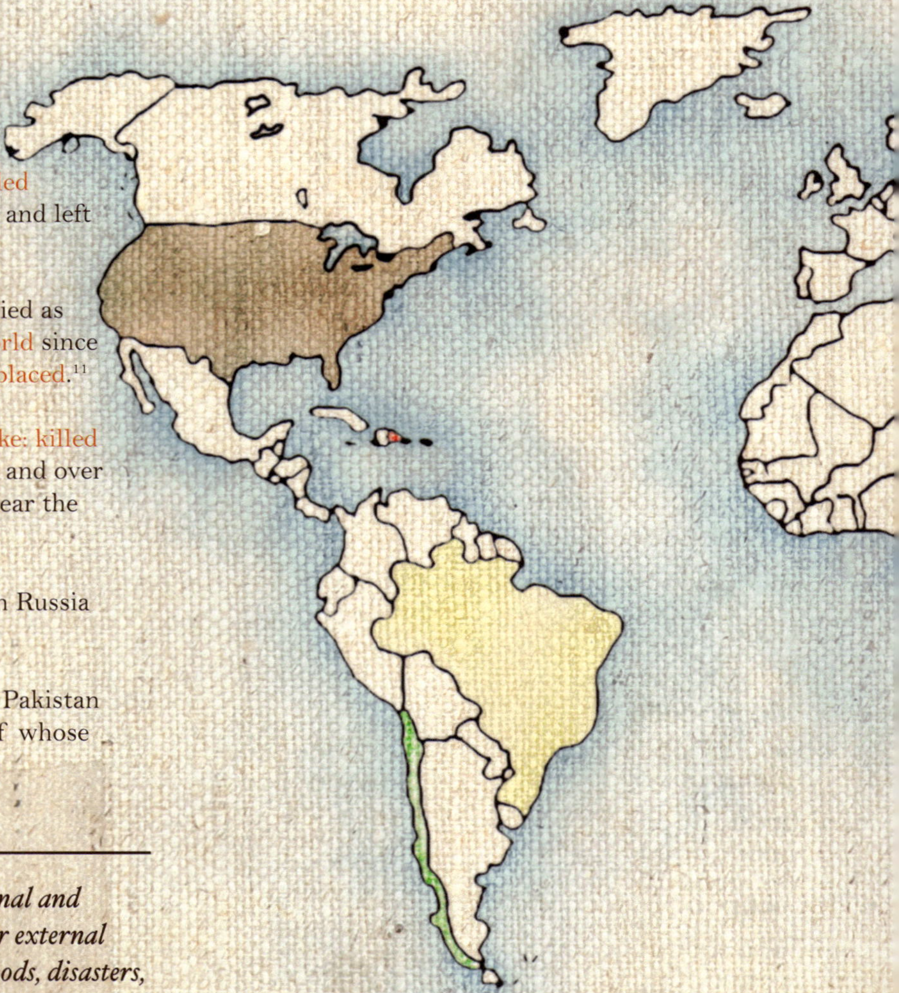

2010

January 12 – Haiti 7.0 Earthquake: Killed 220,000 people, wounded over 300,000 and left 1.5 million people homeless.[10]

February 27 – Chile 8.8 Earthquake: Tied as the 5th strongest earthquake in the world since 1900, more than 1.5 million people displaced.[11]

April 13 – Central China 6.9 Earthquake: killed at least 2,064 people, with 175 missing and over 12,000 injured.[12] Over 85% of homes near the epicenter collapsed.[13]

July through September – Heat wave in Russia killed at least 56,000 people.[14]

July through September – Flooding in Pakistan affected over 18 million people, most of whose homes have been destroyed.[15]

"There are two big forces at work, external and internal. We have very little control over external forces such as tornadoes, earthquakes, floods, disasters, illness, and pain. What really matters is the internal force. How do I respond to those disasters?"

- Leo Buscaglia

Disasters leave people vulnerable and at the mercy of the world. Families are often torn apart by loss, and their sense of security is demolished. Long after the storm or drought has passed, they suffer the consequences of what it means to be left without a home.

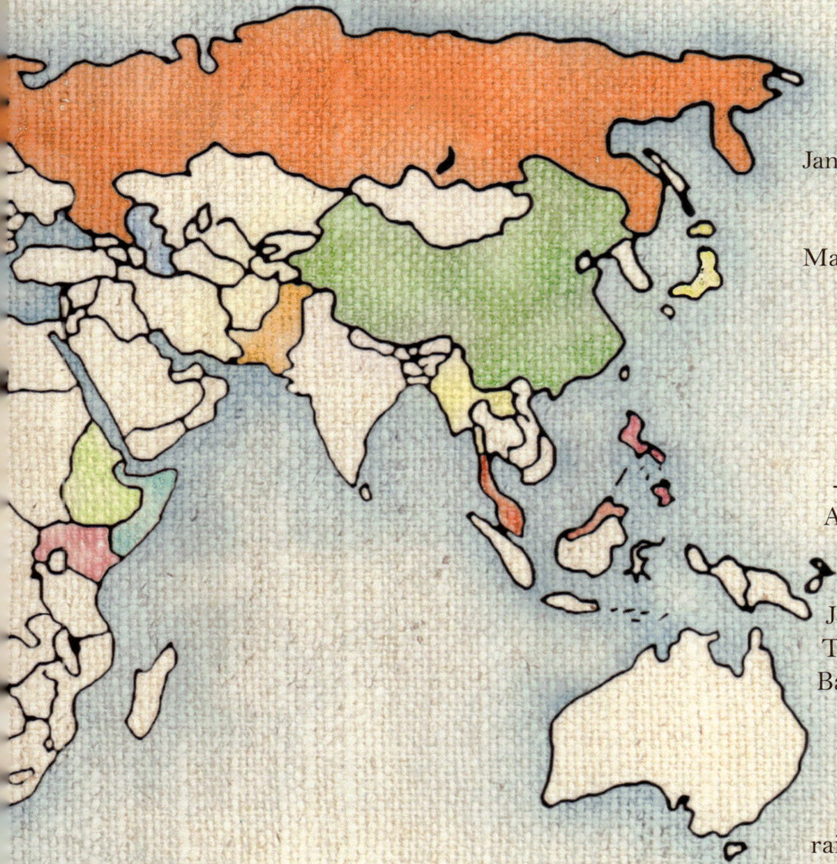

2011

January 12 – Flooding in Brazil: killed over 830 people and left more than 20,000 homeless.[16]

March 11 – Japan 8.9 Earthquake and Tsunami: One of the strongest earthquakes ever recorded, killing over 10,000 with 17,400 missing.[17]

July to Present – Drought in East Africa: Kenya, Somalia, Ethiopia, Eritrea & Djibouti - Considered the worst drought in 60 years.[18] An estimated 10 million people are at risk and 30,000 children have died.[19]

July through December – Floods in Thailand: The worst flooding in 50 years swept through Bangkok, killing 800 and affecting over 12,000 people.[20]

December 16 – Typhoon in Philippines: Tropical Storm Washi dropped 8 inches of rainfall in less than 12 hours, triggering deadly floods and landslides that killed more than 1,200 people. Over ½ million have lost their homes.[21]

January through December – Storms in the United States: Killed more than 700 people, making 2011 one of the worst years of natural disasters in the history of the United States.[22]

Red·Light

an urban area containing
many brothels, strip clubs and
sex-oriented businesses

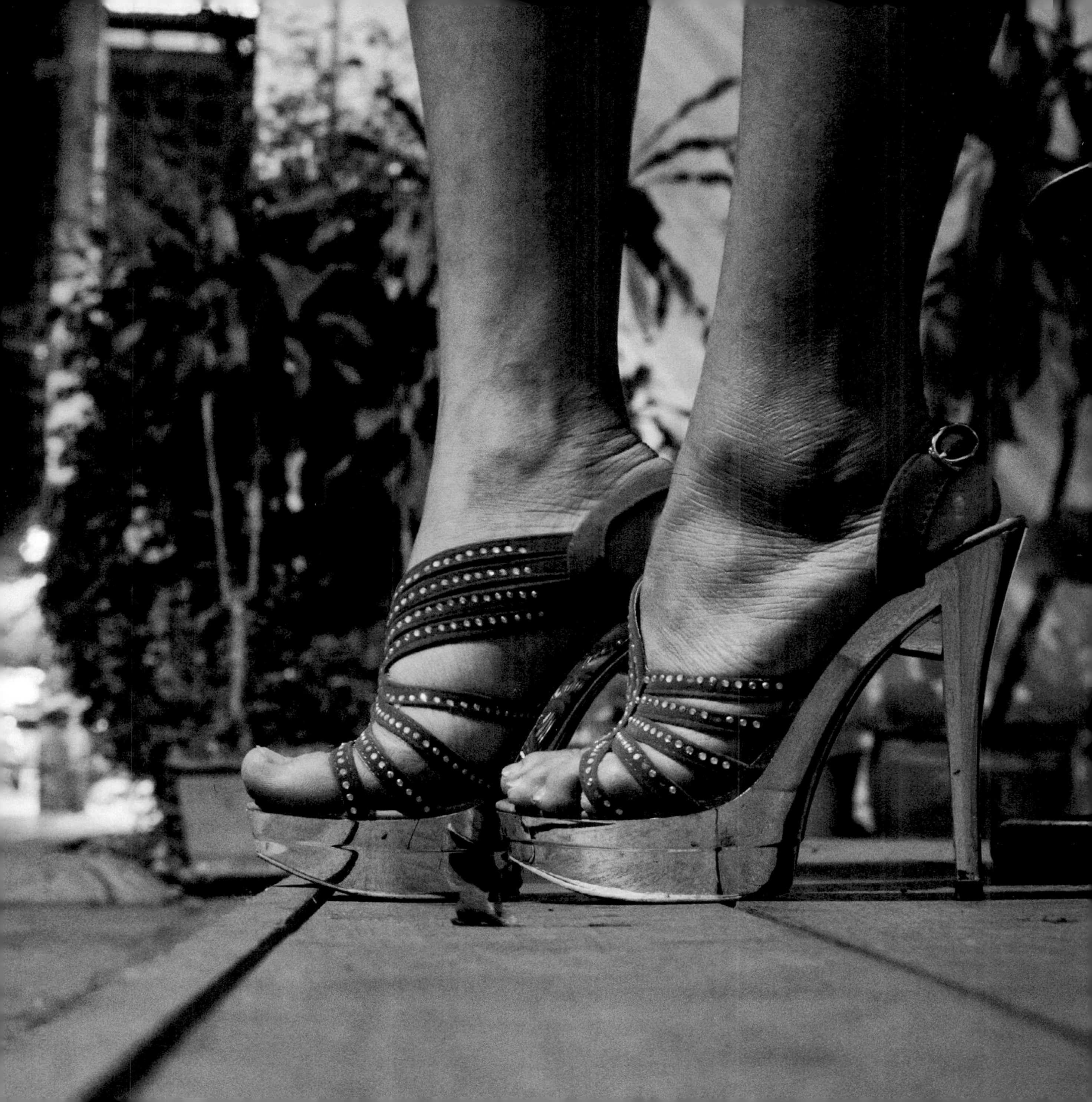

Her short dress, her shallow smile, her eyes darting from face to face on the busy street. Intoxicated, May is in no state to talk, her attention divided and diverted. Just a few hours earlier she had been a different woman with all the pretenses gone and the mask peeled off. She wept, she worried, and she was real. The demand from her family to send home an unrealistic amount of money is more than she can take. How can she be expected to single-handedly support a mother, a father, two brothers, a sister, and a son? The pressure is what drives her to this bar and to this life.

The street just outside the bar is flooded with hundreds of men - Australians, Europeans, Americans, and Canadians. They look like friends, brothers, fathers, grandfathers. Normal looking men, wedding rings on their hands, are walking with young teen girls in tow. As the music blasts its way into the night, the hard beats overpower May's soft voice, drowning out any screams of protest. Her face is conflicted as she gives us a hug, clinging to the hands of love and kindness. "I have to work now," she yells. Then she is gone, dancing her way across the bar. As a group of men claim her attention, an aged hand moves up her thigh, naming a price for that which was never meant to be sold.

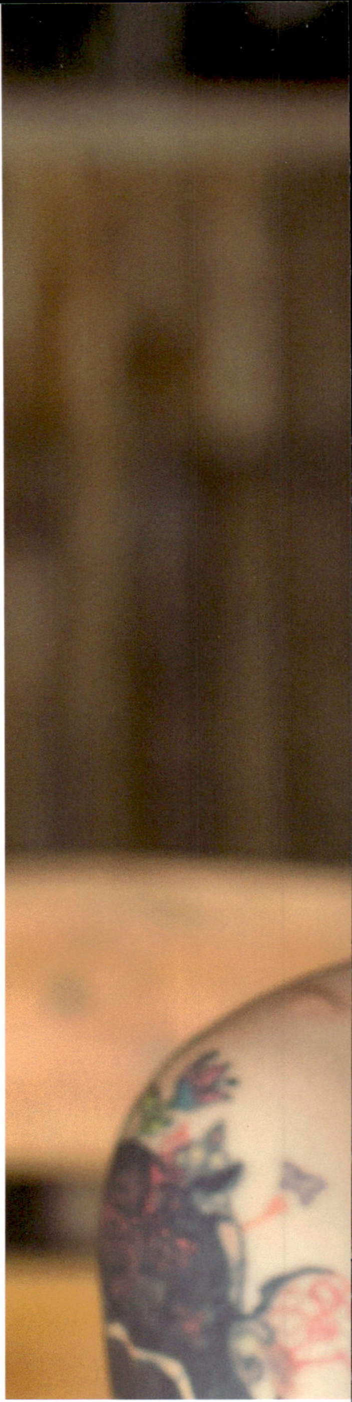

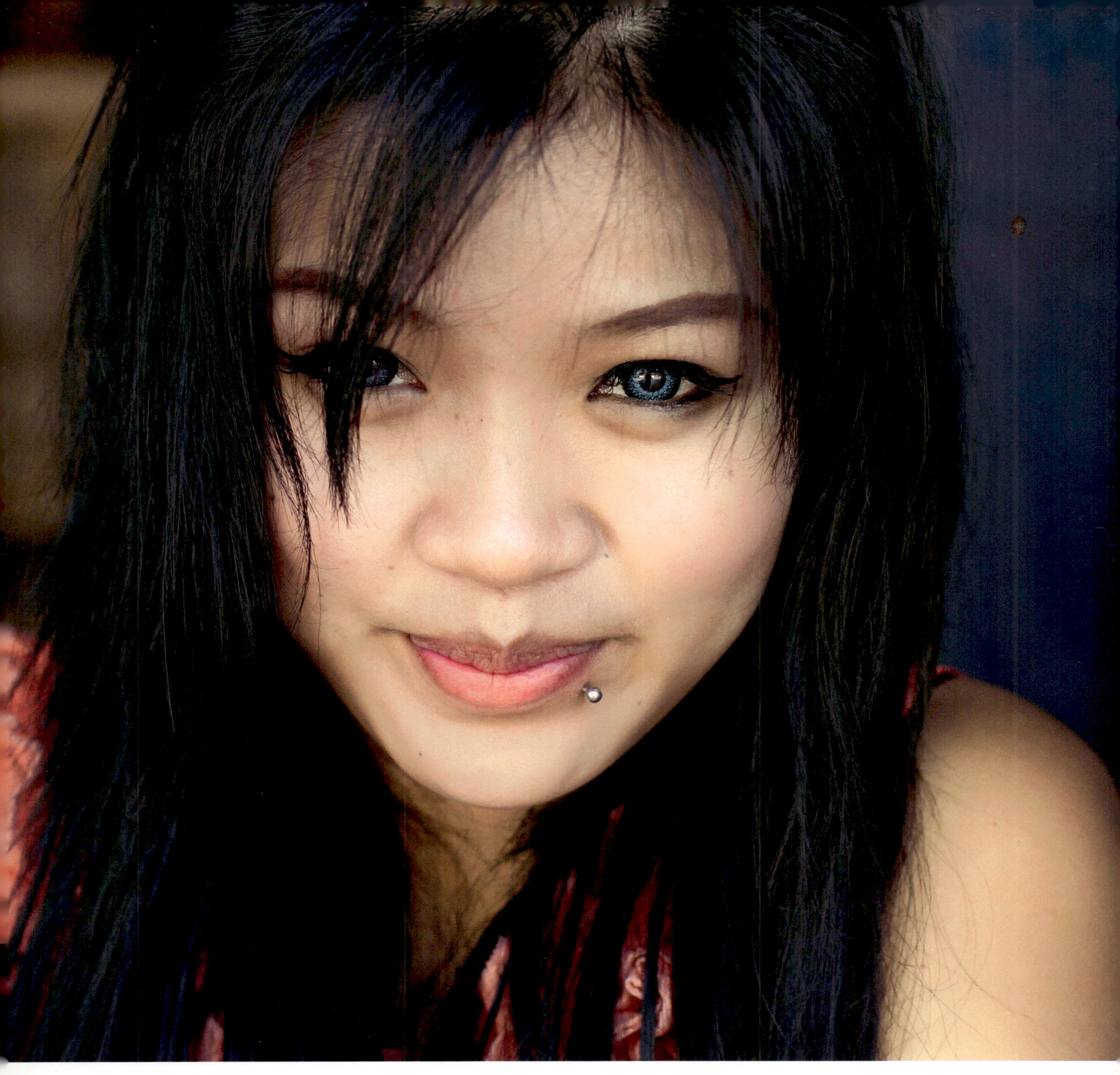

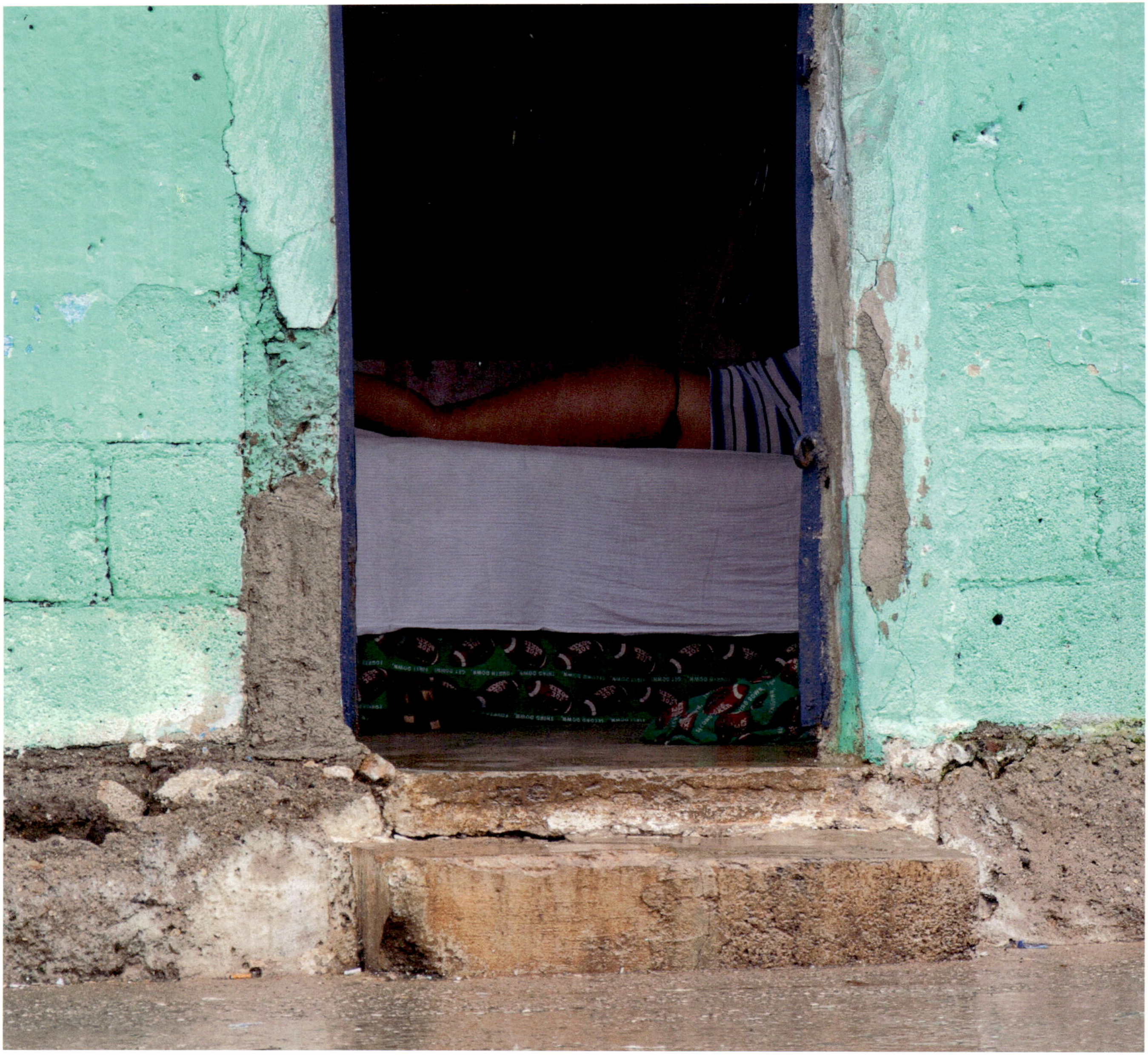

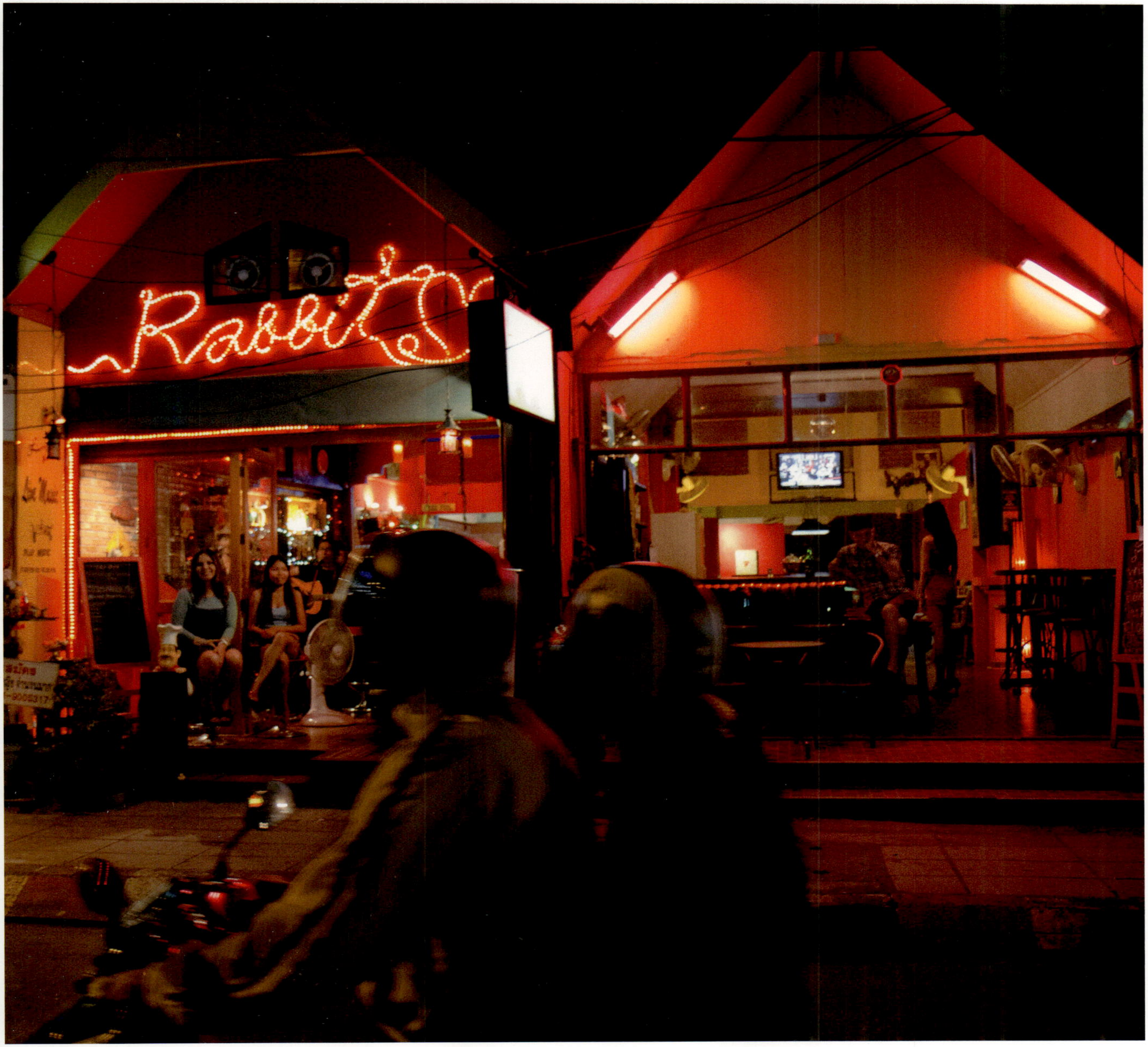
Rabbit

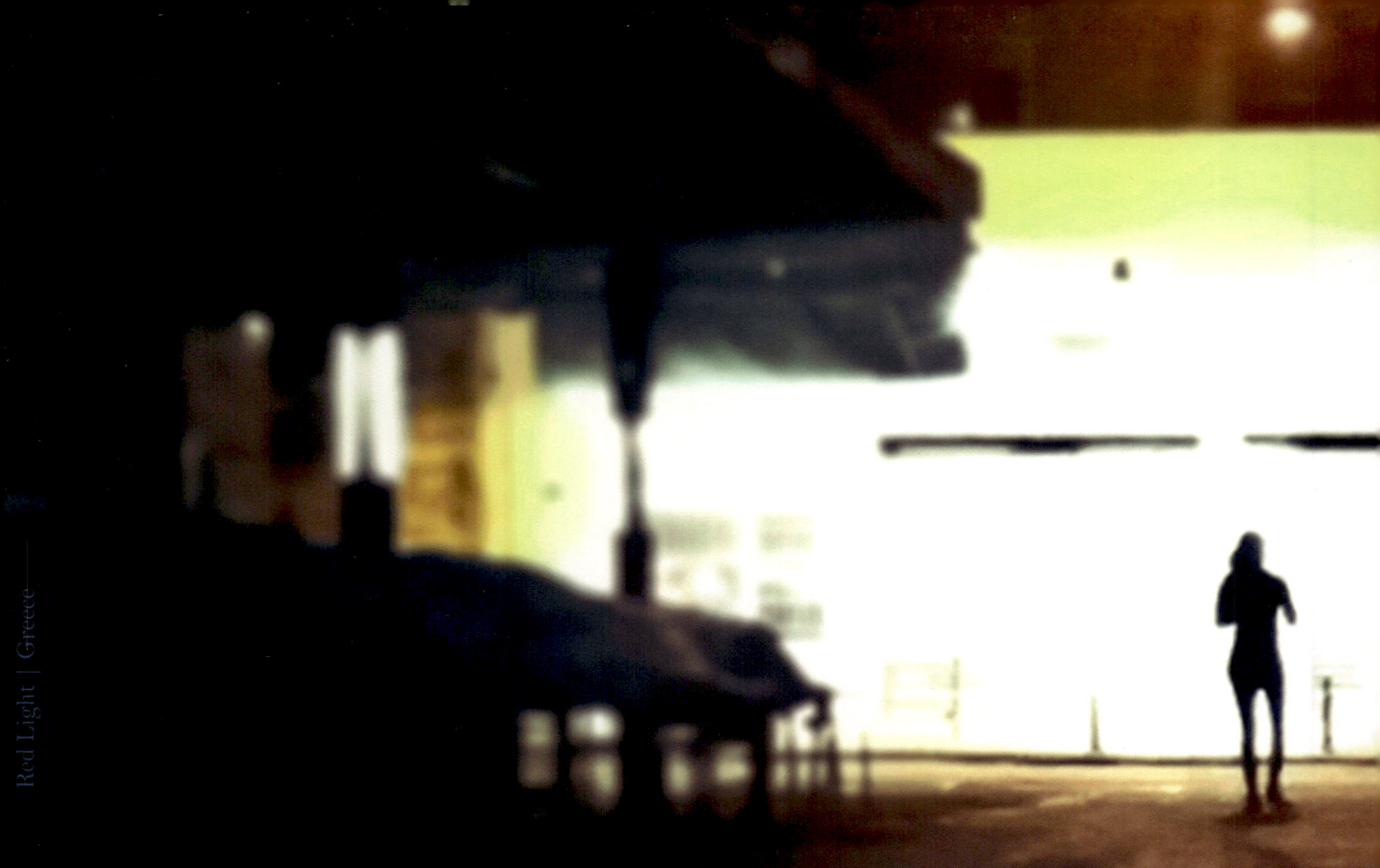

11pm: The glass doors open, a wave of heat blasts us awake as we walk out onto the crowded sidewalk. There are men everywhere; huddled together they stop their conversation to stare as we pass. We look straight ahead and ignore the comments and crude noises directed at us. As we continue on our way, the sidewalk becomes increasingly littered with needles and reeks of urine. Bodies line the street, people passed out in drunkenness while others stand or pace in various drugged-out states. As we round the corner we come upon a group of young women gathered on the side of the busy street. Cars and motorbikes slow as they pass, men staring intently – shopping. Girls as young as seventeen, almost all trafficked from Nigeria.

1am: We meet Deborah standing on the street corner like all the others, with braided hair and minimal clothing, absolutely stunning in the dim street light. Despite her appearance, a childlike innocence becomes more and more clear as we sit on the curb and talk. Men pass, but she makes no effort to catch their eyes, clearly not in the mood to work tonight. She tells us about her family, how much she misses them; how she worries she may never see them again. She begins to speak of her dream of an education, of a husband who would treat her well – of a better life than the one she is living.

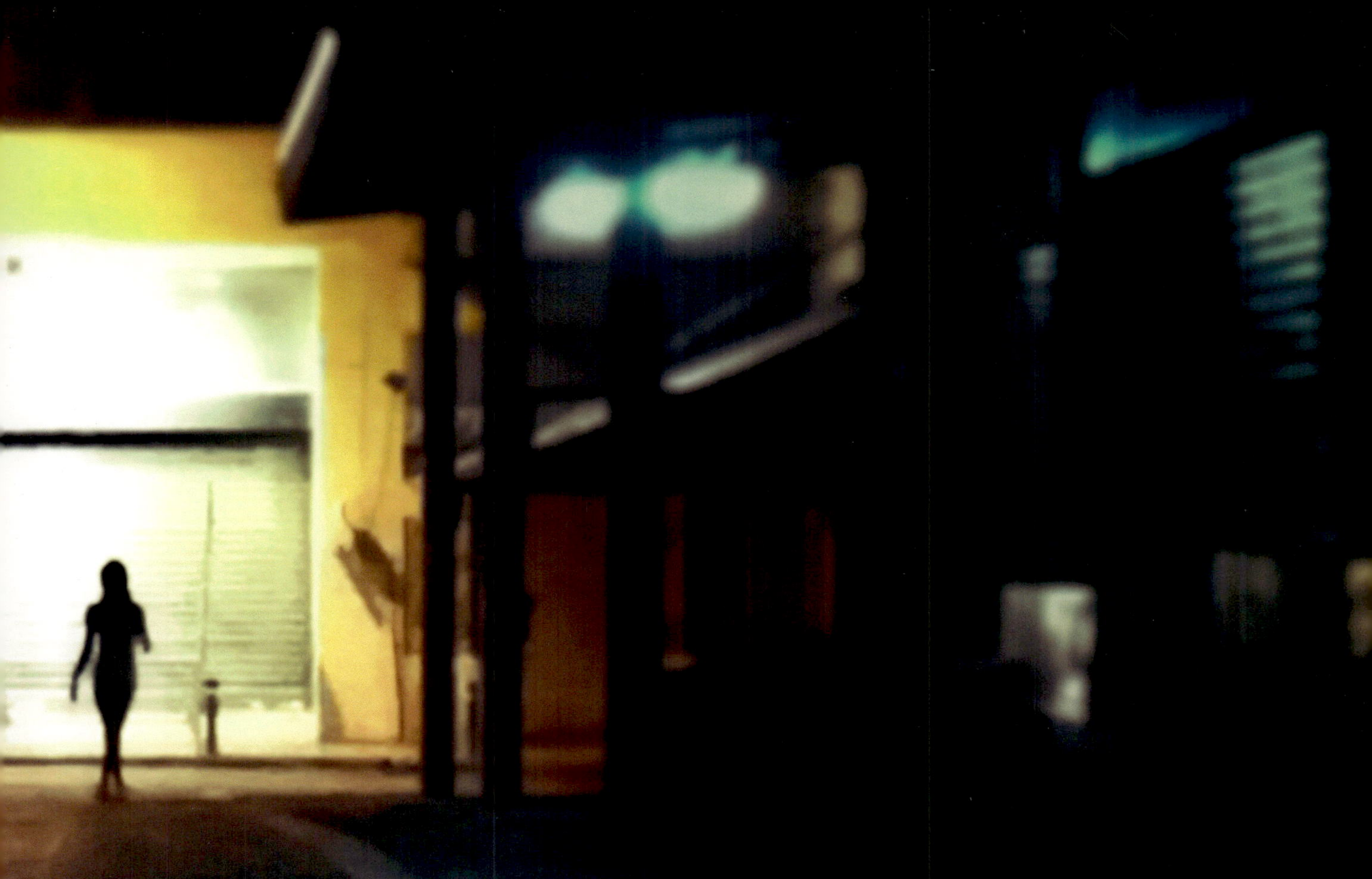

Deborah, like many of the Nigerian women in Greece, has been tricked and bonded into a life of street prostitution. Uncles, cousins, or boyfriends will present an opportunity to go to Greece and work in a "hotel," a job that will pay well and help support their families. Coming from the extreme poverty of Edo, a southern state of Nigeria, Deborah says, "It is a very tempting offer." A black magic curse referred to as the "juju," is then placed on them, binding them to future pimps and to life on the streets. We ask Deborah what will happen if she leaves the streets. She looks confused then replies, "I can never leave. The juju is too strong. My family or I will die." Deborah arrived in Greece with no documents, no money, and told she owes 50,000 euros - a debt she will never pay off. And so she stands on the street corner, night after night, bound to her cursed reality.

As of 2011, **sex trafficking** is the **2nd most profitable** illicit business globally.[23]

Born to single mothers by passing johns or sold to pimps by their desperate families, the children in the red light districts of Mumbai are viewed as a commodity, at best. Women enslaved to pimps, and pimps enslaved to money - neither can afford to view these children as anything other than potential wage earners. Minimally cared for until they reach a "working age" and completely disregarded by the government, the children of sex trafficking in India are left to fend for themselves.

From the room where these children spend their days, men can be seen walking up and down the alley looking for women of their choosing. On the ceiling, curtain rods once used to partition the area are reminiscent of the brothel it once was. Now transformed into an open space, it has become a safe haven for the children of the sex slaves, a way to get them off the streets during the day.

Though giggles erupt from every corner, there is a noticeable lack of children above the age of twelve. When they reach this age, they will be expected to pay their own way, no longer viewed by their parent or pimp as a dependent, but as an employee. They will be introduced to "the line," where their innocence will be sold for 150 Indian rupees, the equivalent of three US dollars.

In a room identical to the one they play in now, their laughter will be replaced by pleas for mercy. They will be raped, again and again. They will be broken, beaten, and exploited. They will be sold multiple times a day and expected to hand over their earnings. Born into this cycle of horror, these children become entrapped in the same harrowing fate. This is the reality of sex slavery.

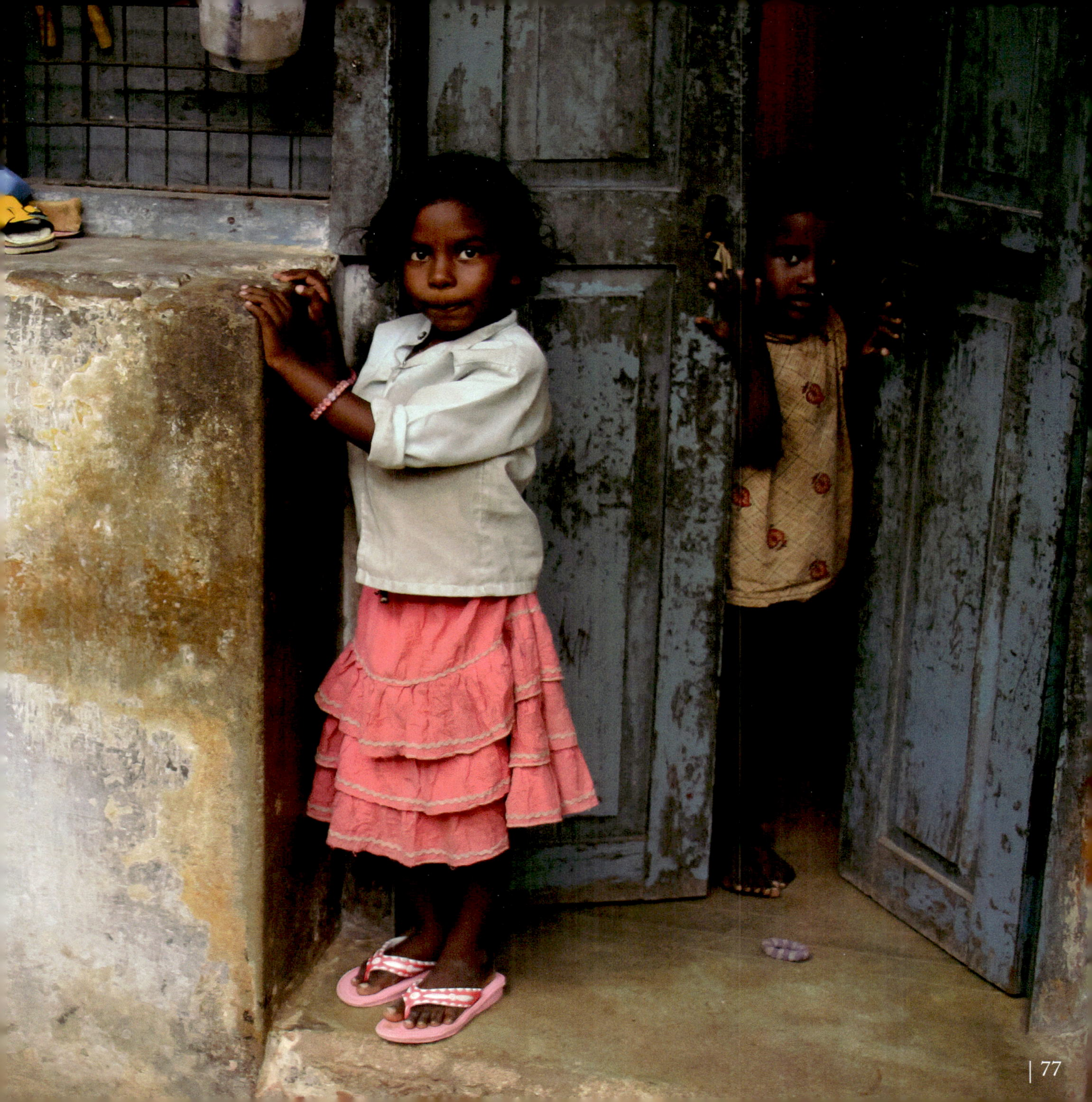

No·mad·ic

a group of people with
no fixed home, constantly
moving from place to place

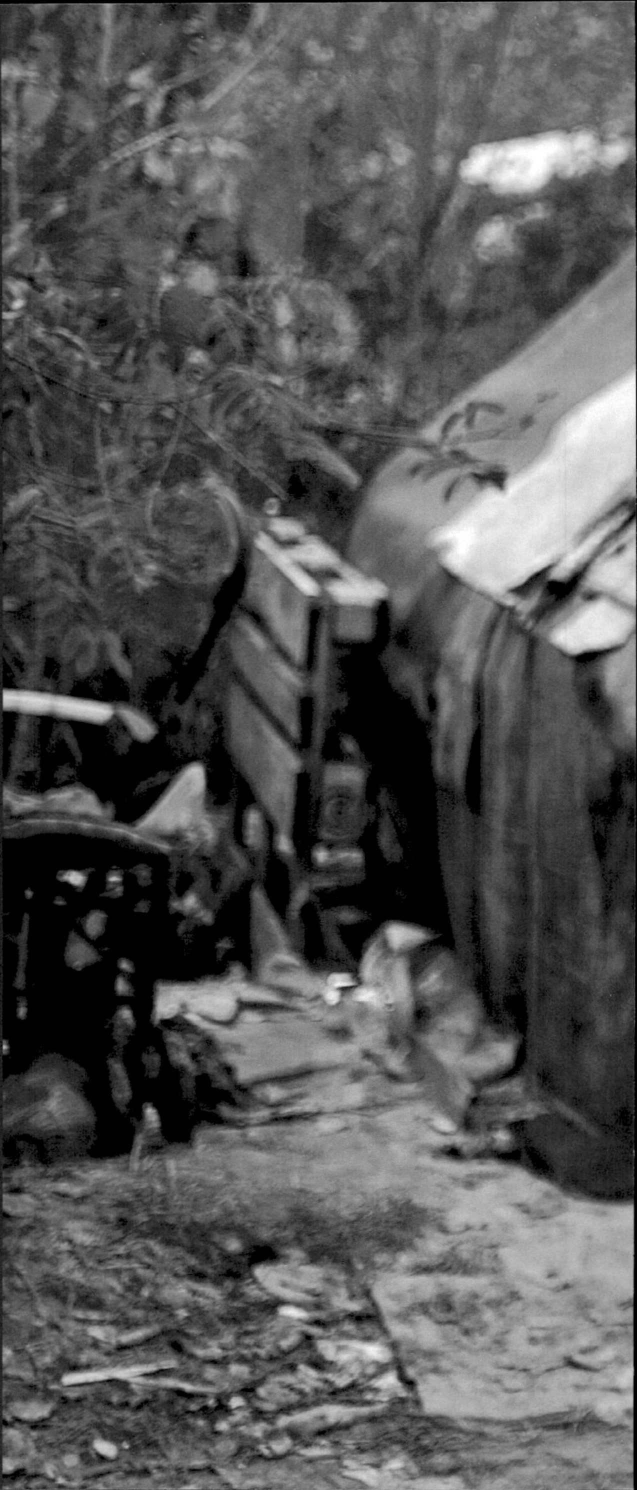

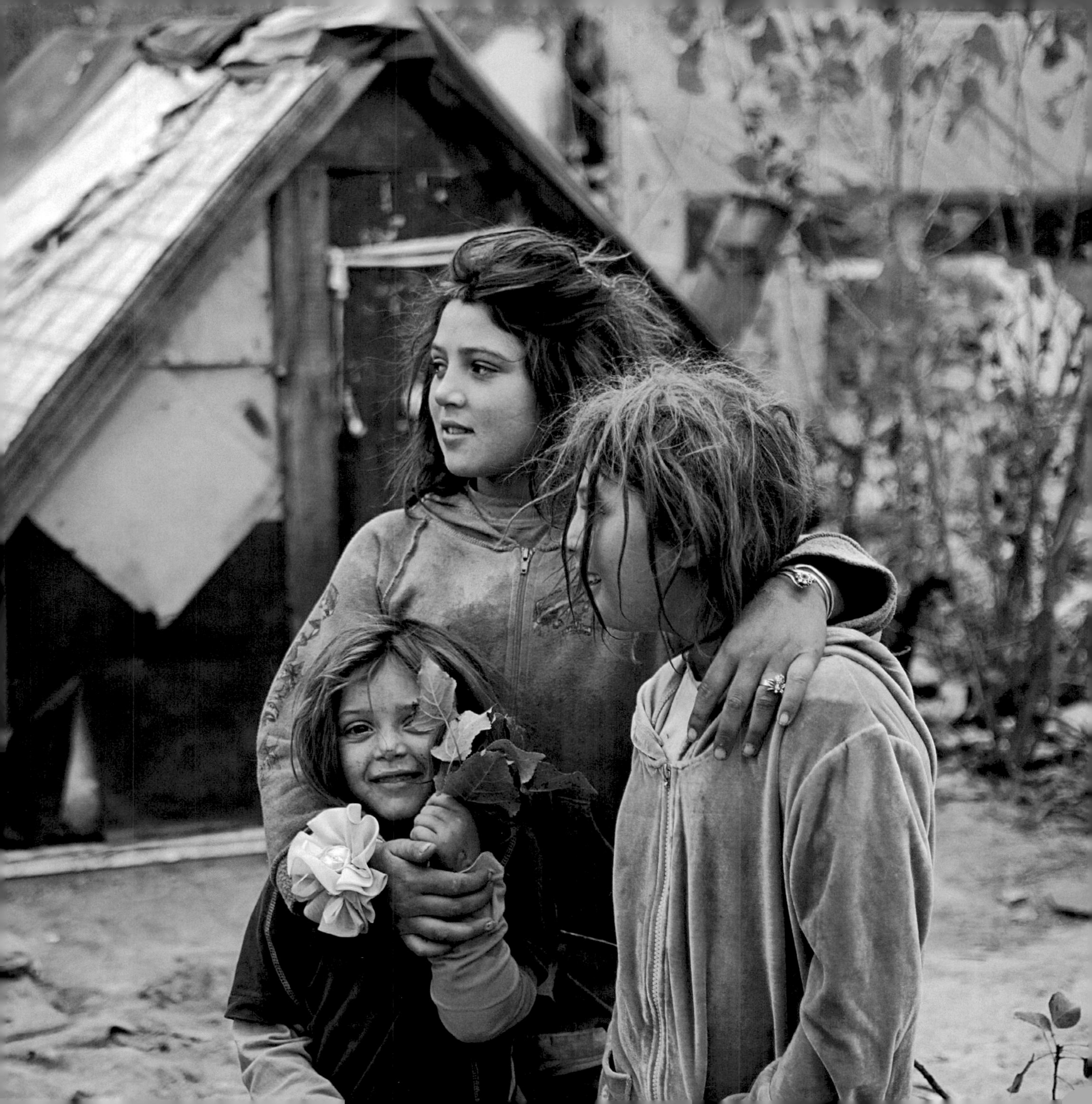

Behind the bushes and thin forestry that conceals the small village, a Gypsy community lives off the side of a highway slightly outside of Kyiv, Ukraine. As we ventured away from the muddy path, we began to see little shacks appear in the distance. The children greeted us first with wide smiles, curious eyes, and heads full of lice. Though winter was fast approaching, they wore only meager amounts of clothing and ran barefoot on top of icy grass.

In this abject and desolate area, the scattered houses were made of scrap material squandered by the Gypsies. Inside the shadowed doorway of an overcrowded and dwarfed house, was a mother with nine children and a crying newborn in her arms. The floor was littered with a mixture of trash and humble belongings. Two tiny beds with ratty blankets sat in either corner of the dwelling that was suffocating in its smallness.

How could a family of eleven survive crammed together in such a little house without heat or a place to lay their heads? These are a people disregarded because of their reputation, social class, and nomadic lifestyle. They are pushed and concealed to the outskirts of society, struggling to survive - scarcely resembling the mythical gypsies we have read about in fairy tales.

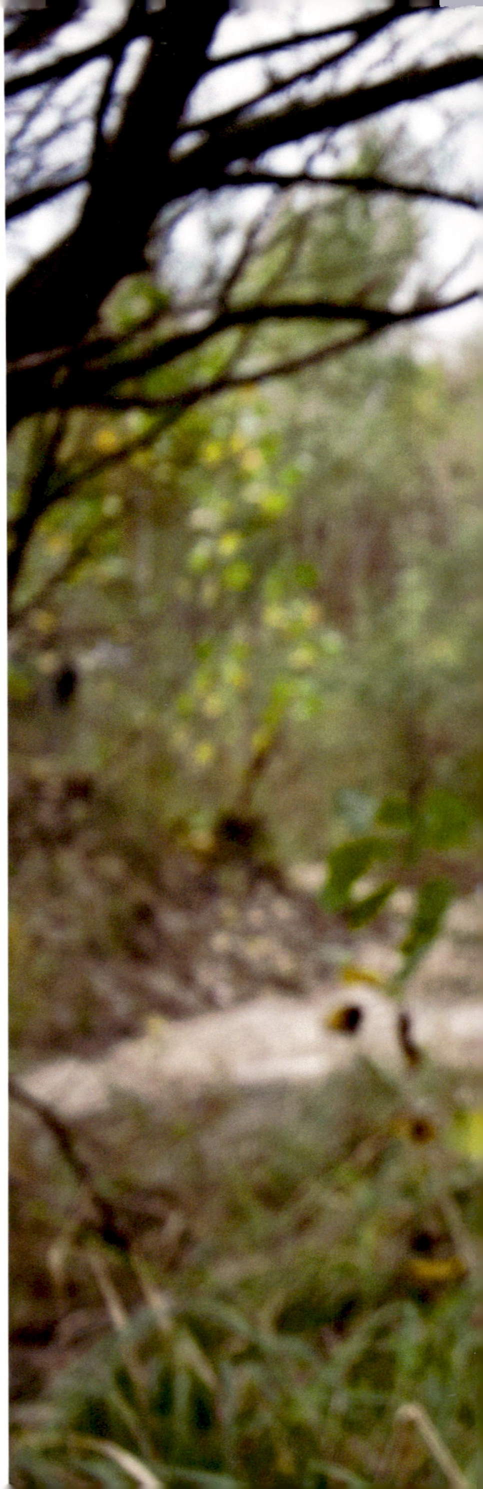

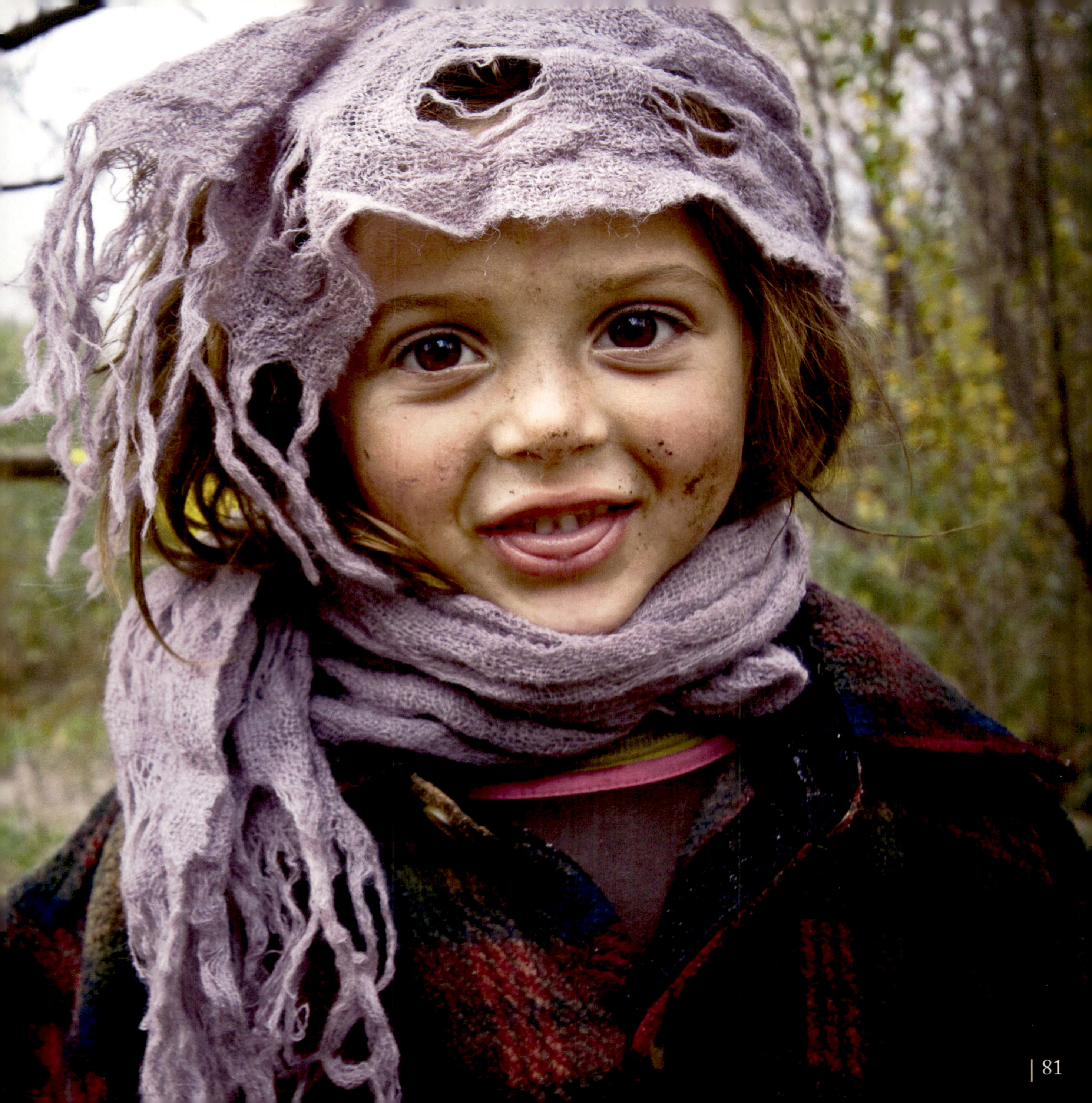

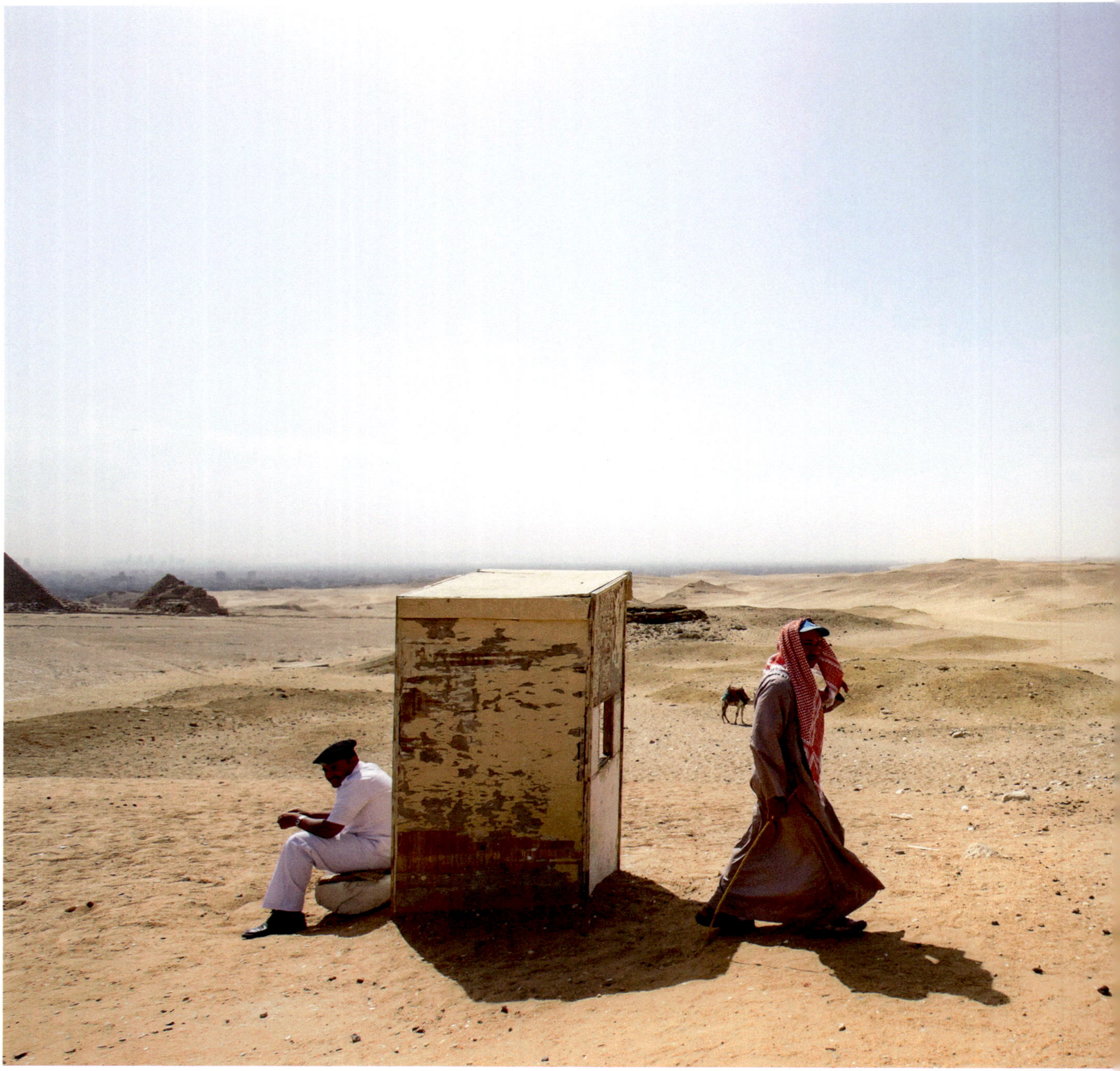

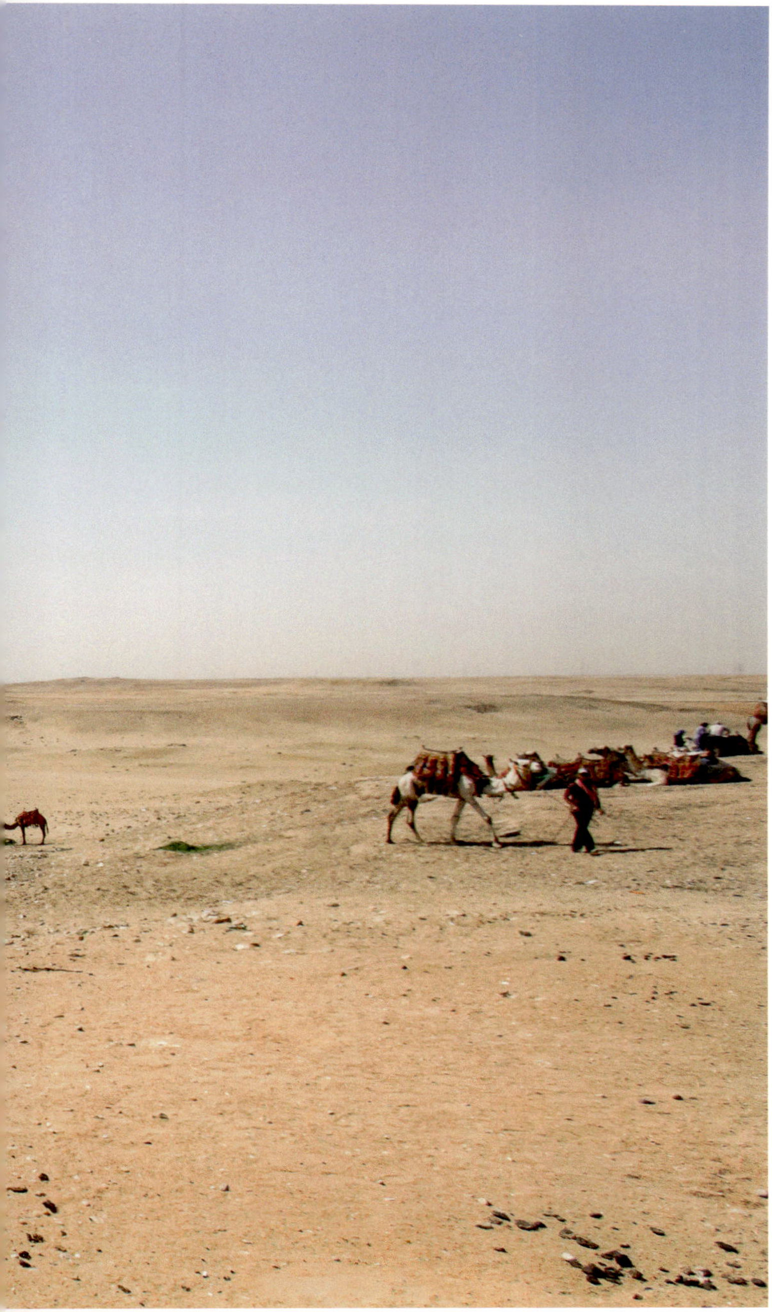

We drove deep into the night trying to make our way through the Egyptian desert to Mount Sinai for sunrise. We arrived around two in the morning, engulfed in darkness, and began hiking up the massive mountain terrain. Soon we came across a herd of camels clumsily lying on the ground off the side of the sandy path.

Out of the darkness, a Middle Eastern gypsy, known as a Bedouin, asked if we wanted a camel ride and began eagerly bargaining prices. Already exhausted and cold, a couple of us happily accepted the offer and climbed onto our camels. Abruptly lifted high into the air by the massive, graceless creatures, we began to climb the steep mountain with our new Bedouin friend, Mohammad.

As we ascended the expansive landscape, Mohammad began to describe his life as a nomad of the Sinai desert. "We are constantly on the move with our herds of camels, goats, and sheep. We have no permanent homes, so the only real attachments we have are to our families. They are all that matter."

We began to understand the depths of the commitment Bedouin have for their family when Mohammad began to speak of his children, saying proudly,

"I walk up and down this mountain seven times a day. I do it for my kids, so they don't have to."

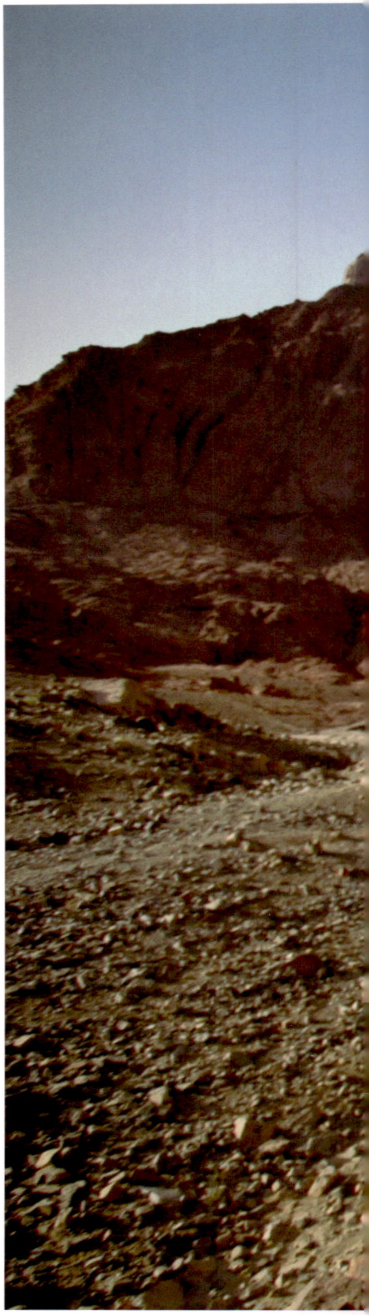

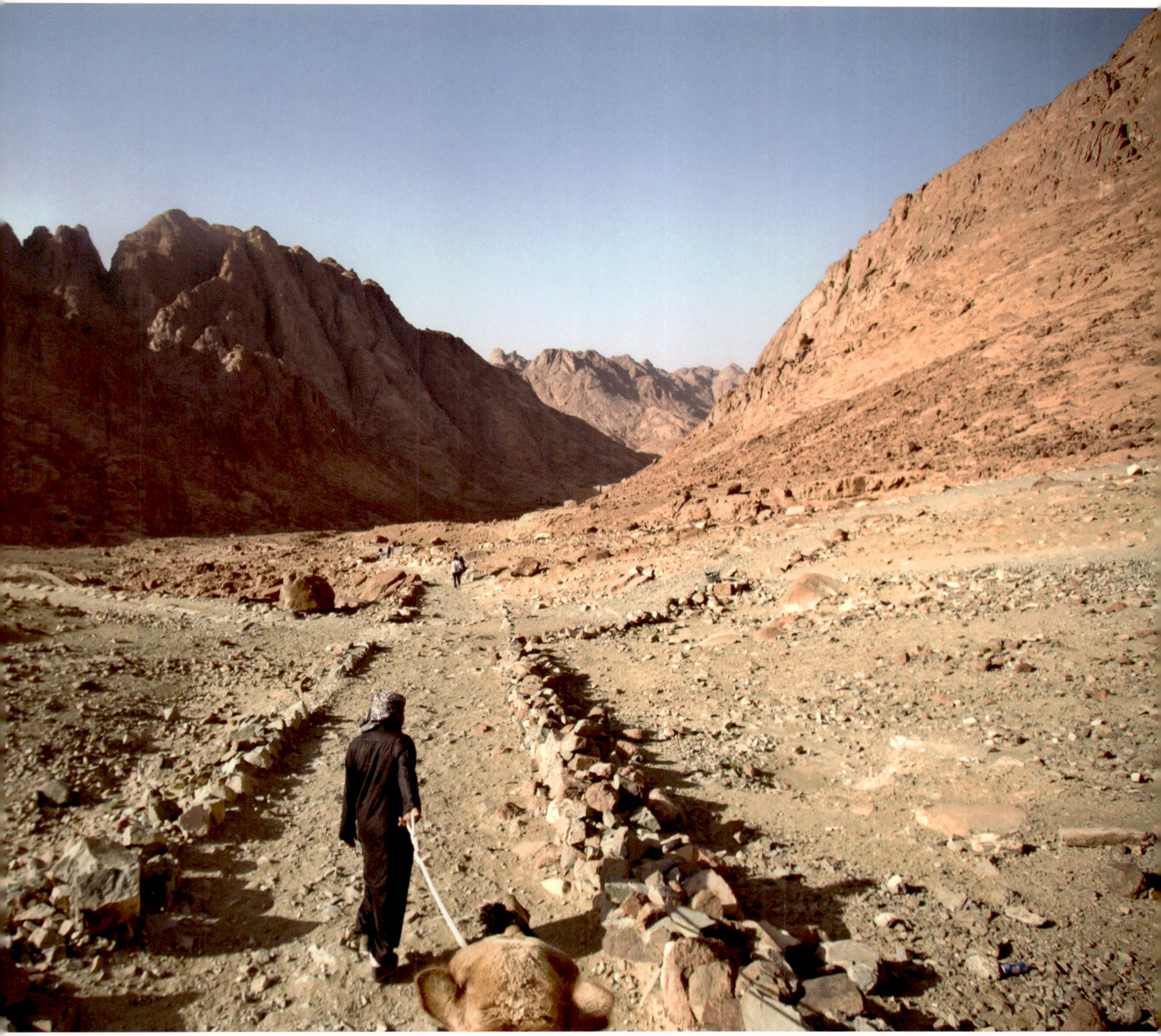

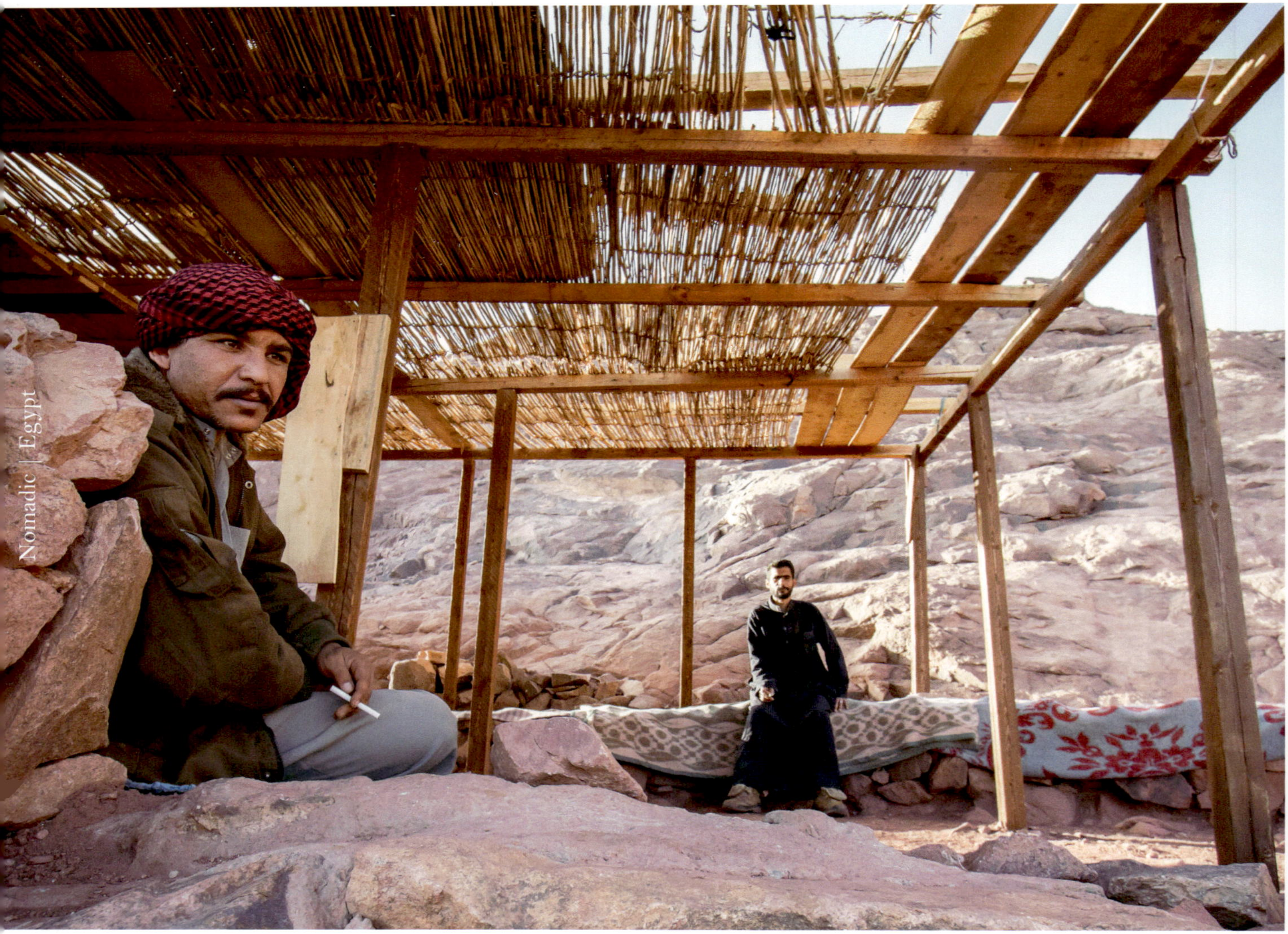

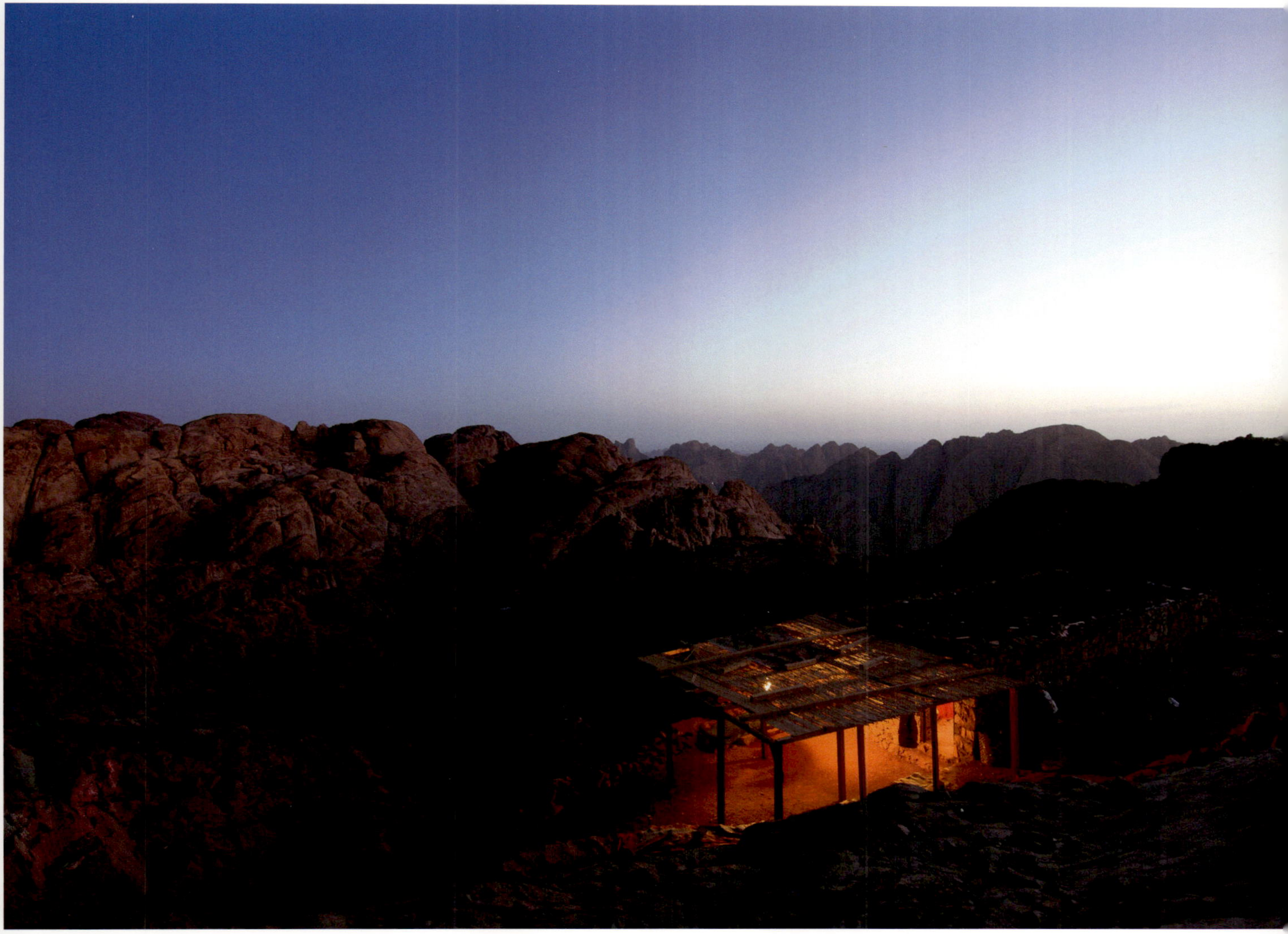

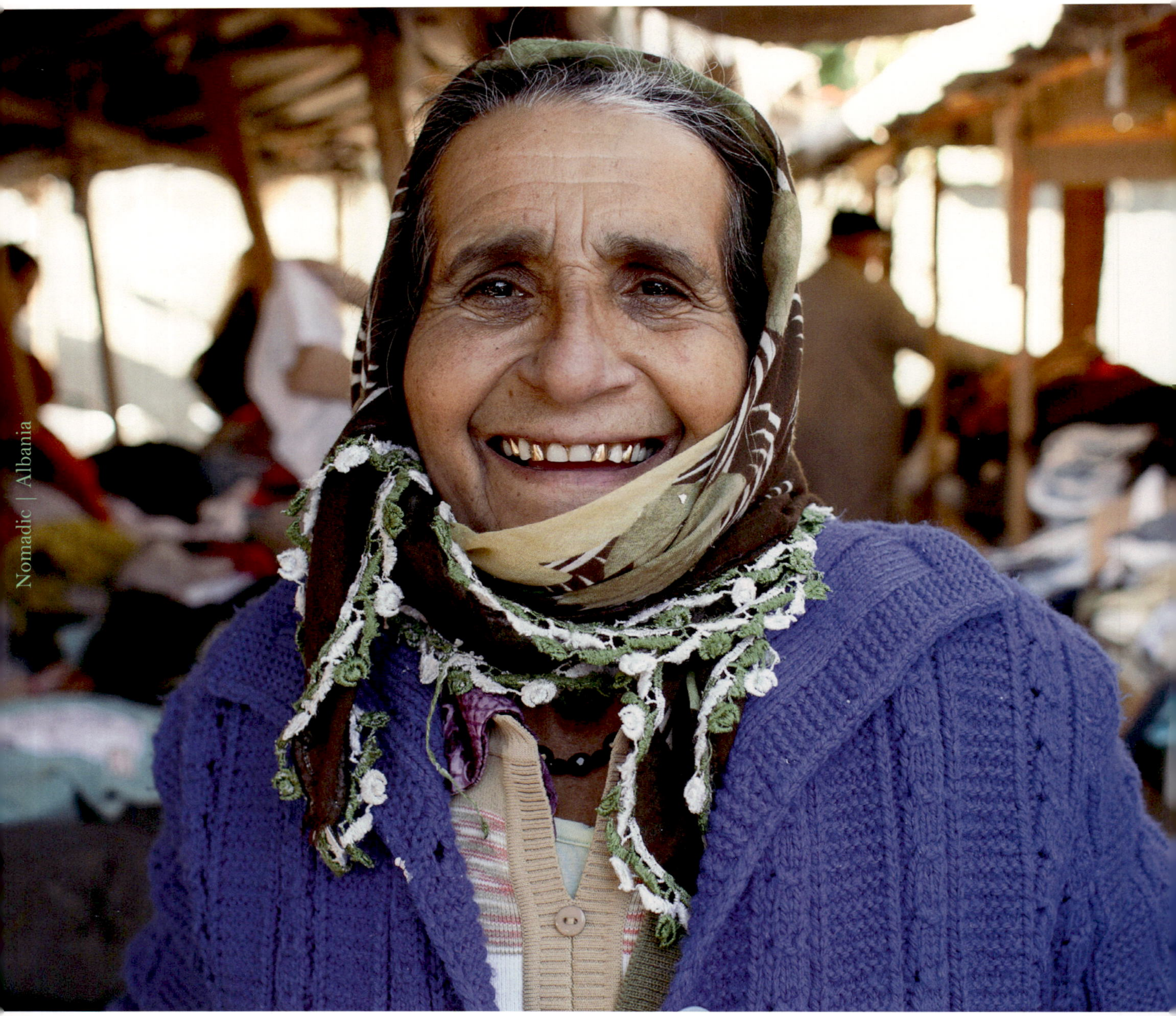

Ragi sits in the corner of the crowded room, his laugh bouncing off the enclosed walls. There is a confidence and authority about him that reaches far beyond his sixteen years. He says in a firm voice, "I wish to someday be a leader in my community, to represent my people." Knowing we want to hear more of his story, he looks our way and smiles, "First, I must start by explaining who we are."

Ragi is an Albanian Romani, known to most of the Western world as a Gypsy. "During the reign of communism," Ragi begins, "we were forced into a stationary lifestyle after years of surviving as nomads. Now in the rise out of communism, we have become a settled people still living within a nomadic mindset, struggling to move forward while staying true to our culture."

Most Romas are pressured into arranged marriages by the time they are thirteen; they are pulled out of school and pushed into life as a husband or wife. It is a tradition that perpetuates illiteracy and results in unemployment. "In turn this causes the poverty we find ourselves stuck in." Ragi says, "I have already resisted two arranged marriages. I want to stay in school, to complete high school and even university if I can, but it's not going to be easy." He is the only Roma in his school, facing racial violence and discrimination from his Albanian classmates. Alongside the pressure from his family to quit, Ragi states,

"The opposition is overwhelming at times, but I am determined. I want my children to have more opportunities and support than I do. Some parts of our culture need to change if we are going to thrive, but this will not happen with just one. It will take many more to change the way we live and think."

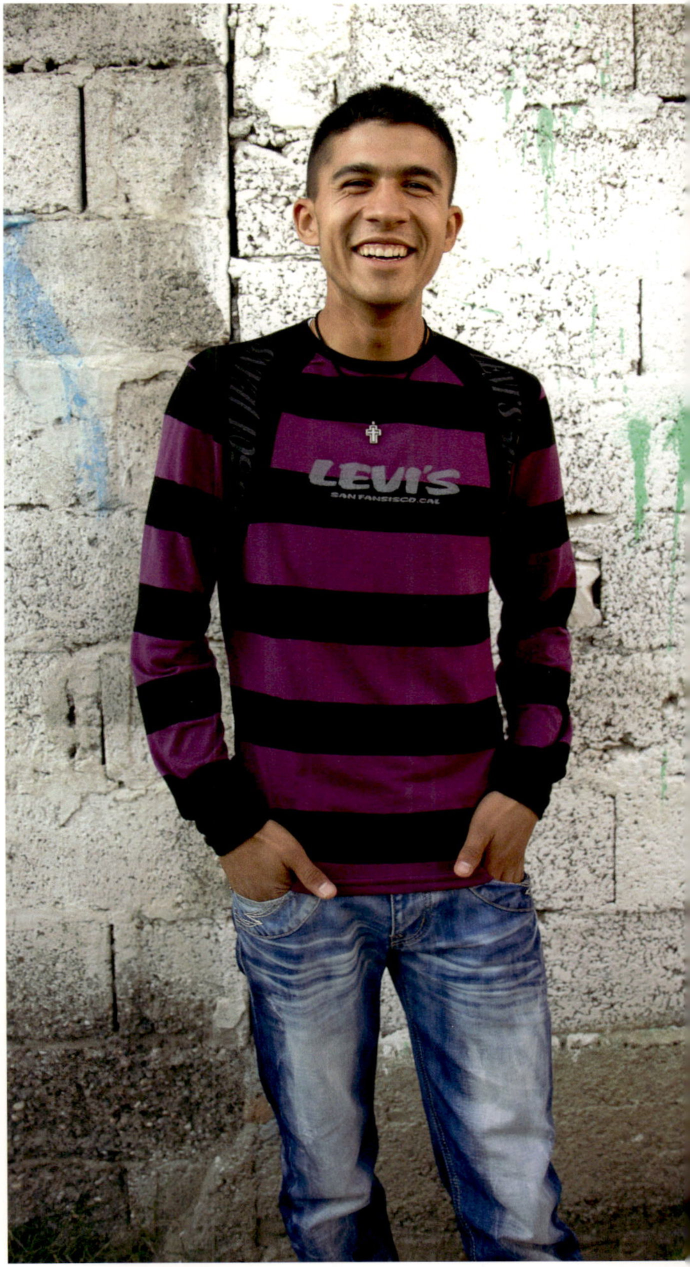

Slums

heavily populated urban areas characterized by substandard housing and squalor

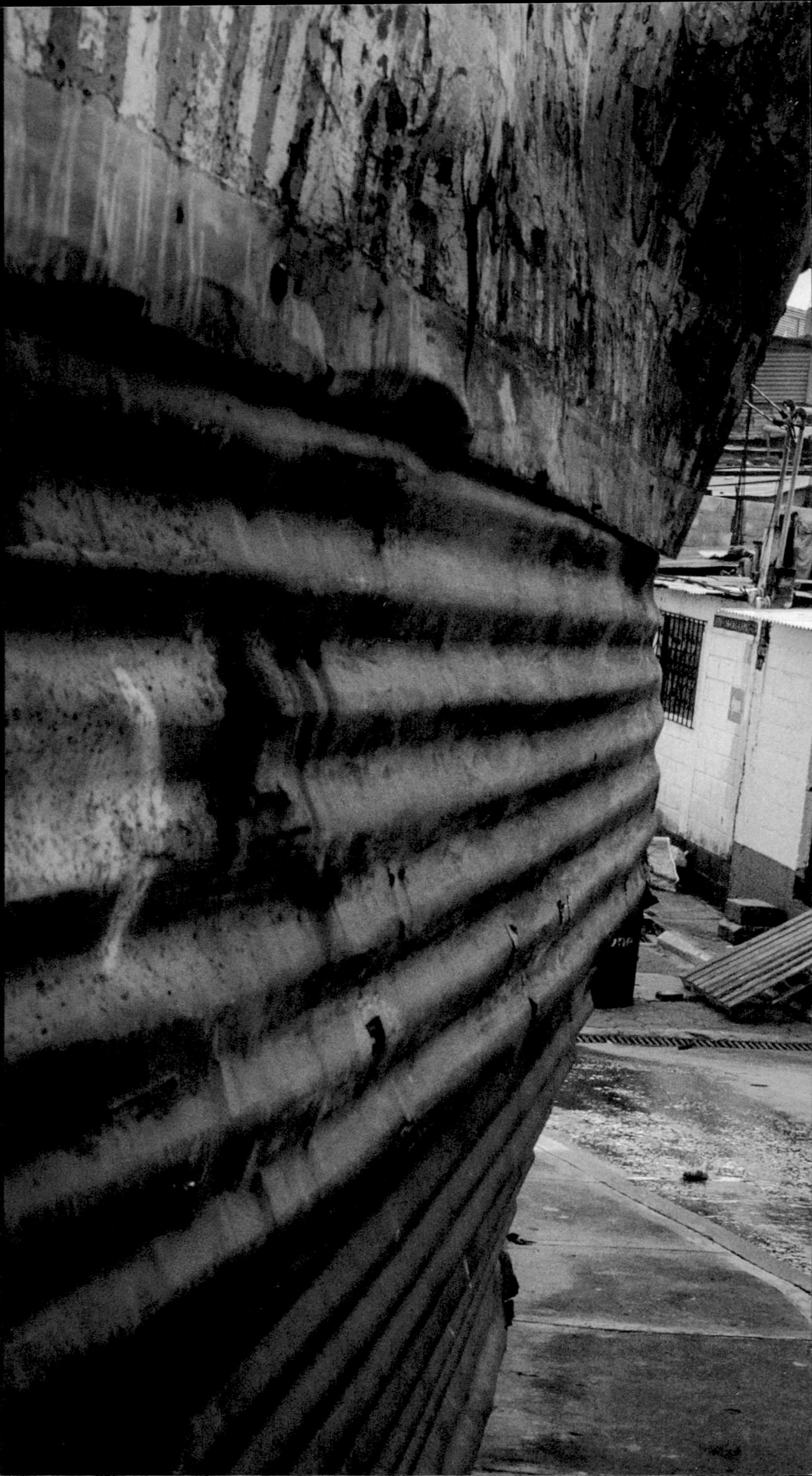

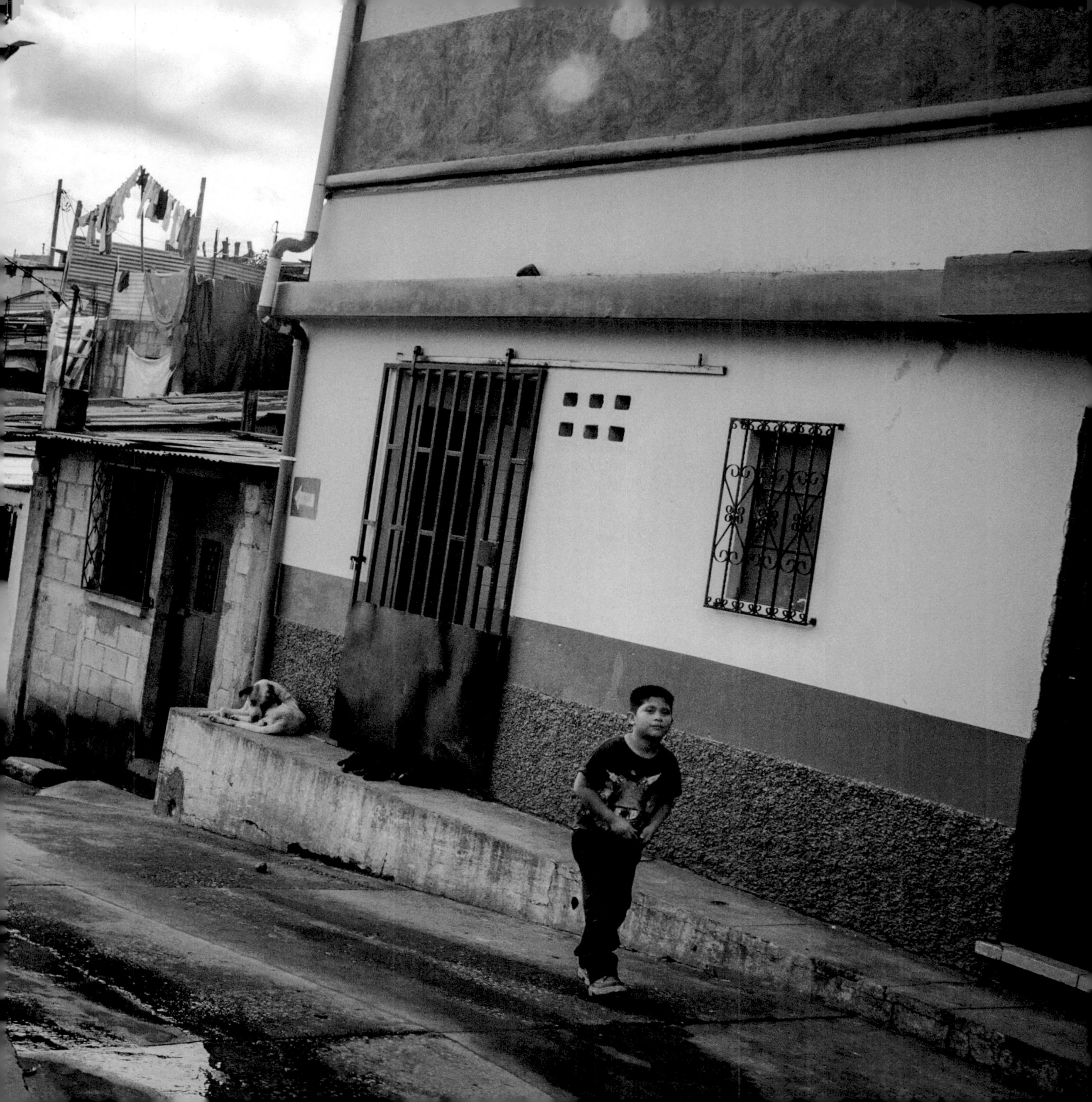

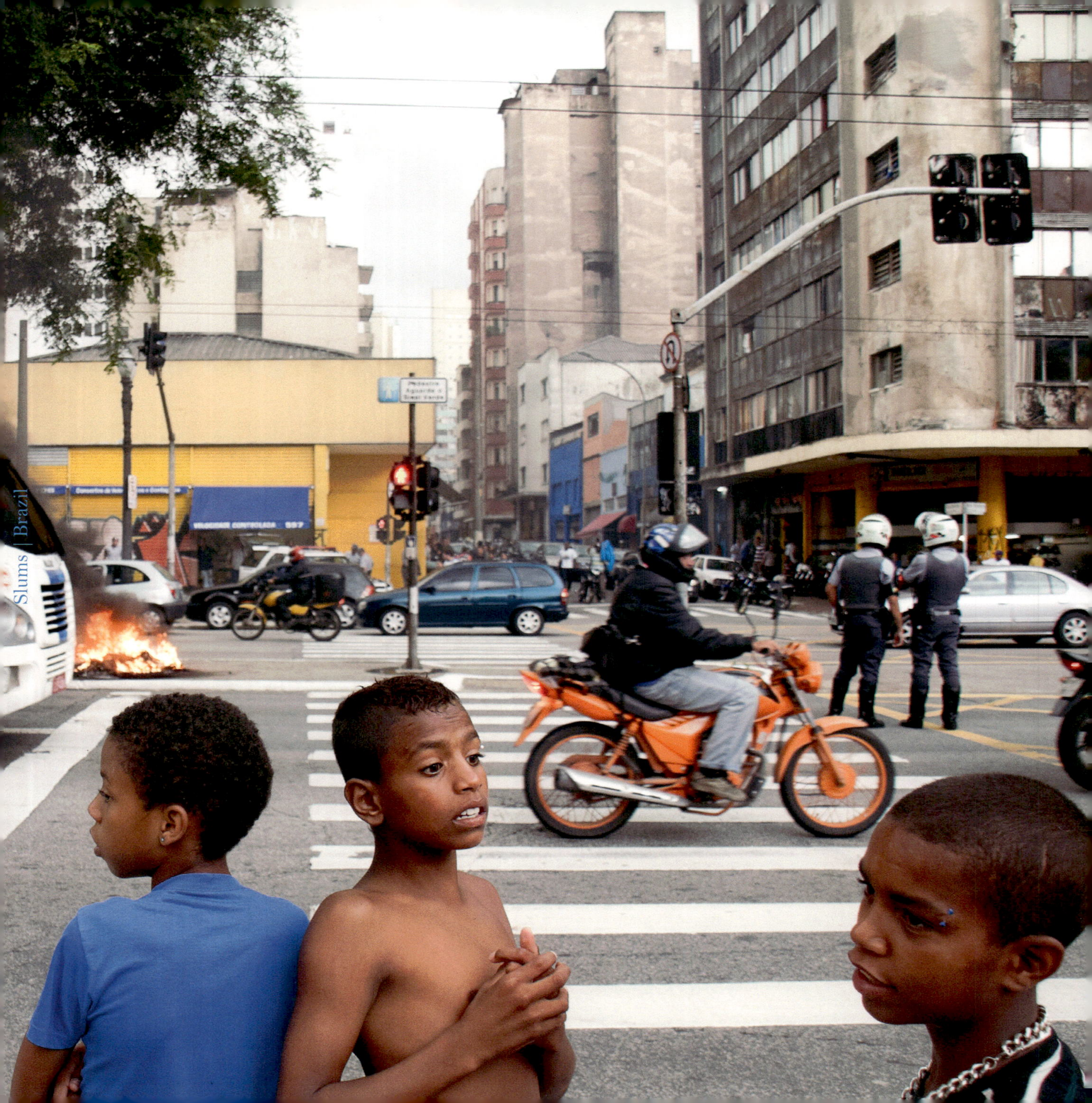

Children as young as nine to adults well into their fifties line the streets. They are skin and bone, teeth rotted by the copious amount of drugs they have inhaled. Their sockets are deep, housing eyes that stare into the void as we pass.

Found in the center of the city of São Paulo, Brazil, Cracolândia is known for widespread drug trafficking and use, squatters, homelessness, and prostitution. Within a corner of the slum is a place squatters gather and set up makeshift homes in deserted buildings. It is here we watch as a twelve-year-old boy melts down black tar heroin into a rusty spoon with a torch lighter. His eyes are fixated on the liquefying substance as he tries to steady his shaky hand. He loads his syringe and ties the tourniquet around his arm. Surveying his skin for a few seconds he finds a protruding vein and sticks it without hesitation. As the drug travels through his bloodstream his whole body convulses, mouth beginning to foam. He rocks back and forth on his chair, straining to see what is behind him. He suddenly gets up, shakes his head, walks in small circles, sits back down, and then repeats the cycle. As hallucinations begin to invade his mind, he visibly drifts in and out of reality.

This is routine life in Cracolândia, where the gangs and drug dealers that control the area supply children a few free hits so they quickly become addicted. It is not long before the desperation to obtain their next fix leads these young adolescents to do whatever the dealers demand in exchange for drugs and protection. Their addictions lead them into a web of violence, prostitution, and severe poverty, all within this six-block radius of misery.

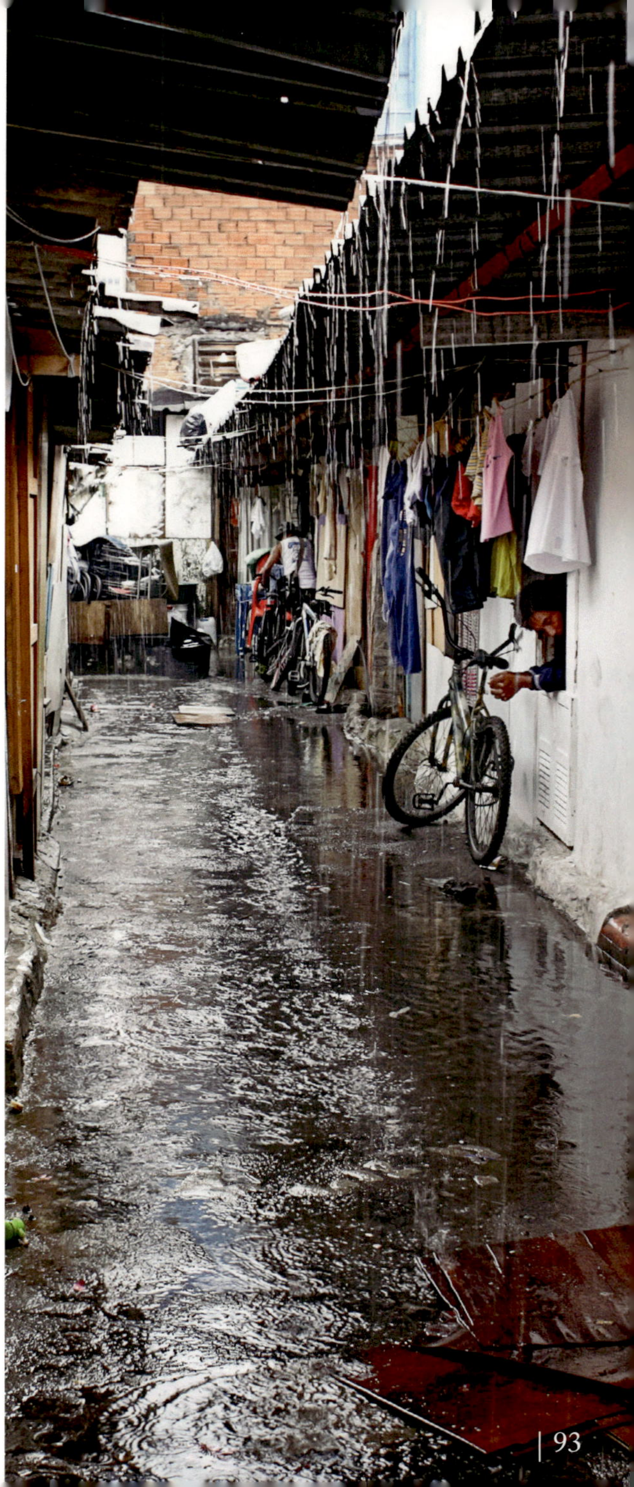

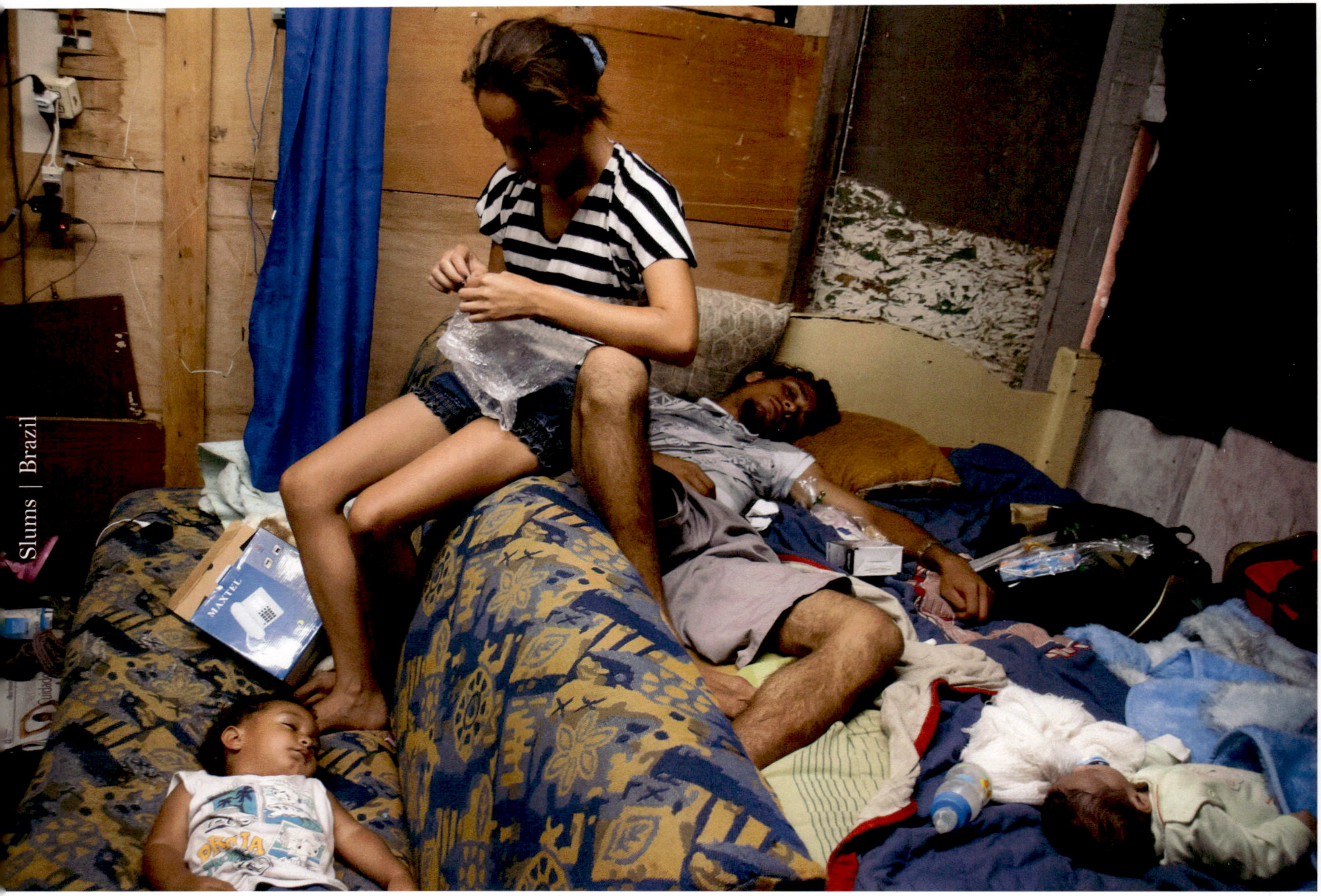

"A slum is not a chaotic collection of structures; it is a dynamic collection of individuals who have figured out how to survive in the most adverse of circumstances."

-Kalpana Sharma, Journalist

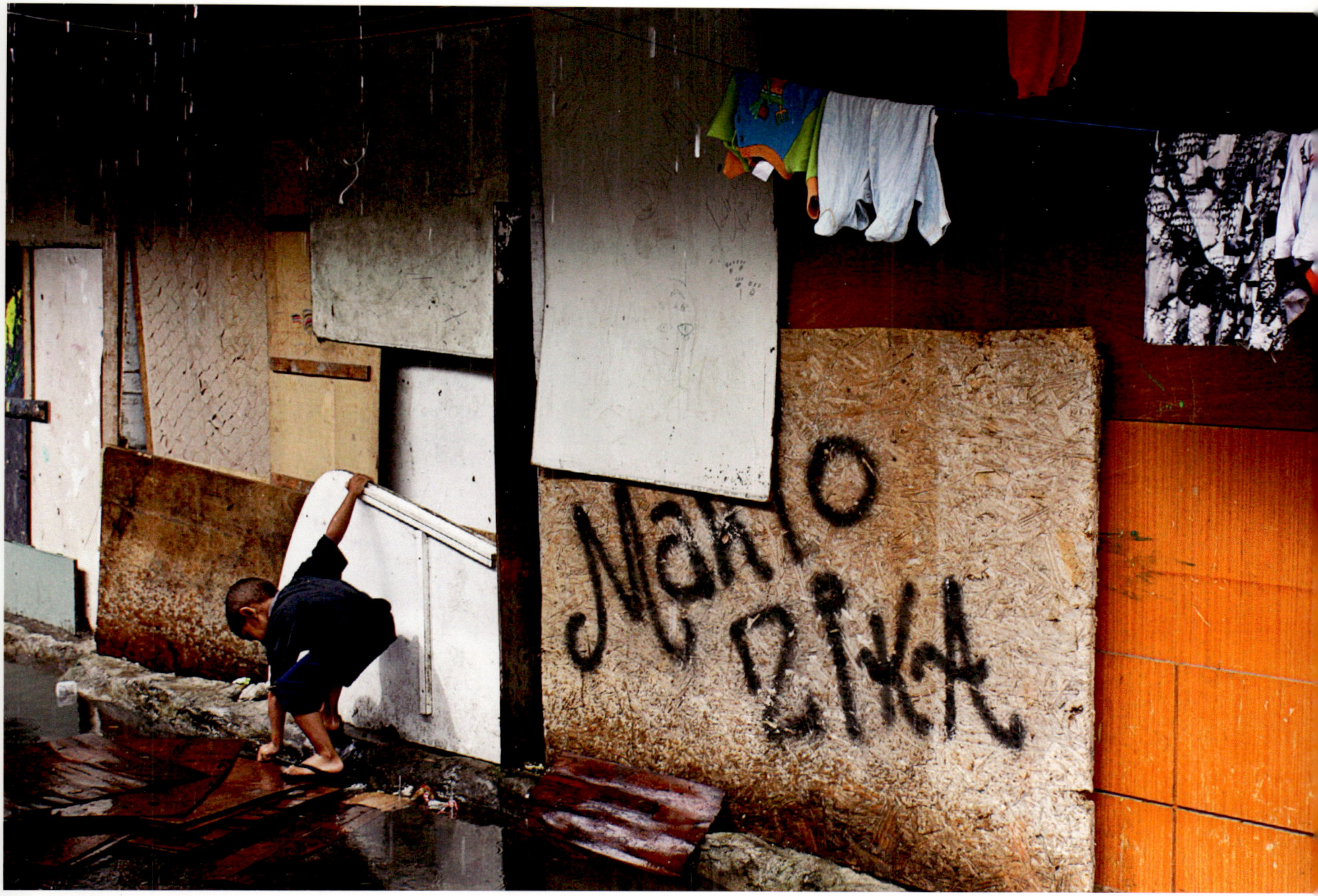

One out of every three city dwellers – **nearly a billion people** – **live in a slum** and that number is **expected to double** in the next 25 years.[24]

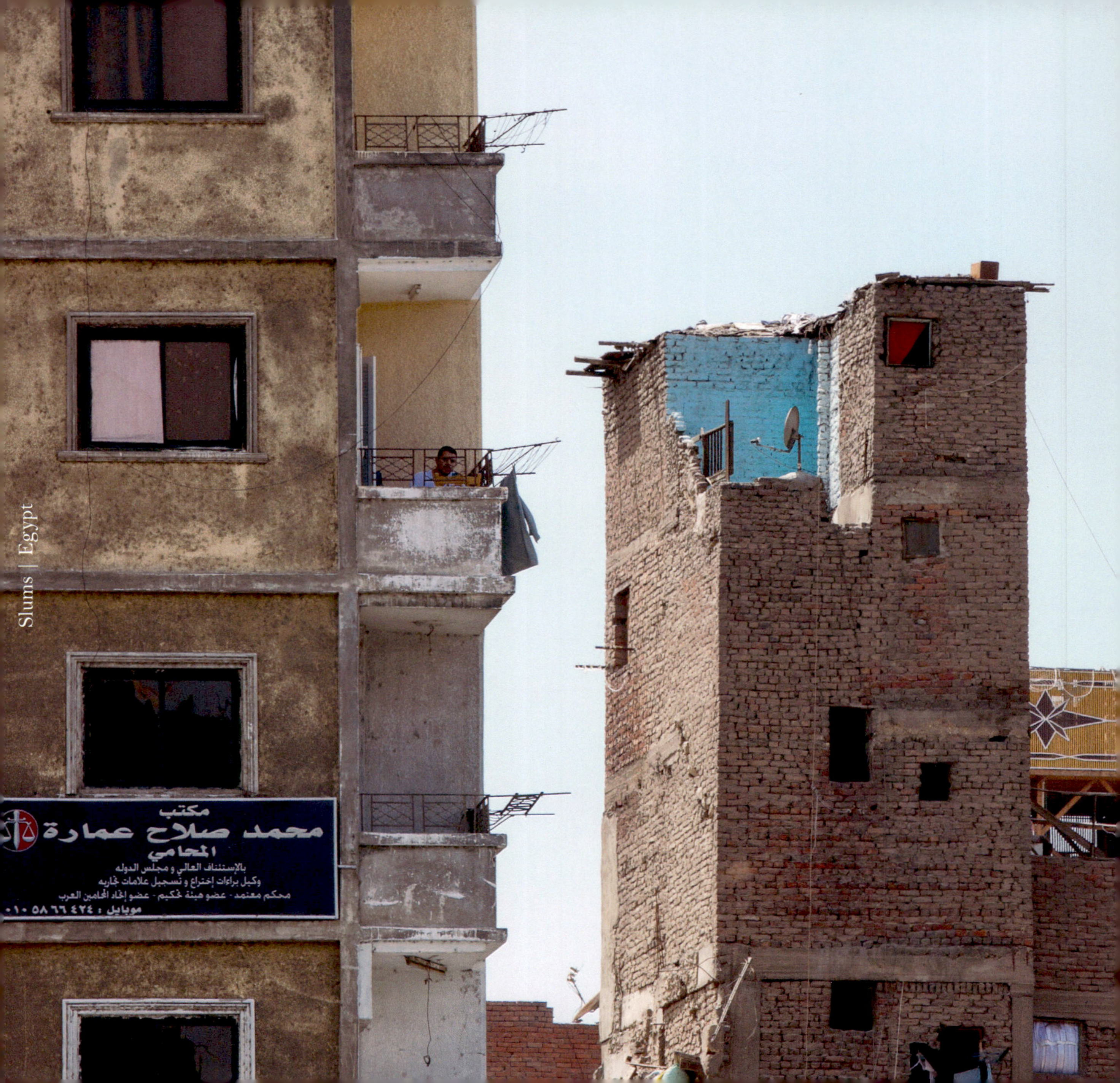
مكتب
محمد صلاح عمارة
المحامي
بالإستئناف العالي و مجلس الدوله
وكيل براءات إختراع و تسجيل علامات تجاريه
محكم معتمد - عضو هيئة تحكيم - عضو إتحاد المحامين العرب
موبايل : ٠١٠٥٨٦٦٤٢٤

The stench is almost unbearable, rising with the heat in waves. Garbage is all that can be seen, stacked in the streets, piled as high as the buildings, overflowing from an endless source. Though just a few miles from the Great Pyramids of Giza, this area remains unseen by most.

Magdy's words are full of emotion as he speaks of Manshiyat Naser, Arabic for "Garbage City." As Cairo's largest slum, it is home to the Zabbaleen, those who collect and sort the city's garbage as a means to survive. Magdy sighs, "The Zabbaleen don't know anything else. They have no way of knowing or seeing another way of life. The Western world is so driven by materialism, by a hunger for more...always more. There is no such thing here."

In passing, we see families in rooms waist high with trash, sorting the unsellable from the sellable. "This has been their way of life for years, a cycle passed down the generations." Magdy explains, "If they can make enough to get by today, to feed their children a meal, then they are happy. This home is all they will ever know."

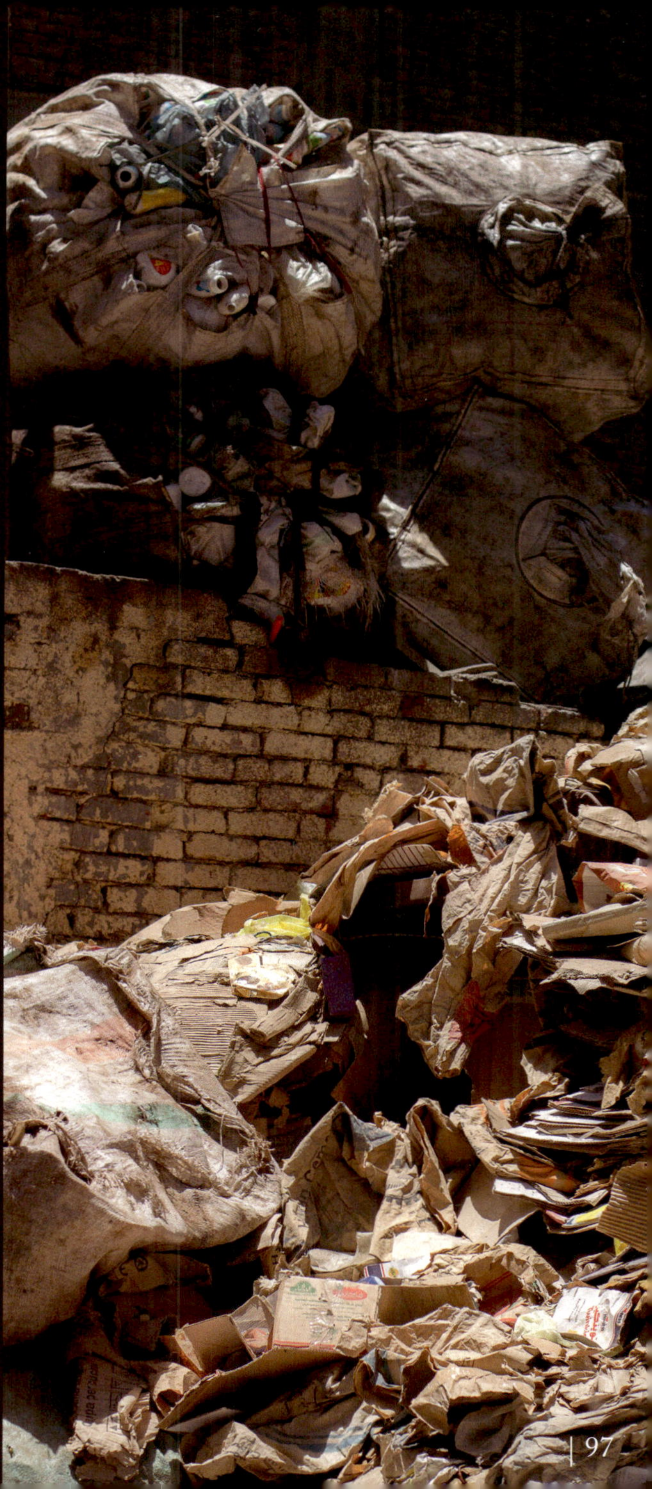

A·bus·ive

causing mental, emotional or physical injury to another

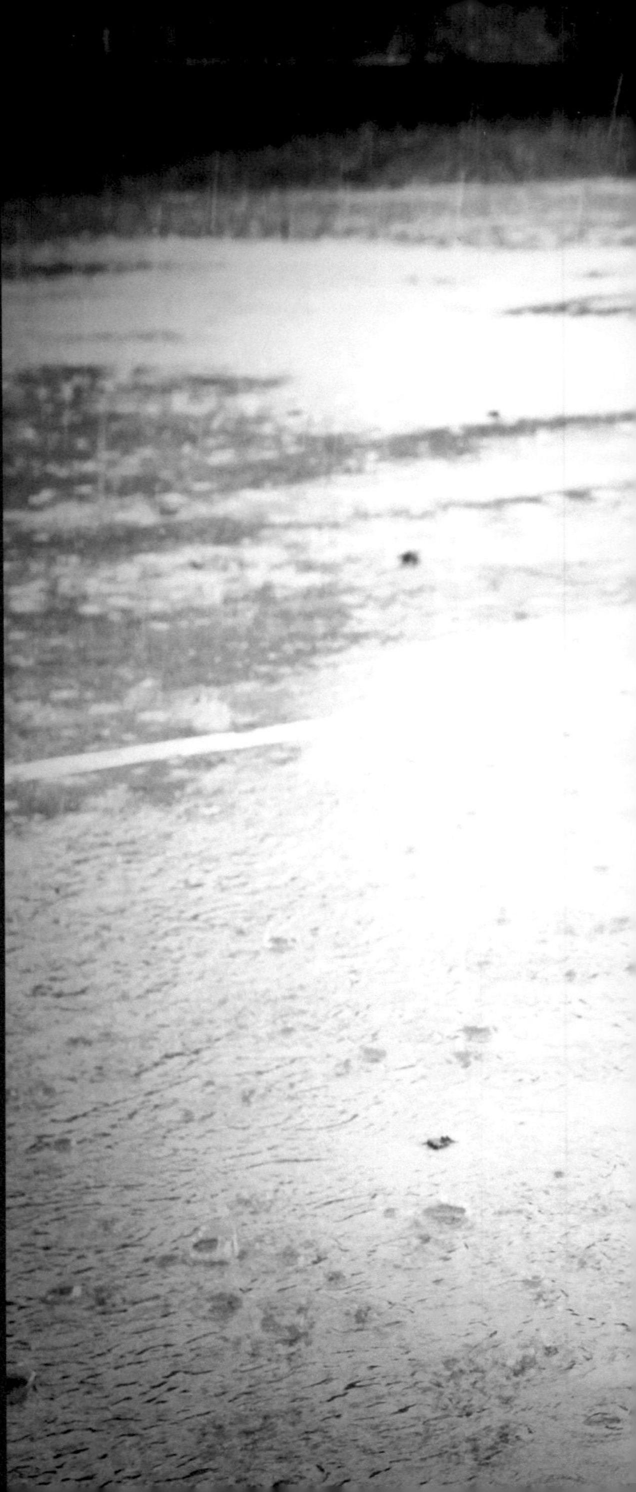

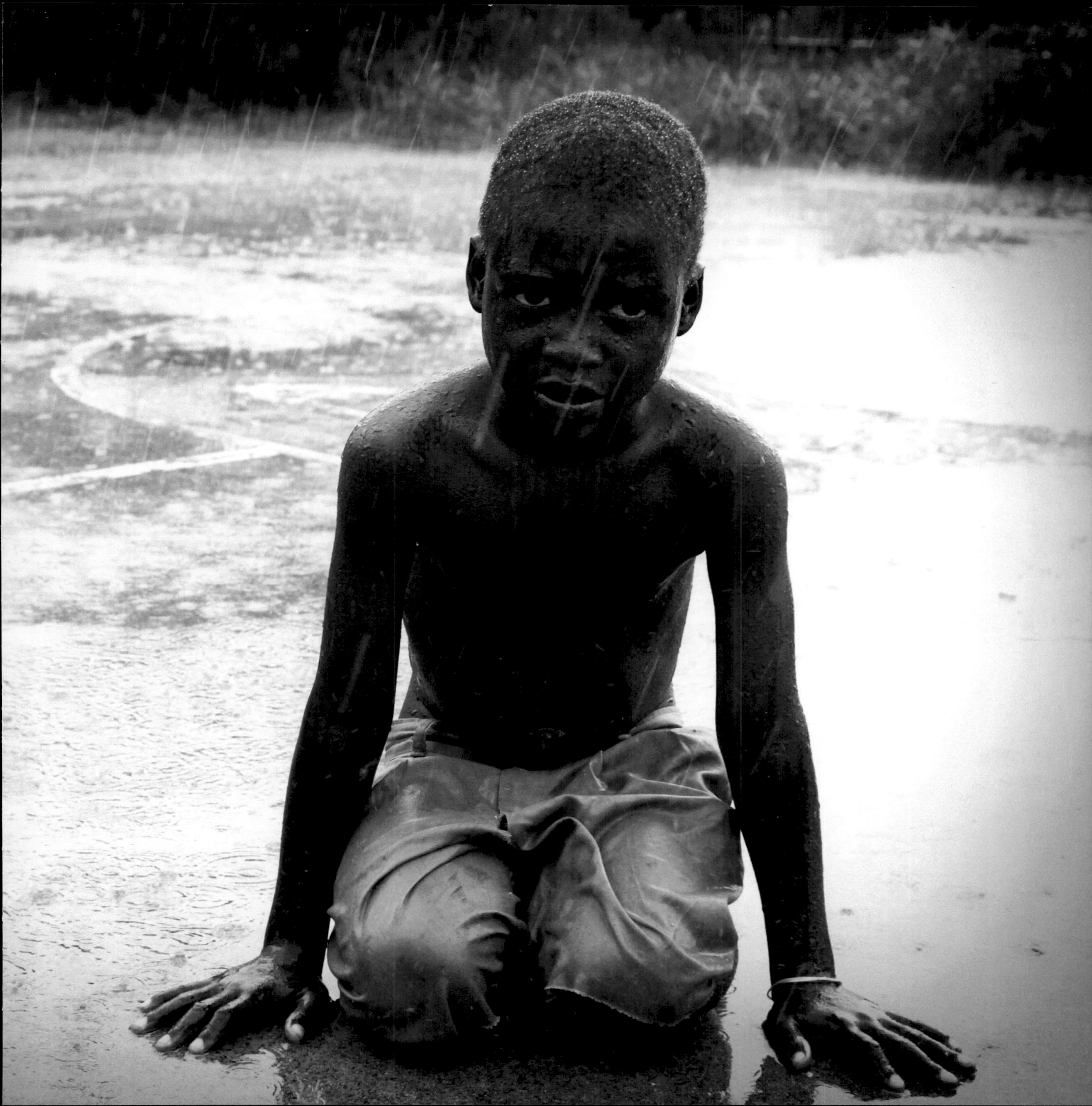

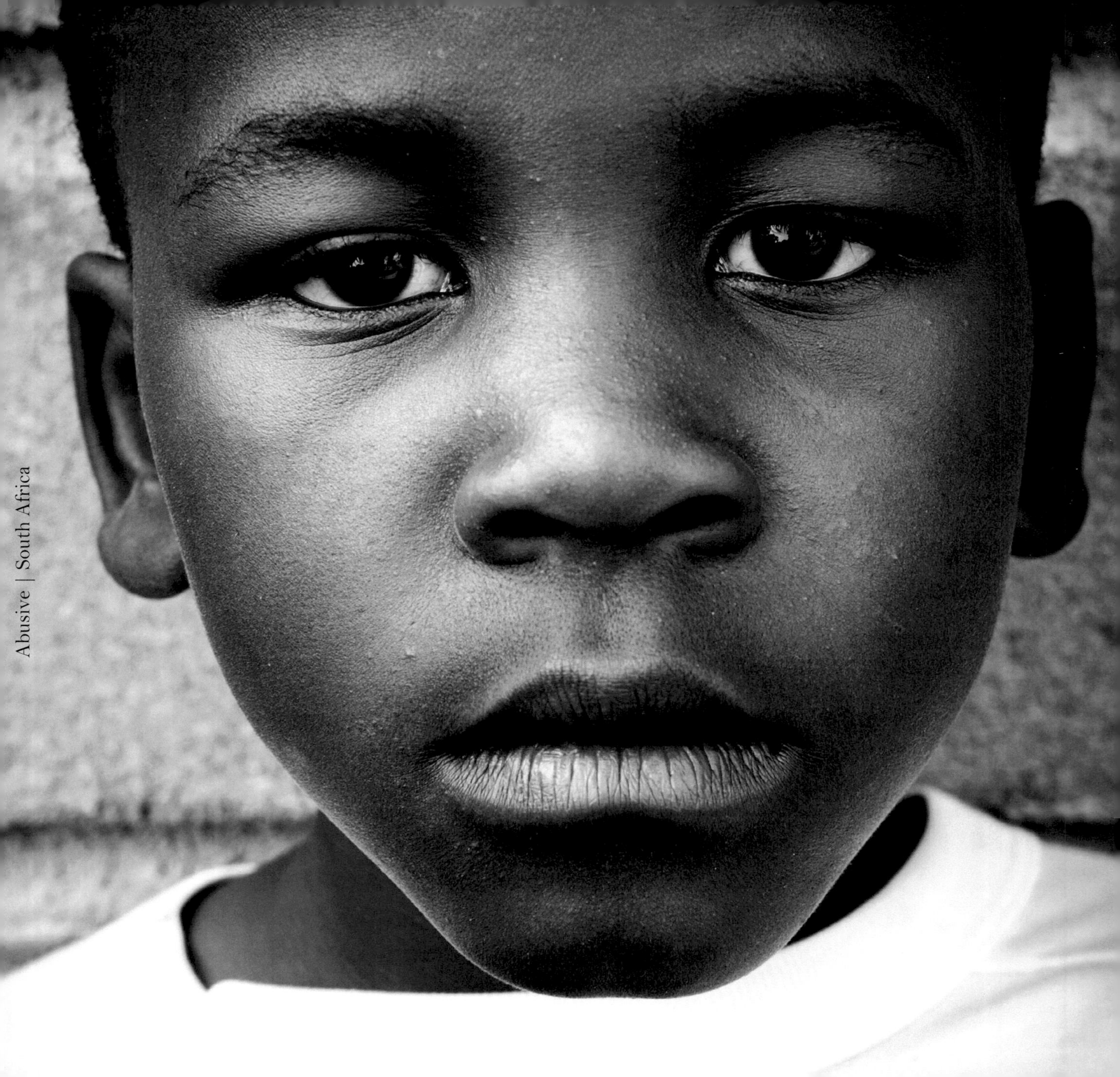

Abusive | South Africa

The mountains were lush and the streets were dusty, uneven, and scattered with modest homes made of cinder block and tin. As we explored the landscape of South Africa, we became focused on a family across the street.

A young boy was running in circles around his mother, joyfully entertaining himself. When he abruptly stopped and began to cry for her attention, her swift hand landed him flat on his back in a matter of seconds. She bent over and began to hit and punch the child. The teenage boy sitting nearby broke out into laughter as he observed the scene unfolding in front of him.

There appeared to be a normalcy to this moment that surpassed our understanding. The circumstance of their lives is one of accepted abuse, both given and taken - abuse that is seemingly deserved and casually laughed at.

Pain breeds pain and abuse begets abuse. It is a cycle for those who have been in it, one they may not even identify as harmful or destructive. When violence is the only language someone has learned, can we expect them to speak differently?

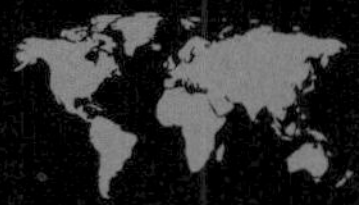

Worldwide, approximately **40 million children** are **subjected to child abuse** each year.[25]

Philippines | Ethiopia

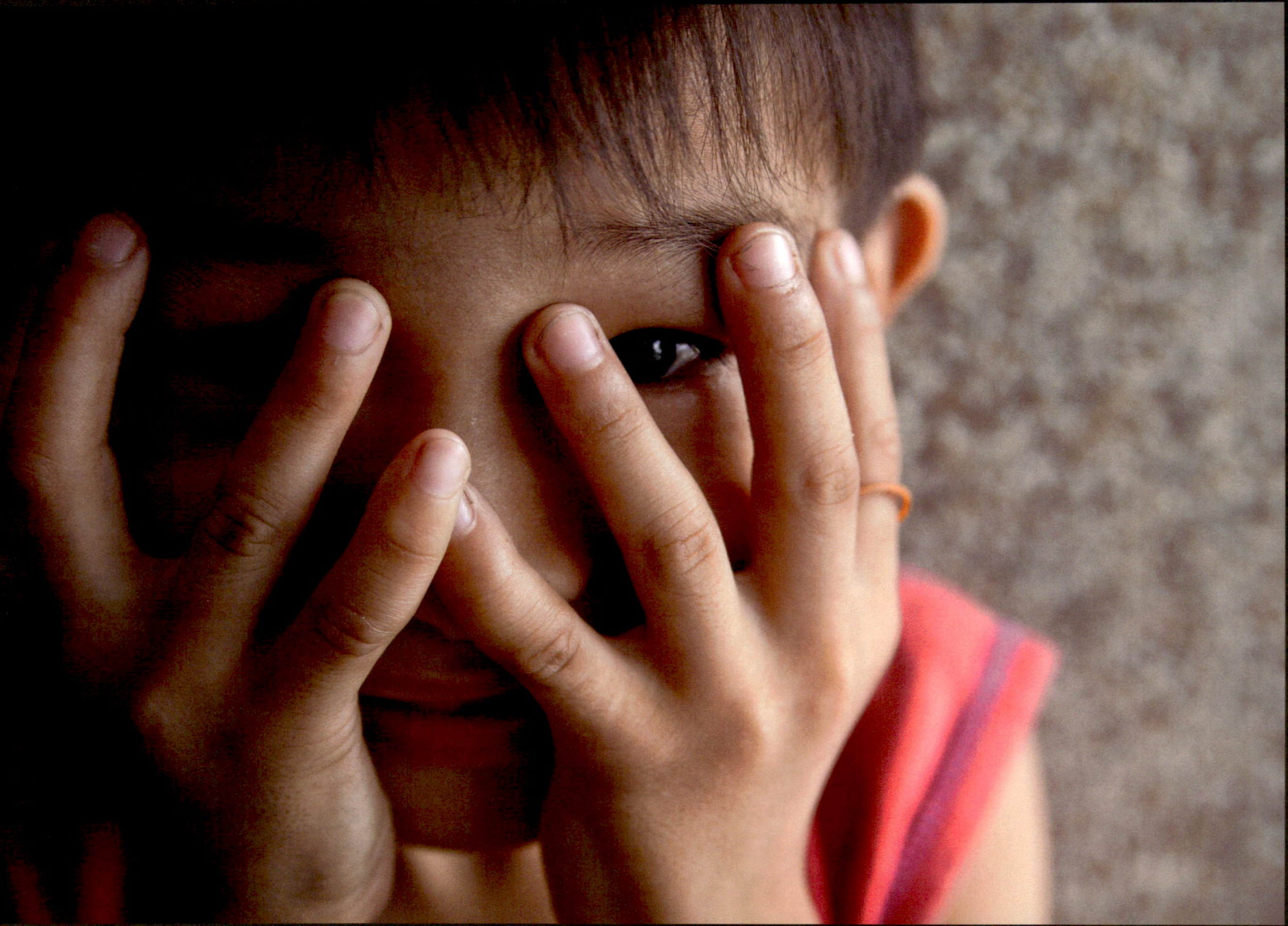

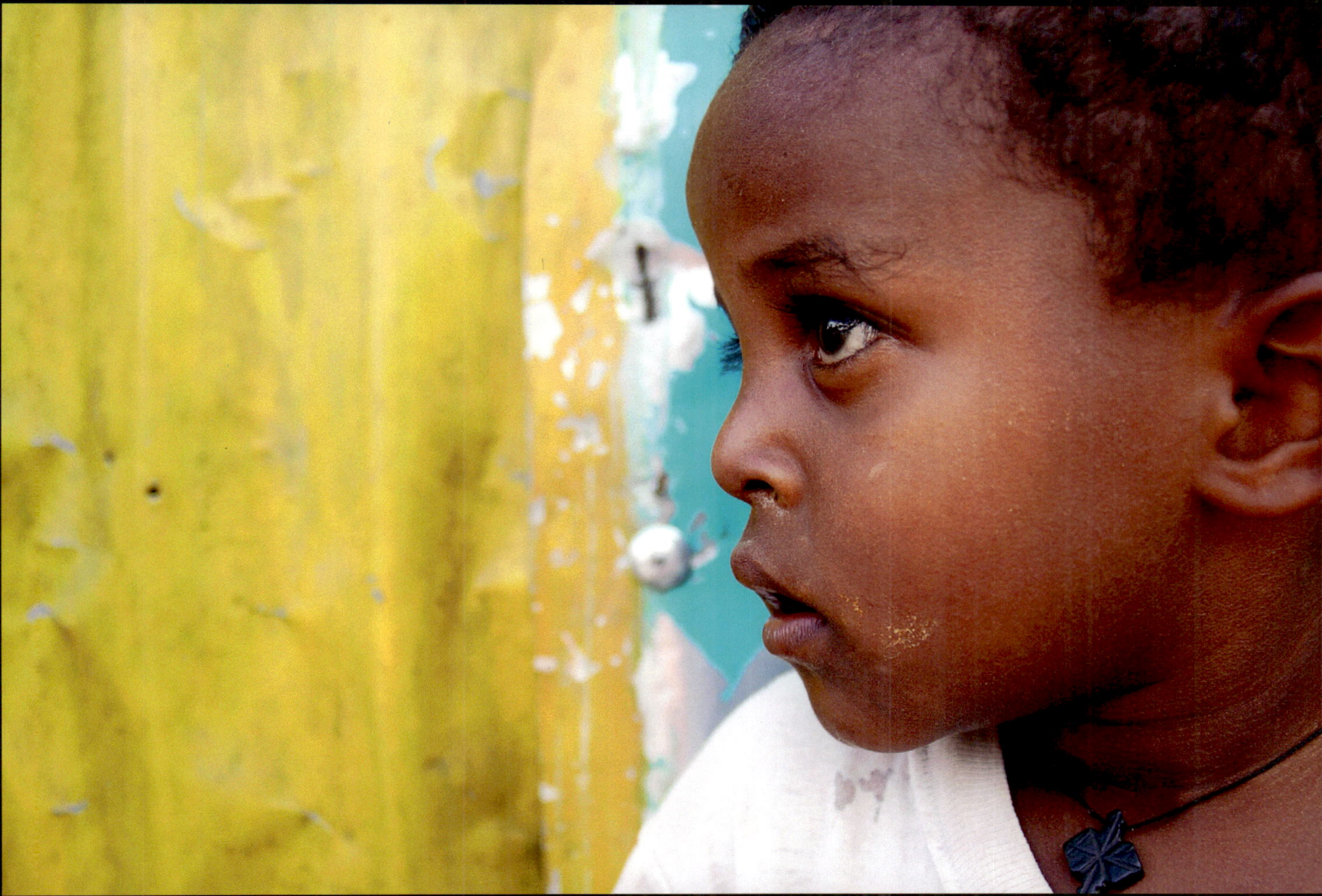

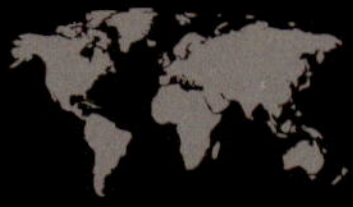

Between **133 and 275 million children** worldwide are estimated to **witness domestic violence** annually.[26]

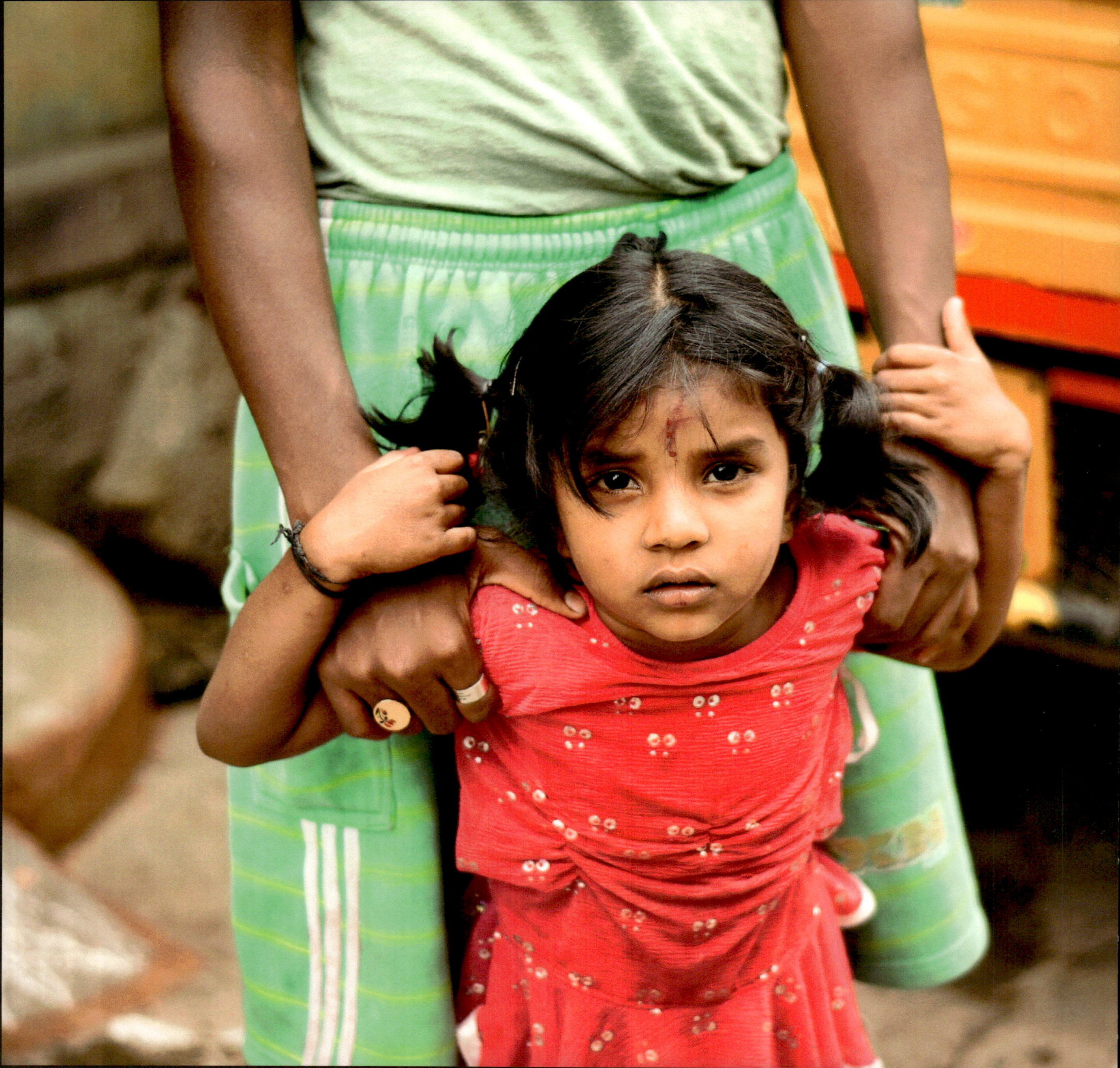

Abusive | India

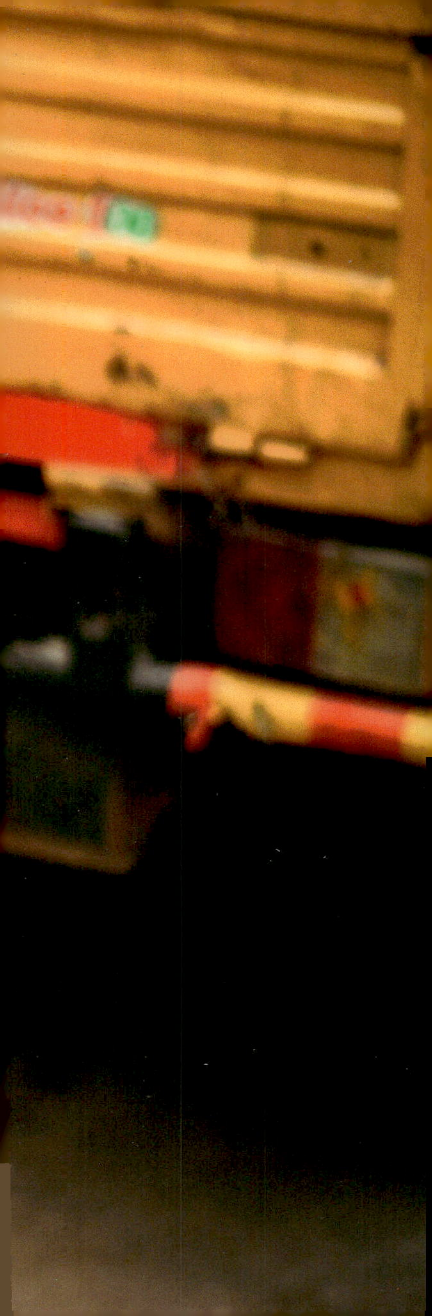

Up all night, anxiously peering out the window, ten-year-old Giovanni learned to be resilient at a young age. He has grown up in constant fear of the volatile, life-threatening rage of his alcoholic father.

Disappearing for days at a time, Giovanni is never certain when his father will return or what level of violence he will bring through the door. Knowing he is small and utterly defenseless, Giovanni stands in the gap, fiercely committed to protecting his mother and sister.

Each day as the sun goes down, he must leave behind the boy he is to become the man he is forced to be.

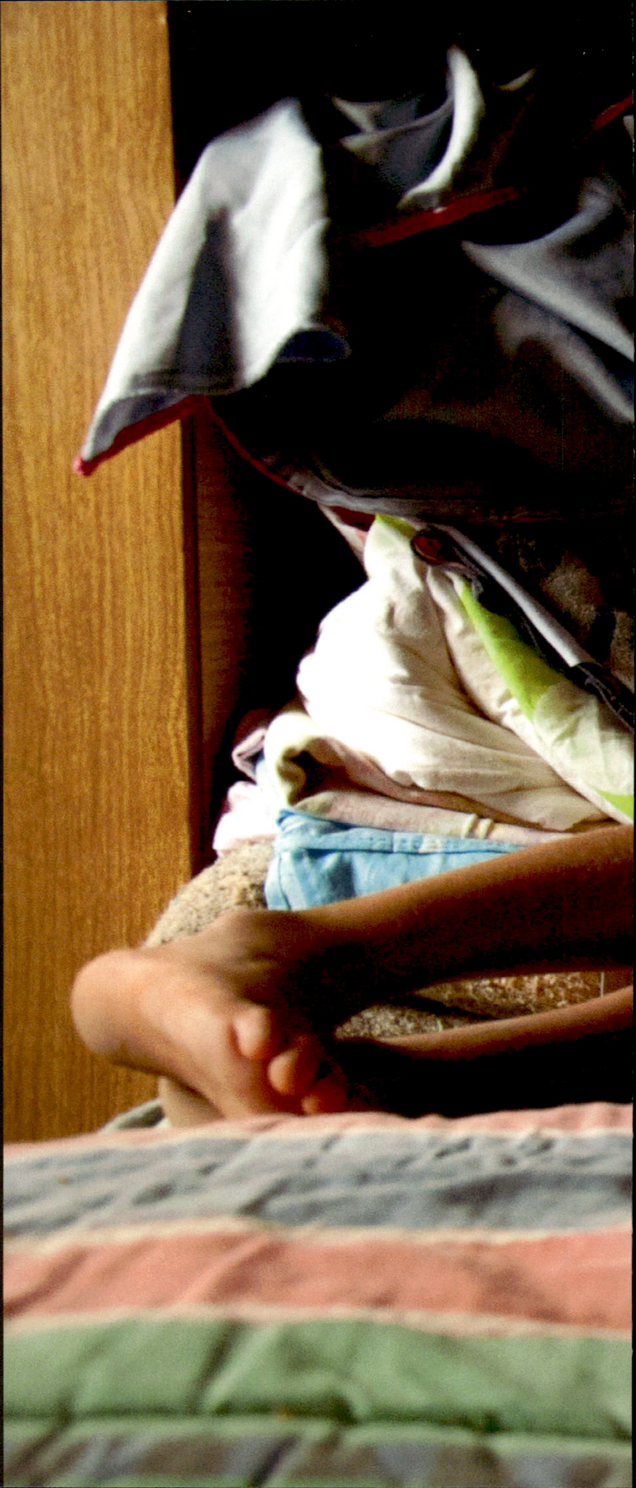

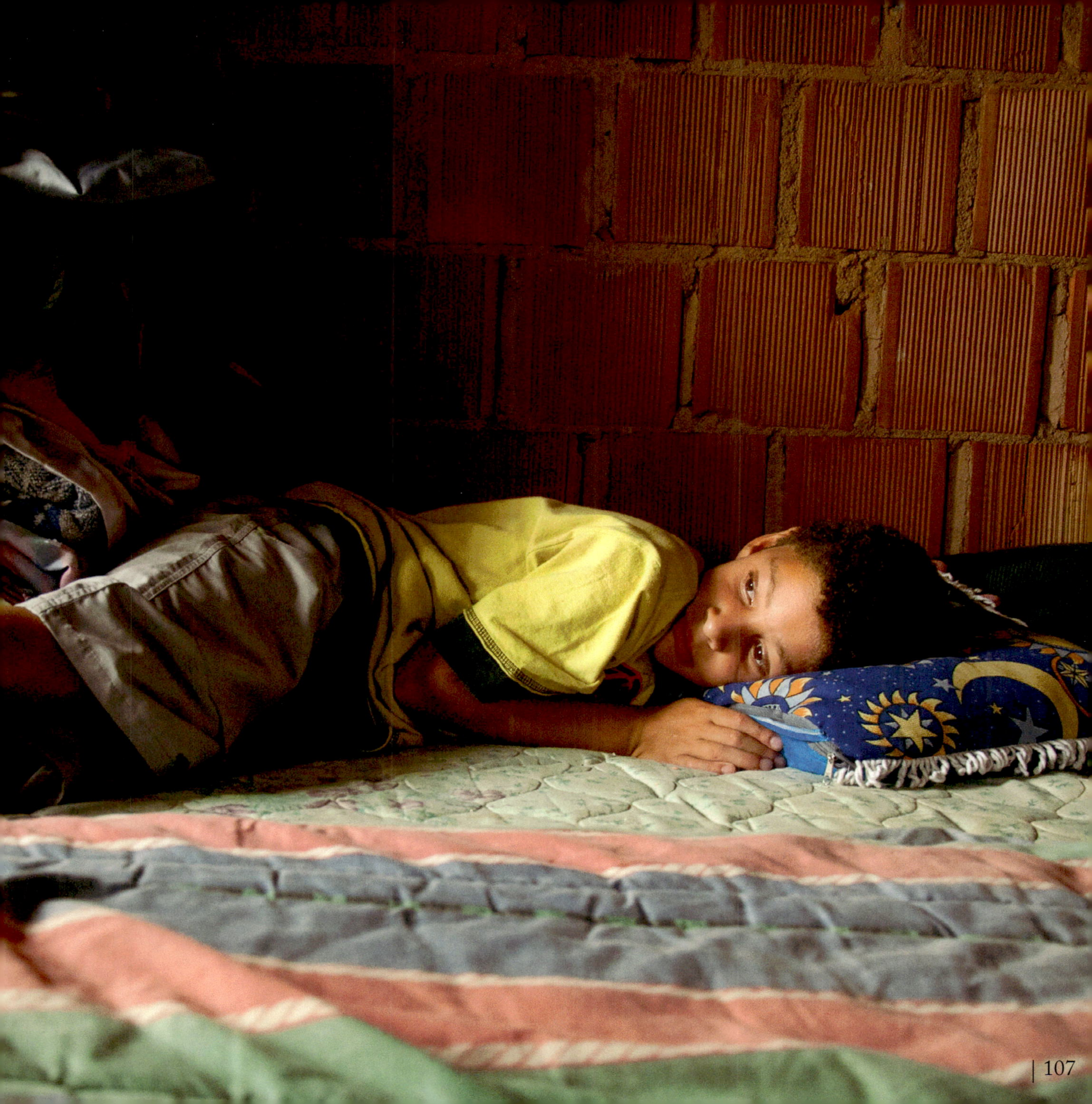

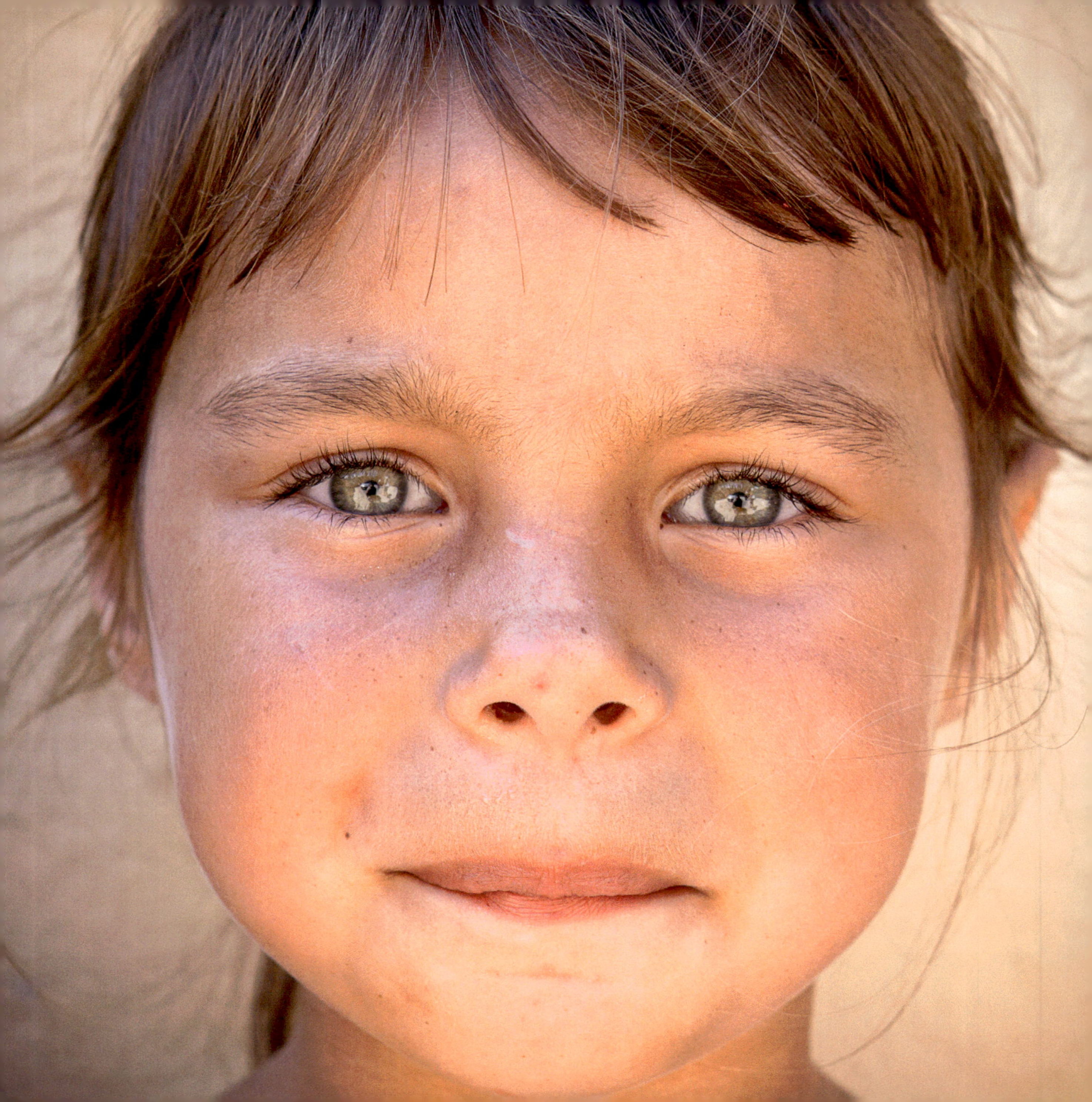

A Call

to restore the house of **Humanity**

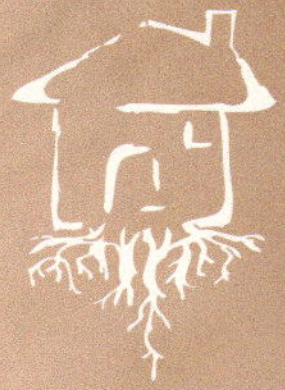

We embarked on this journey around the world passionate about discovering the reality beyond the comforts of our own lives and homes. Every step of the way, we came face to face with both beauty and breakdown. We believe God is the creator of all things and that his heart is deeply grieved by the state of the world and the brokenness of humanity. We also acknowledge that he asks us to care for one another; to love, protect and serve each other. It has not been the neglect of God that has led us to this state of destruction and depravity, but the result of our own selfishness, pride, and ignorance. In our role as brothers and sisters in this world, we have let each other down.

All too often we like to point the finger anywhere other than toward ourselves, especially when it comes to issues of global injustice. We have become detached from personal responsibility; we like to blame God, blame the government, blame him, her - anyone. Yet, in our everyday choices, in the simple small decisions, we shape the world. We shape what is normal within our own hearts and homes and in turn those norms change cultures and countries with each passing day.

Every small decision adds to the sum total of change. One person's choice to buy a sexually explicit magazine or click onto a pornography website directly affects sex trafficking around the world. One person's choice to physically abuse their child has a domino effect that reaches far beyond the abused person or household. Every time we hold onto anger and bitterness by refusing to release someone from their mistakes, we add that anger and bitterness to the landscape of the world. When we choose to put our finances and our resources solely toward improving our own lives, we contribute to the deprivation of other people.

"We worship choice and prioritize our right to personal happiness, regardless of how it impacts anyone else." [27]

The progression of self-worship, of self-focus, is a growing epidemic around the world and is becoming the foundational soil in which humanity is being rooted. We must combat our self-focused mindsets by becoming responsible for our decisions, realizing that our actions have consequences beyond our own lives. We must stop believing that it is enough to contribute to the solution - we must admit that we are part of the problem.

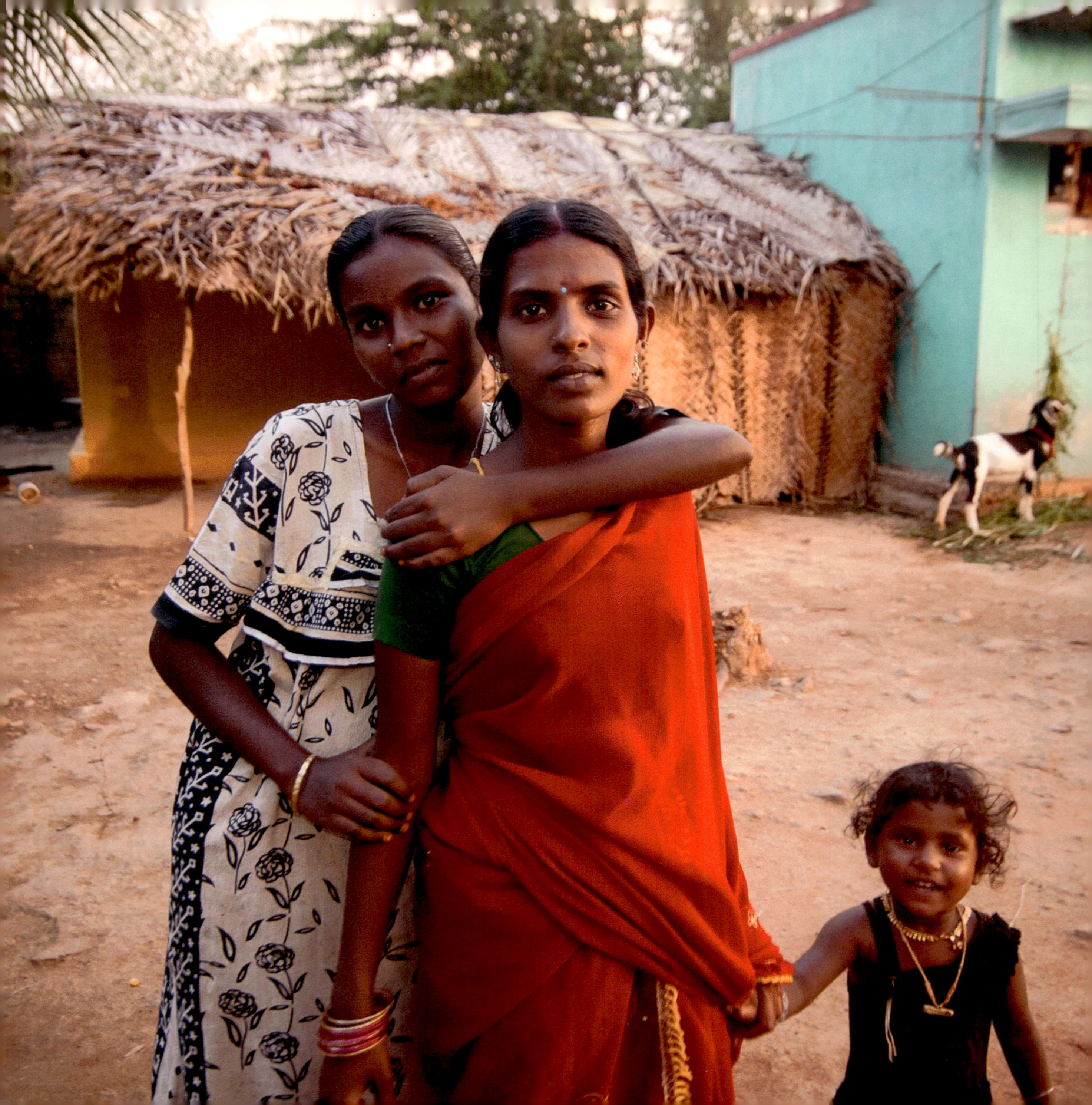

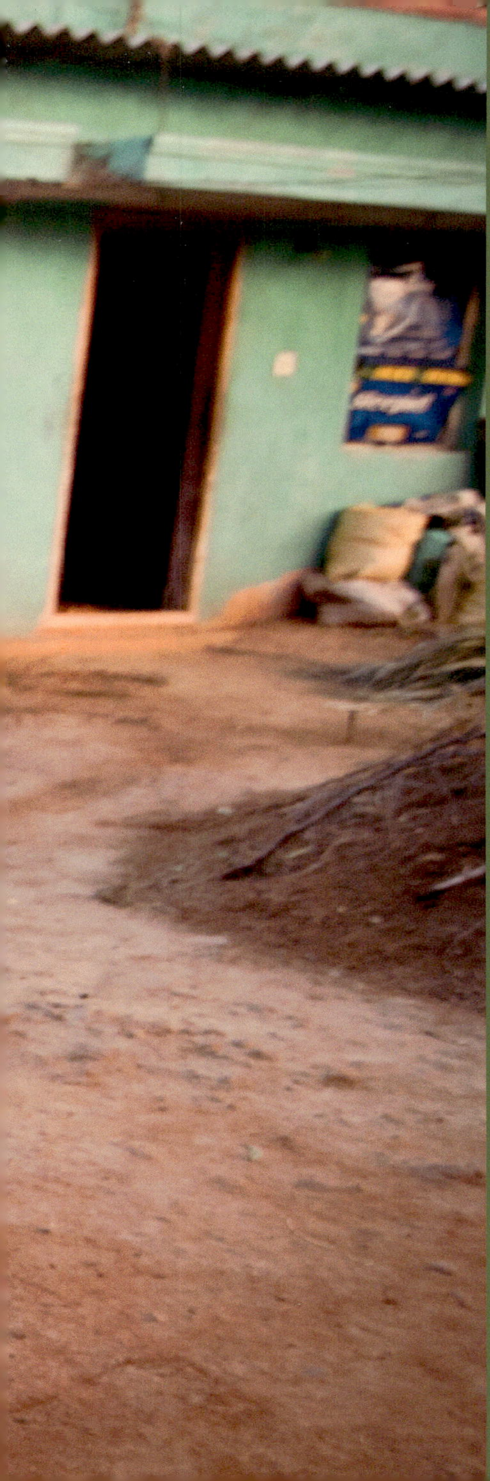

As the trend of individualism grows, the basic structure of family continues to crumble, finding itself amongst the rubble of our broken lives. Breakdowns occur on a daily basis within our own families and

simple miscommunications can lead us into a place of isolation and silence.

If we are not intentional about addressing our hurts, problems, or needs, the distance between us grows and the walls within our homes become thick with bitterness.

Over the past fifty years, divorce, abandonment, abuse, disease, and poverty have been increasing, leaving families shattered and basic needs unmet. People become vulnerable and the cycle of broken homes continues when one looks outside the family for worth, refuge, or a sense of belonging that he or she should find within the home.

A healthy, functioning family is a critical component in changing the world. If we are committed to each other, in our marriages and roles within the family, we can bring about true change. If we remain faithful and self-controlled, choosing to model sacrificial love, patience, kindness, and forgiveness, we will pass these values onto our children and in turn reflect them into our societies.

Change begins within the walls of our own hearts

and when it is lived out within the walls of our homes, it penetrates the walls the world has built to divide us from each other. Building families with the ability to forgive and reconcile, be selfless and to take ownership of the consequences of one's choices, will bring lasting change. Though we are only one person, one family - we are part of one people, one world that makes up **the house of humanity.**

Living It Out

"We think sometimes that poverty is only being hungry, naked and homeless. The poverty of being uncared for is the greatest poverty. We must start in our own homes to remedy this kind of poverty."

-Mother Teresa

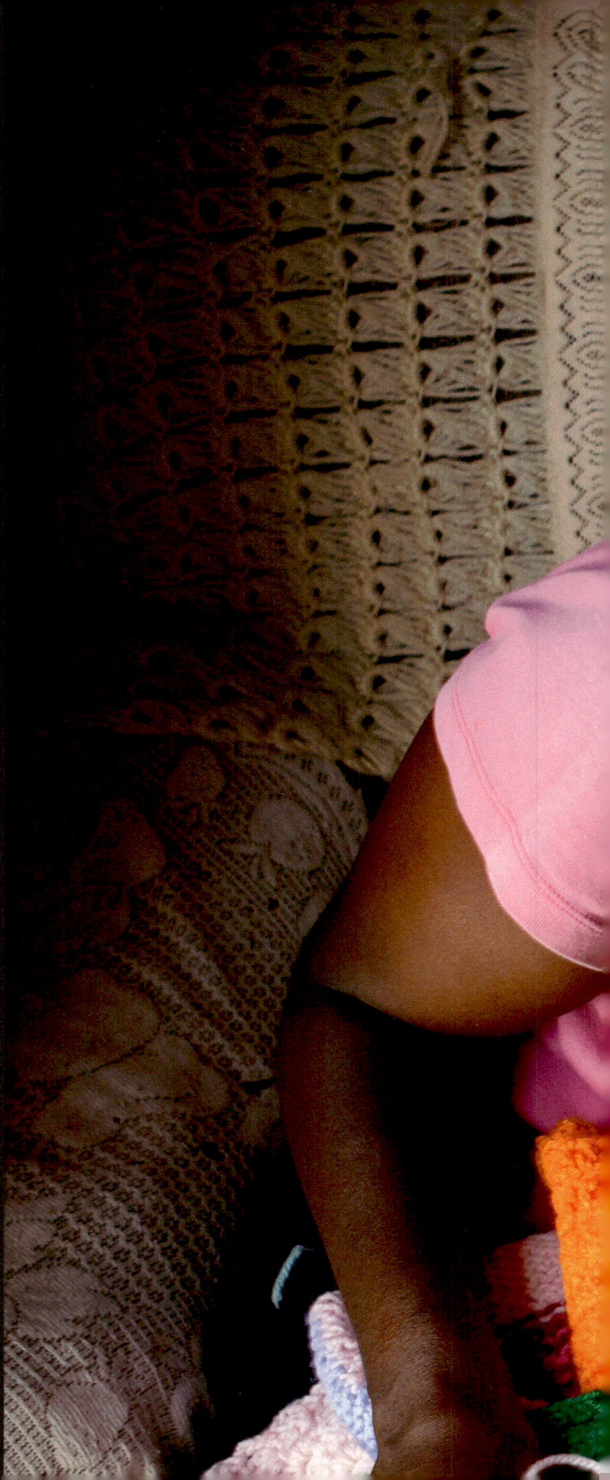

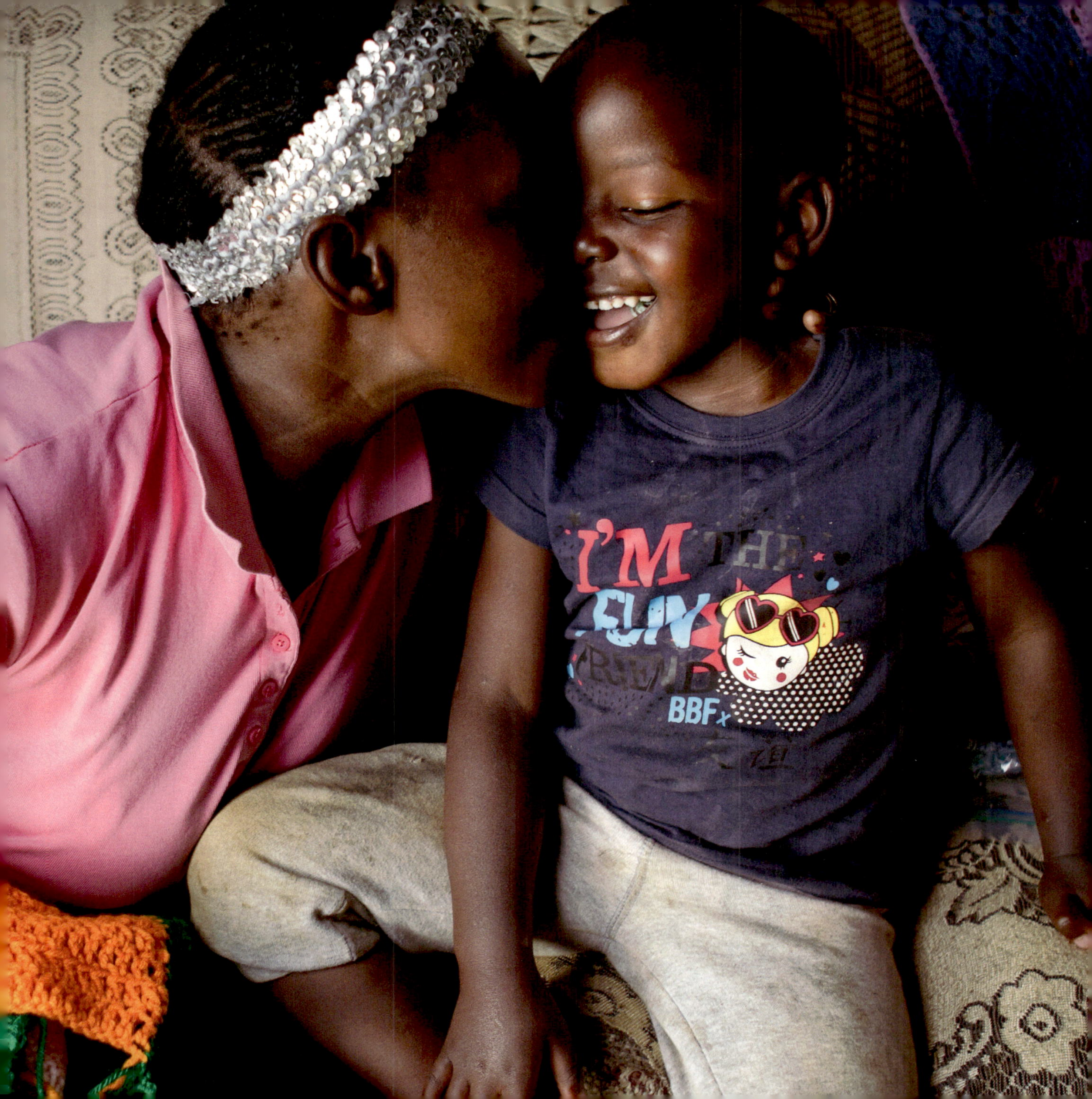
I'M THE
FUN
FRIEND
BBFx

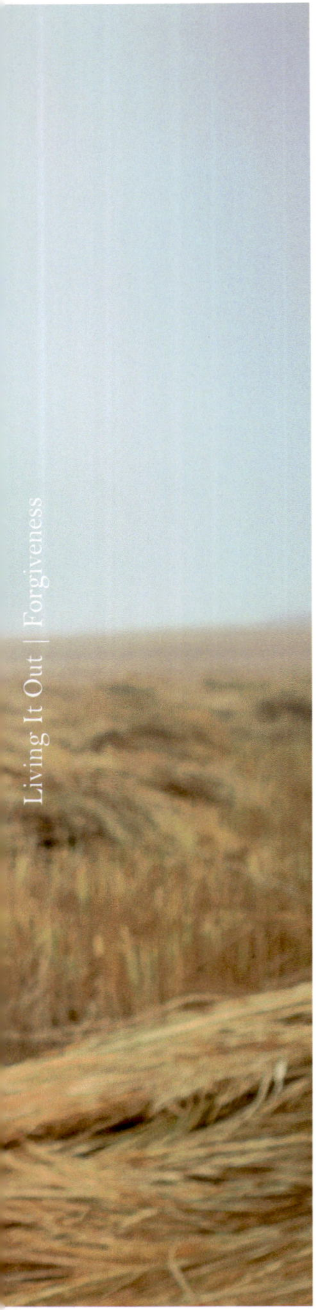

Emmi was born in a small mountain town in northern Thailand. When she was three years old, her father suspected her mother of an affair, an act that in Thai culture brings immense shame to the family. In the heat of his anger and despair, he killed her, realizing too late that it was all a misunderstanding. When her father was put in jail, Emmi was left an orphan. Seen as a curse to the family, with a face that resembled her father, Emmi was cast aside with no one willing to take her in. She grew up hating her father, hating that he had taken everything from her. Bitterness crept into her heart, binding her to the past and consuming her future. When she was eleven, her grandfather tried to sell her into prostitution, confirming in her mind that she would always be seen as an unwanted burden to her family. And so she left, running at the first chance she had with the intent to never return.

Years later, in an orphanage just outside Chiang Mai, a European couple discovered Emmi and committed to supporting her. With their help, she started up a sponsorship program to help girls out of prostitution through job training and placement. She worked for years with these women, helping them find hope and healing, all the while carrying the burden of her own past. One day the realization struck her, “Here I am teaching others about grace and forgiveness, and yet refusing to give it to my own family.” So she decided it was time to go home and face the past from which she had been running.

It was not an easy task, to face her father after so many years. It was a choice Emmi had to make, to let go of blame and bitterness, and give their relationship a new start. She soon realized how much her father had suffered as well. He had killed the one he loved, and as a result lost his daughter, his family, his home. He had been hurting as much as she had.

“There is no offense too large to forgive. Forgiveness is a choice. A choice to walk out of bitterness and into reconciliation.”
- Emmi

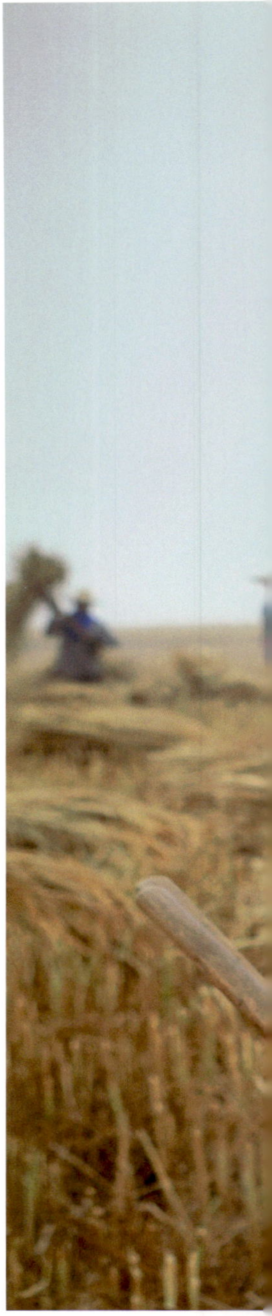

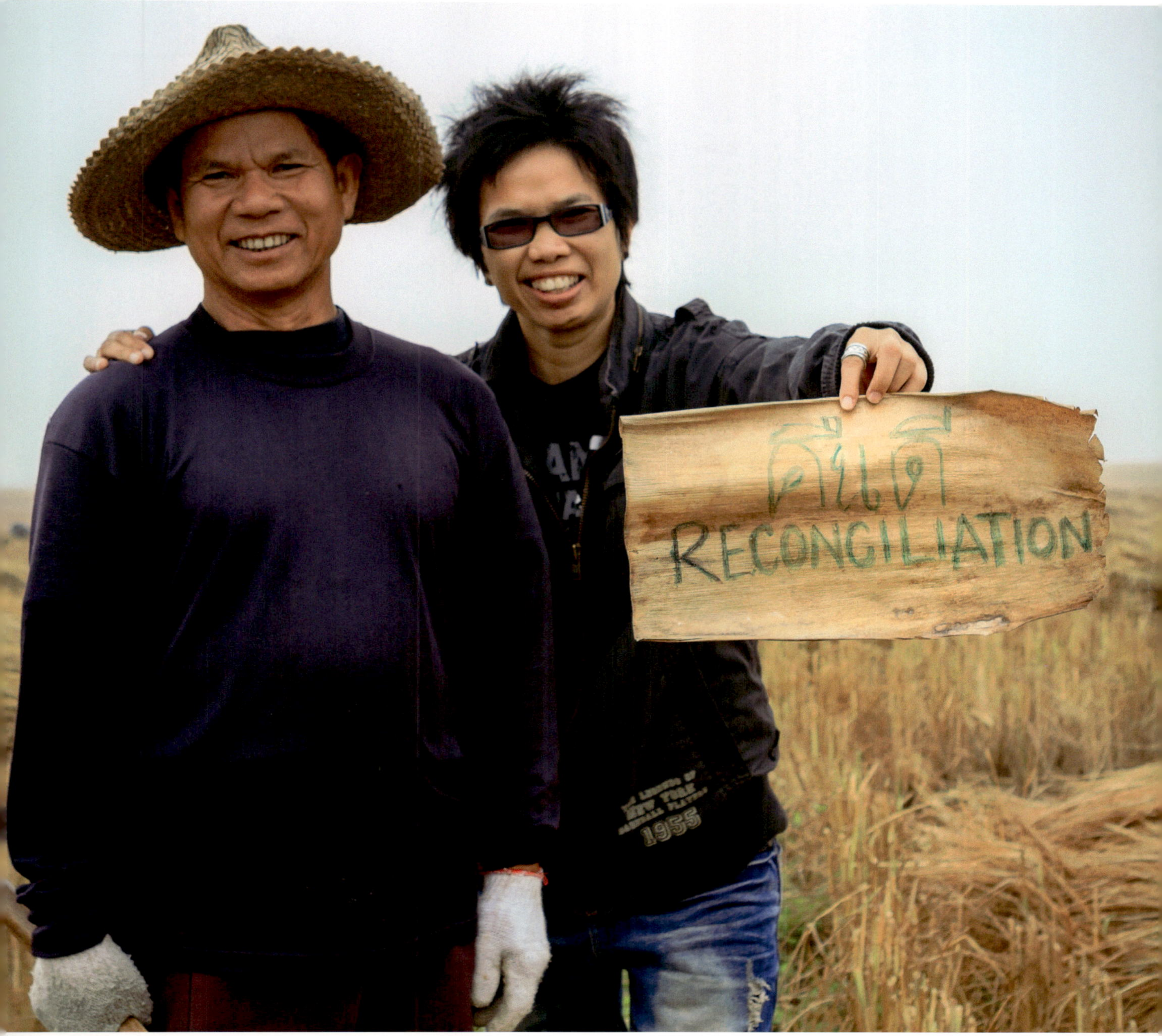

คืนดี
RECONCILIATION

Thirteen smiling but cautious faces appeared from around the corner as we approached the small house made of mud and sticks. Petros and Elizabeth Kunene welcomed us into their family as we crammed into their tiny home to share a meal by candlelight. Varying in age and unparalleled in beauty, these children quickly warmed up to our group of ten strangers. By nightfall, the children were playing games with us around the bonfire and snuggling close to our sides on the mud stoop, singing songs of hope into the midnight sky.

In their home country of Swaziland, 25.9% of adults are HIV positive, that is 1 in 4, the highest prevalence in the world.[28] Coupled with the world's highest rate of tuberculosis,[29] the adult population is dying, leaving over 100,000 children without parental care.[30] When two of Petros' sisters passed away, shortly followed by the death of one of Elizabeth's brothers, seven children suddenly had no one to care for them. Petros and Elizabeth did not hesitate to take them in and their family quickly grew from eight to fifteen.

Though resources are limited and means are scarce, it is clear through their actions that nothing is more important than helping a child succeed. The way Petros and Elizabeth interact with each of the children creates no sense of division between their natural and adopted family. When we asked which children were biologically theirs, a proud smile came across Petros' face as he replied loud enough for the children to hear, "They are *all* mine." In their role as parents, they are deeply committed to giving these children a home that they can truly call their own.

Petros and Elizabeth are an incredible example of what it means to be selfless, to give of what you have no matter how small, to improve the life of another person. They are living out selflessness, loving other people above themselves. In this tiny corner of the world, two people with very little material wealth are giving a gift far more valuable. They are giving home and hope back to children who have lost theirs. High up on the hillside of the vast expanse of Mbabane, Swaziland, the Kunene family refuses to let death be the end of dreams.

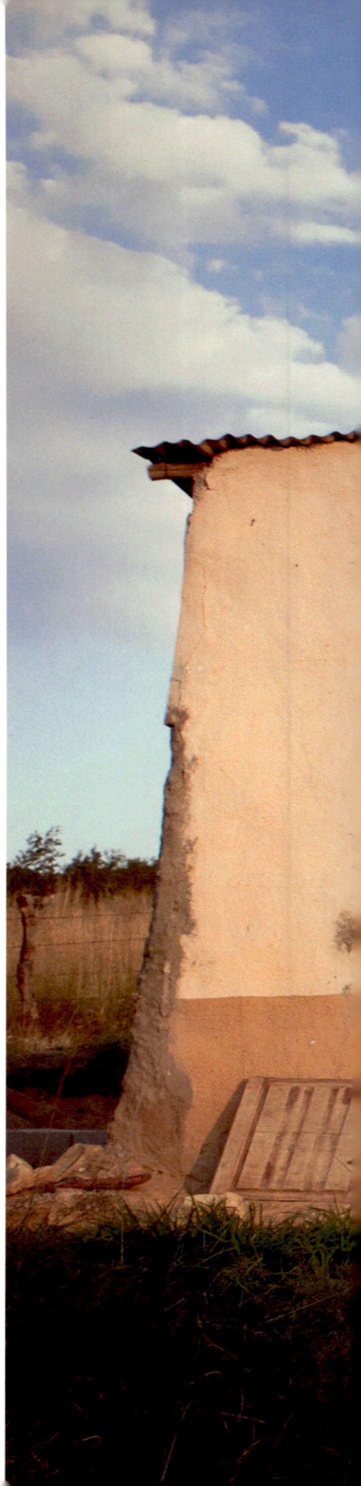

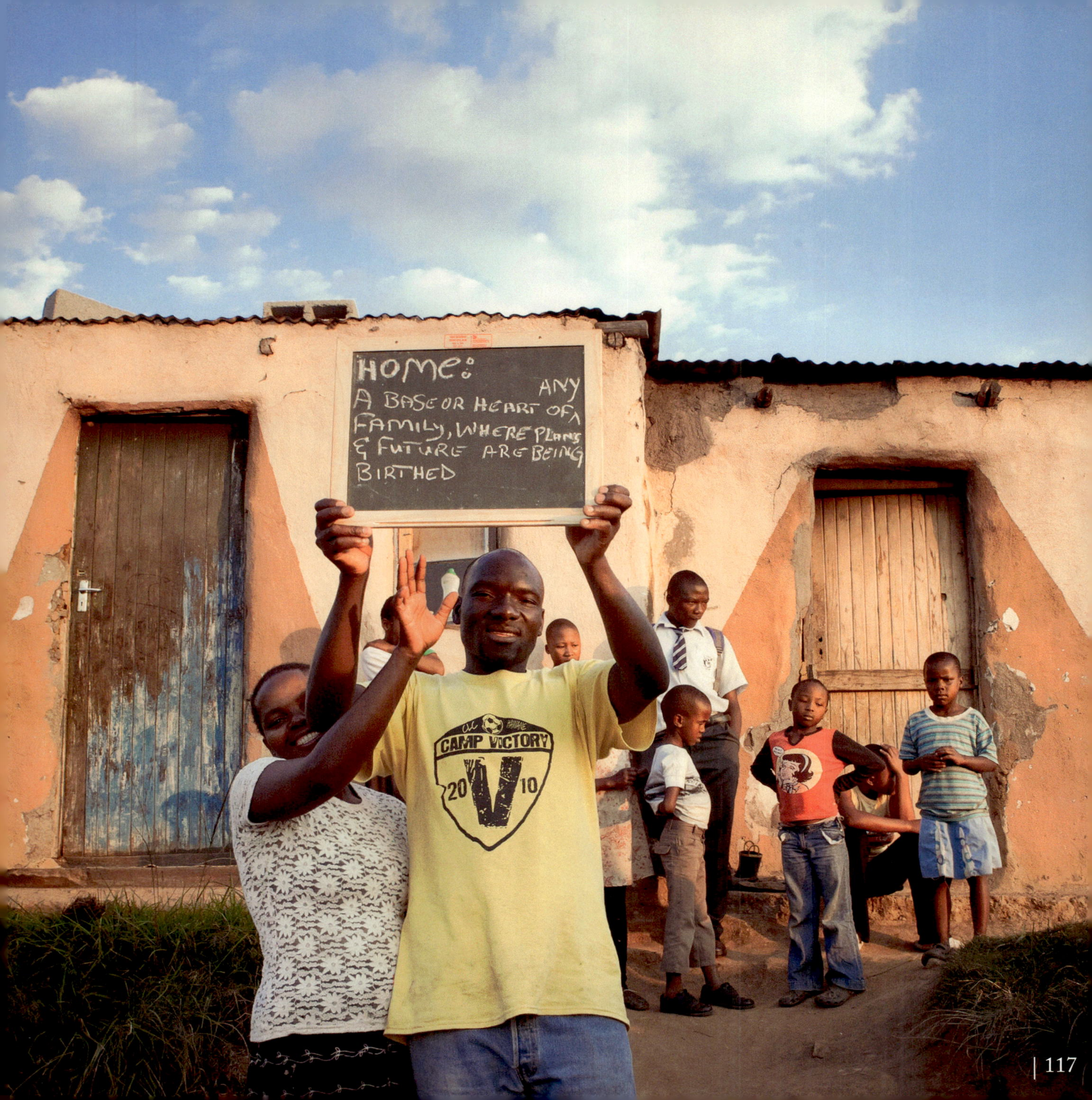
HOME:
A BASE OR HEART OF ANY
FAMILY, WHERE PLANS
& FUTURE ARE BEING
BIRTHED
CAMP VICTORY
2010

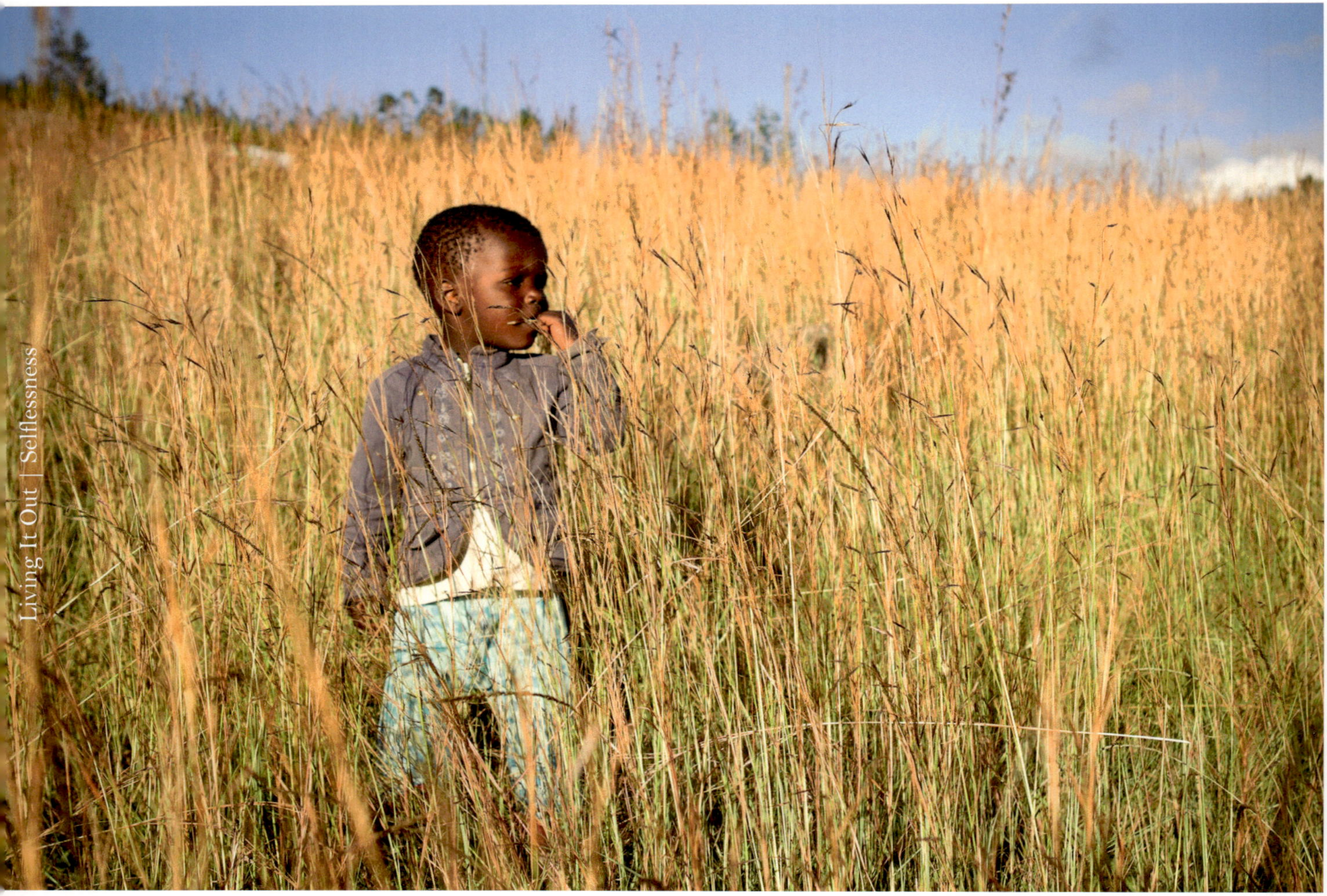

"We want them to feel that this is their place, to feel warm here. I always define home as a place or heart where any family who has plans can develop those plans or those plans can be birthed for the future. Home is a place where you belong, where you can run to and where you can be found. This is the way to their success...

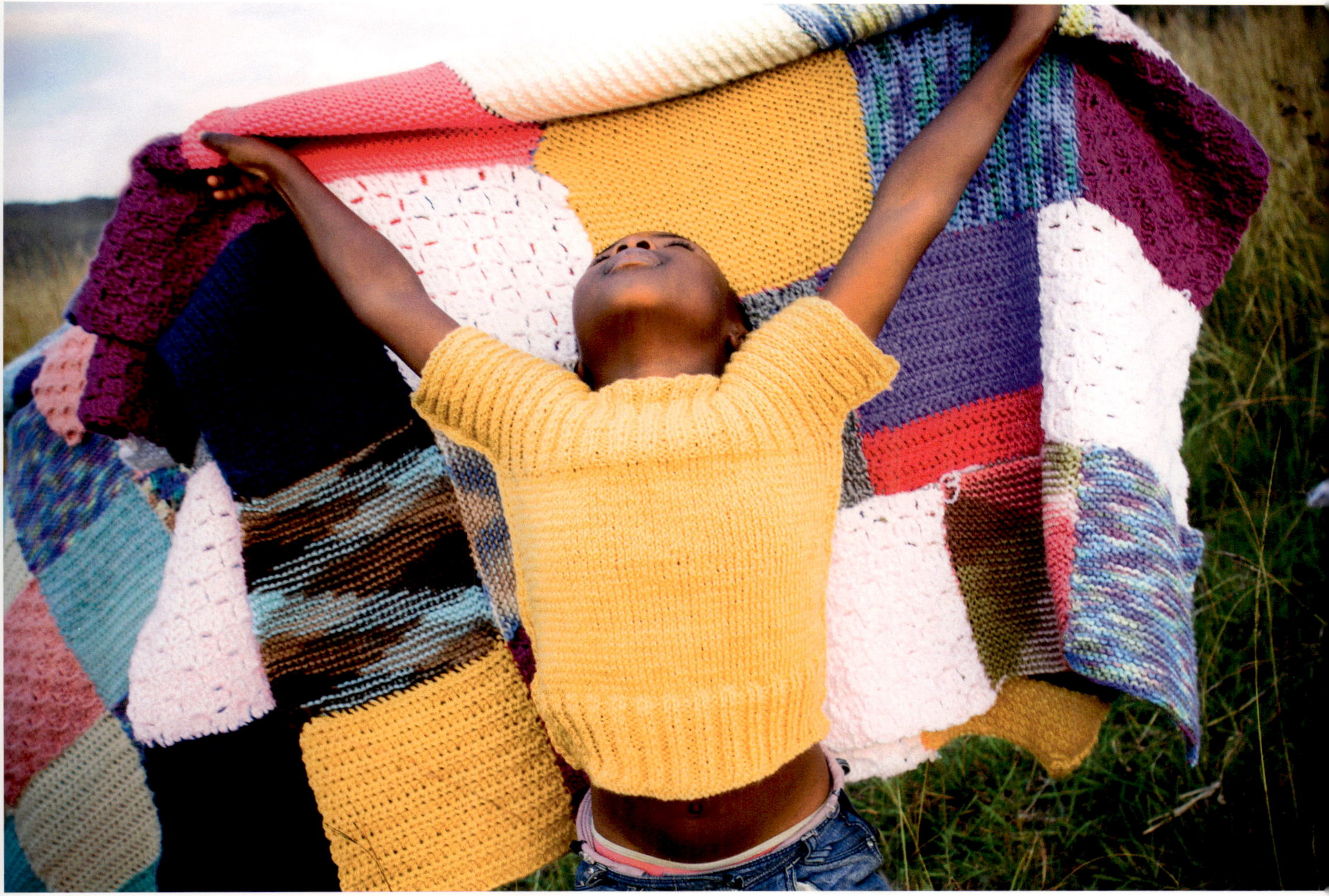

...Our vision is to see the dreams of these children come to reality. We know they have dreams in their lives and after they lost their parents, it's like their dreams had vanished completely. So we are here to revive that, we are here to show them there is still hope."

- Petros Kunene

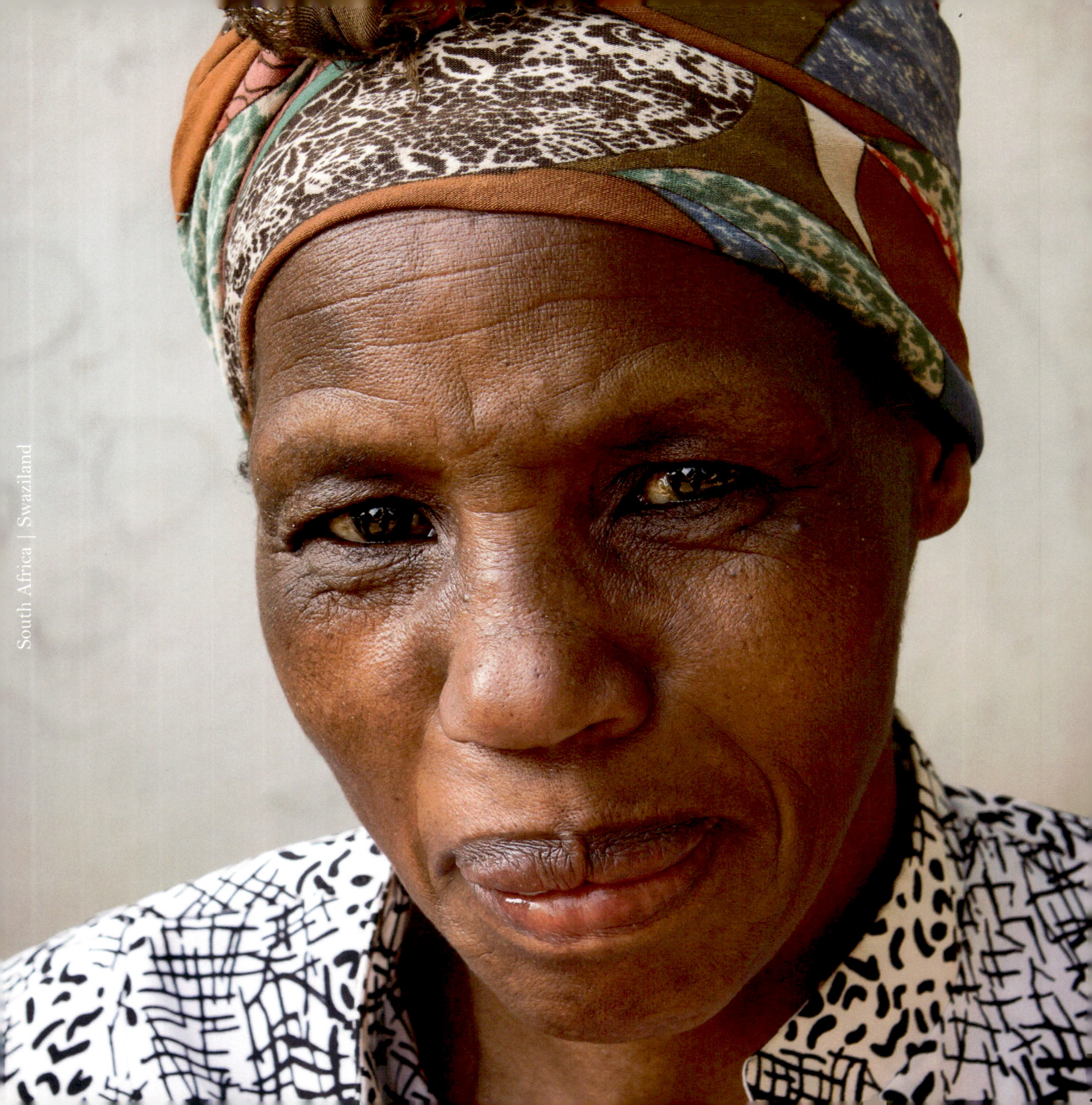

South Africa | Swaziland

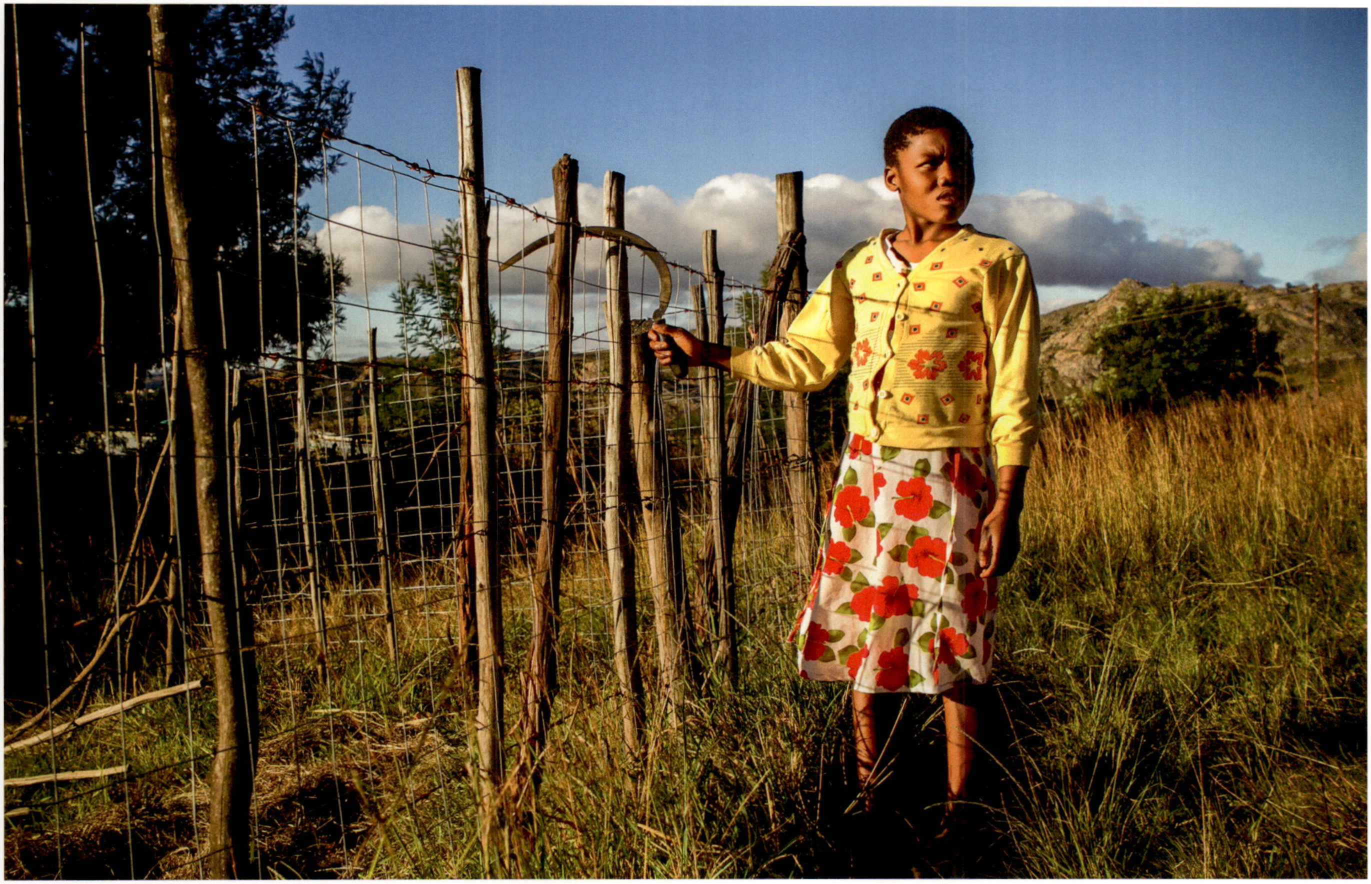

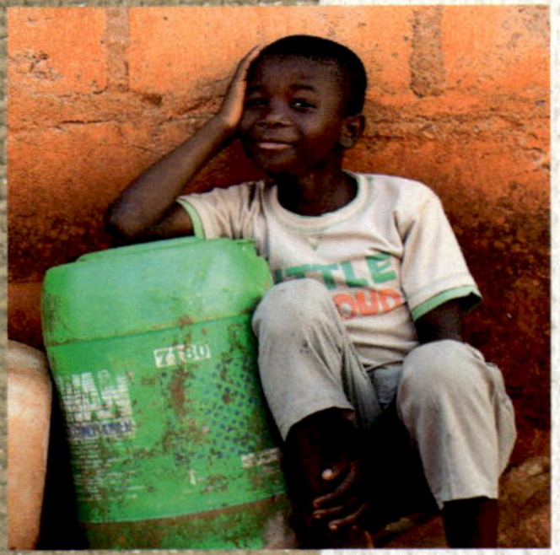

orphaned

- Consider adopting, fostering, or sponsoring a child.

- If you know a child who has lost a parent, give of yourself as a mentor or role model.

- Examine and redefine your role as a mom or dad, making sure that the needs of your child are being met.

www.bbbs.org
www.worldvision.org
www.savethechildren.org
www.tenthousandhomes.org

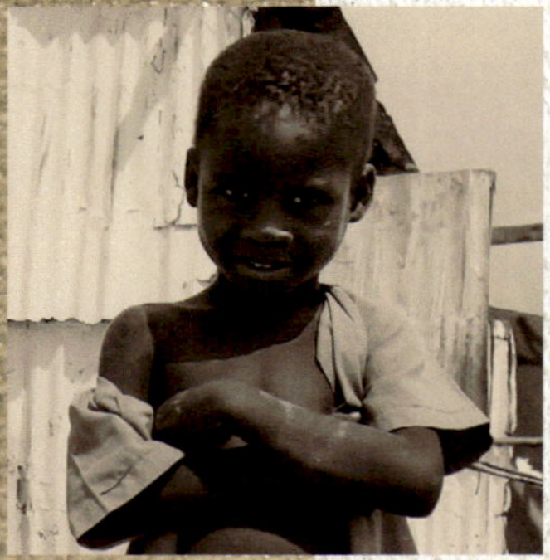

displaced

- When you see someone struggling with language, customs, or directions, help them in any way you can.

- Invite a family who has just moved into your community over for dinner. Help them feel accepted and at home.

- Create an atmosphere within your home where everyone is accepted. Seek to understand those within your family that you struggle with or that may feel out of place.

www.rescue.org
www.refugeesinternational.org

war-torn

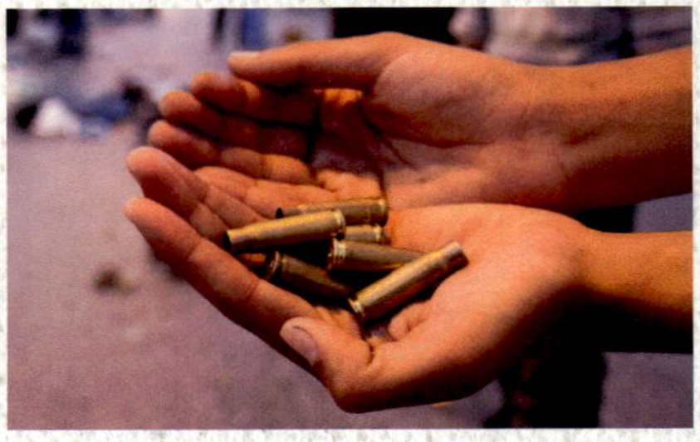

- Identify the person, circumstance, or issue in your life that you are holding bitterness or anger toward. Make a decision to forgive, even if the person or circumstance seems undeserving of forgiveness.

- Have the hard conversations within your home to address the issues of tension, hostility, or disunity within your family. Seek resolution.

- In the difficult conversations, listen more than you speak. Seek to understand rather than to be understood.

- Commit to a no yelling rule within your home and between yourself and your spouse.

www.warchild.org
www.womenforwomen.org

IMPACT

A CALL TO RESTORE THE HOUSE OF HUMANITY

the effect or influence of one person, thing, or action, on another

isolated

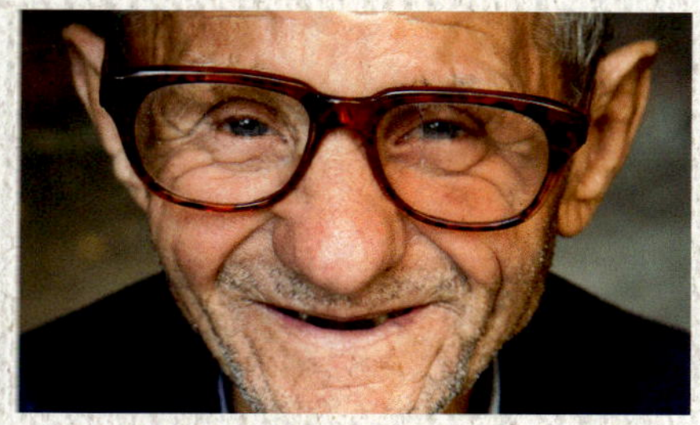

- Visit your grandparents and ask about their story, history, and journey. Write it down. This is your heritage.

- Go to your local elderly home, ask which person rarely or never has a visitor and commit to visiting that person a few times a month. Play cards, read them a story, or let them tell you theirs.

- At your school or workplace, choose to eat lunch with the person that always sits alone. Ask them about who they are. Get to know them.

- If you overhear people making fun of an outcast person or people, stick up for them and refuse to join the conversation.

www.iwgia.org
www.leprosy.org
www.littlebrothers.org

homeless

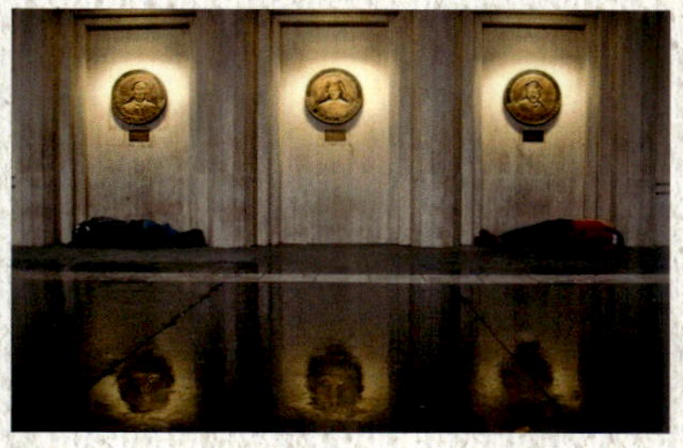

- Make a point of addressing homeless people when you pass them on the street. A smile and a "hello" can make all the difference.

- Take a homeless person out for lunch and ask to hear their story.

- Ensure that the needs of your children are being met inside your home, creating a sense of safety and belonging.

www.salvationarmy.org
www.homelessshelterdirectory.org

ruins

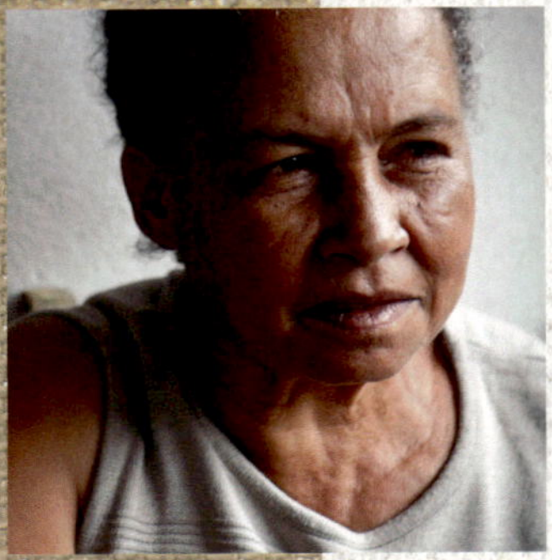

- When a disaster occurs in your area, be willing to take in people who need refuge.
- Identify your personal area of skill and use it to help others in an area of need. For example, knit hats and blankets for families who have lost everything or create a flier to raise awareness.
- Organize a garage sale, bake sale, etc., in your community to raise money for donation to relief programs.

www.dwb.org
www.actionaid.org

slums

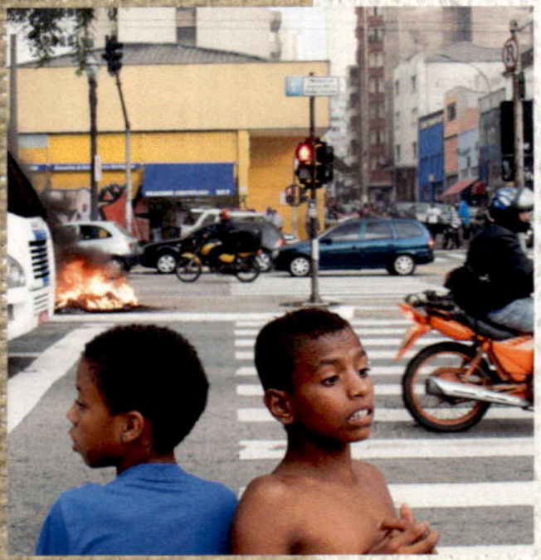

- Research the regions of greatest poverty in your hometown or city and look into local organizations that are assisting them. Find out how you can help.
- As a family, opt out of Christmas gifts and choose to give the gift of food, blankets, or clothing to a family in need.

www.careusa.org
www.samaritanspurse.org

red light

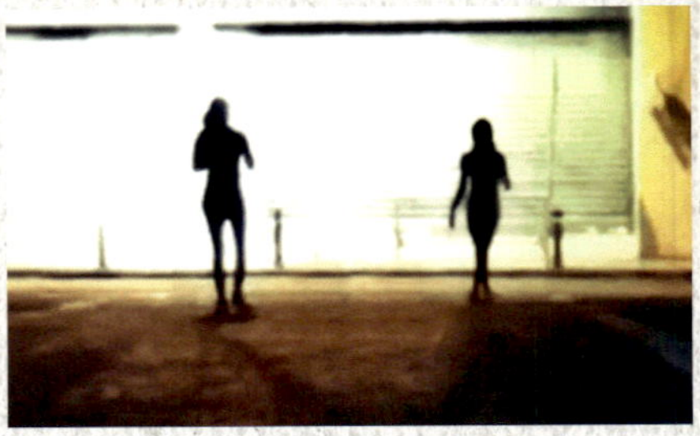

- If you have an addiction to pornography, find an accountability partner or seek professional counsel.
- Install computer software that prevents the viewing of pornography.
- Start a conversation with your family about how the media portrays sexuality. Recognize that if you are not the teacher of your kids in this area - music, magazines, and movies will be.

www.notforsalecampaign.org
www.humantrafficking.org
www.sexandmoneyfilm.com
www.nefariousdocumentary.com

IMPACT

A CALL TO RESTORE THE HOUSE OF HUMANITY

An individual has not started living until he can rise above the narrow confines of his individualistic concerns to the broader concerns of all humanity.

-Martin Luther King, Jr.

nomadic

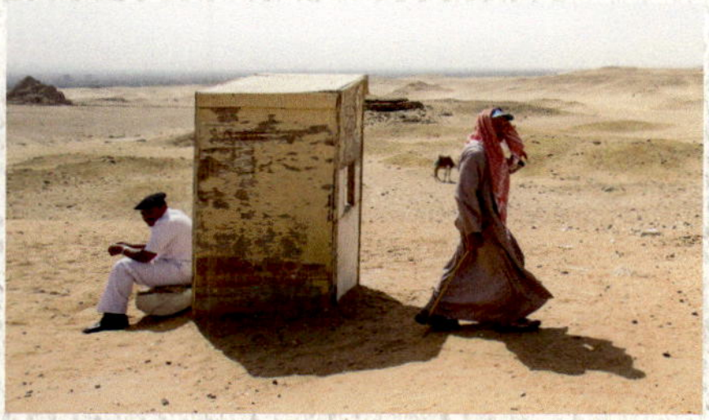

- Take time to understand the culture you come from. Learn traditions, history, and cuisine of your lineage.

- Commit one night a month to celebrate the culture(s) within your home, cook the cultural food, listen to cultural music - connect with your roots.

- Have a game night in your home where communing with each other is the focus, rather than television, phones, or computers.

www.reocities.com/~patrin/orgs.htm

abusive

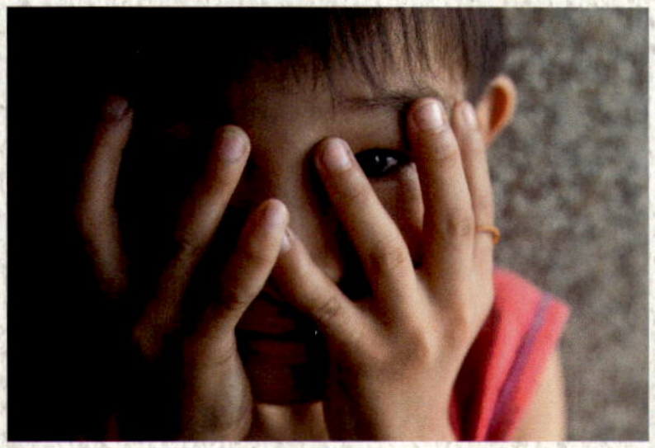

- Recognize that spoken words can be more damaging than physical abuse.

- Have open discussions with your children about bullying, physical, mental, and sexual abuse. Teach them to always be honest with you if they have experienced any of these things.

- Seek counseling through a church or organization that can help you work through issues of violence within your home.

www.standagainstdv.org
www.nnedv.org

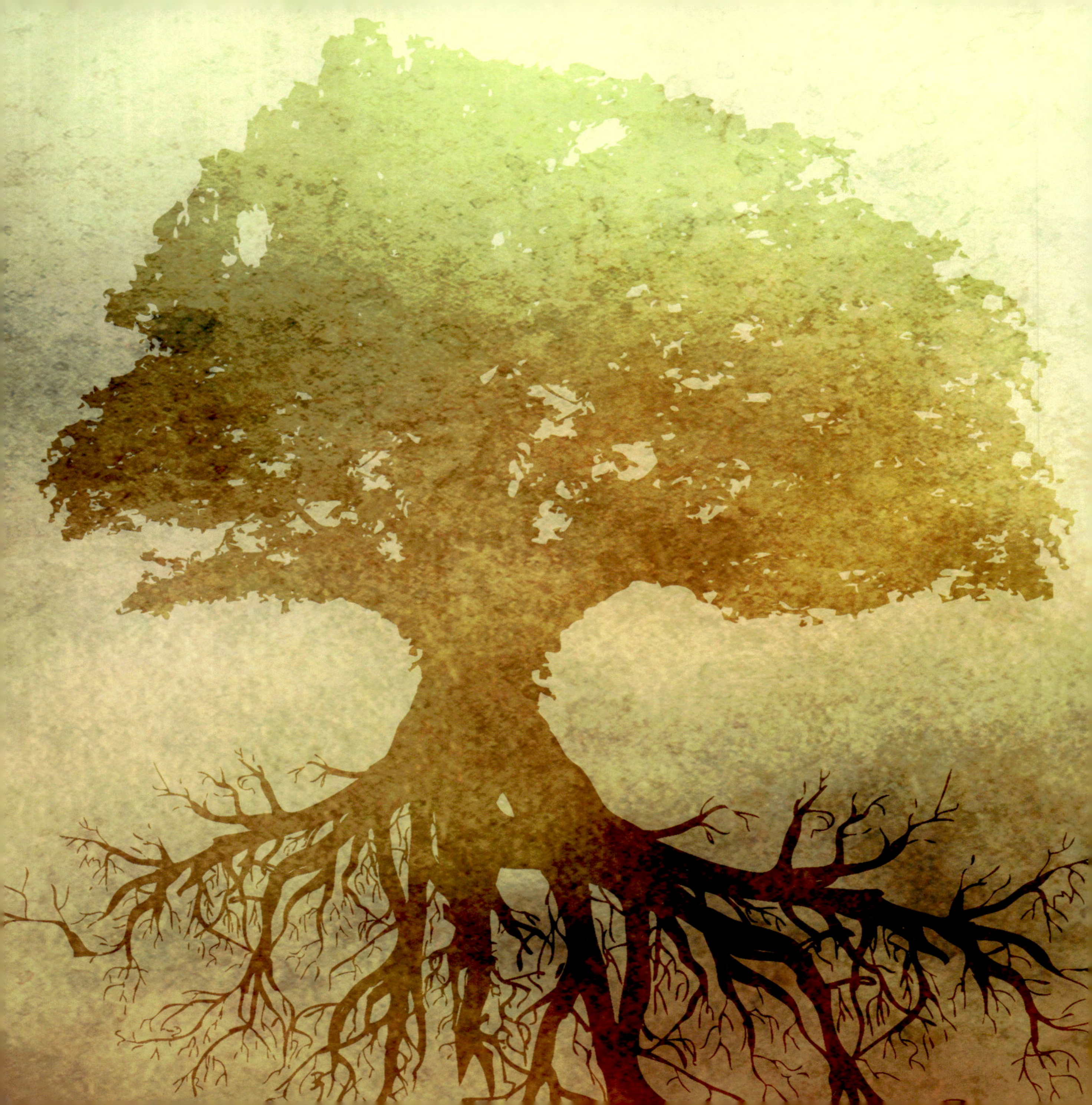

Our hope is that when people begin to recognize their unique role within their homes, families, and communities and begin to live that out with responsibility, forgiveness, and selflessness - the world will truly be transformed.

[love beyond yourself]

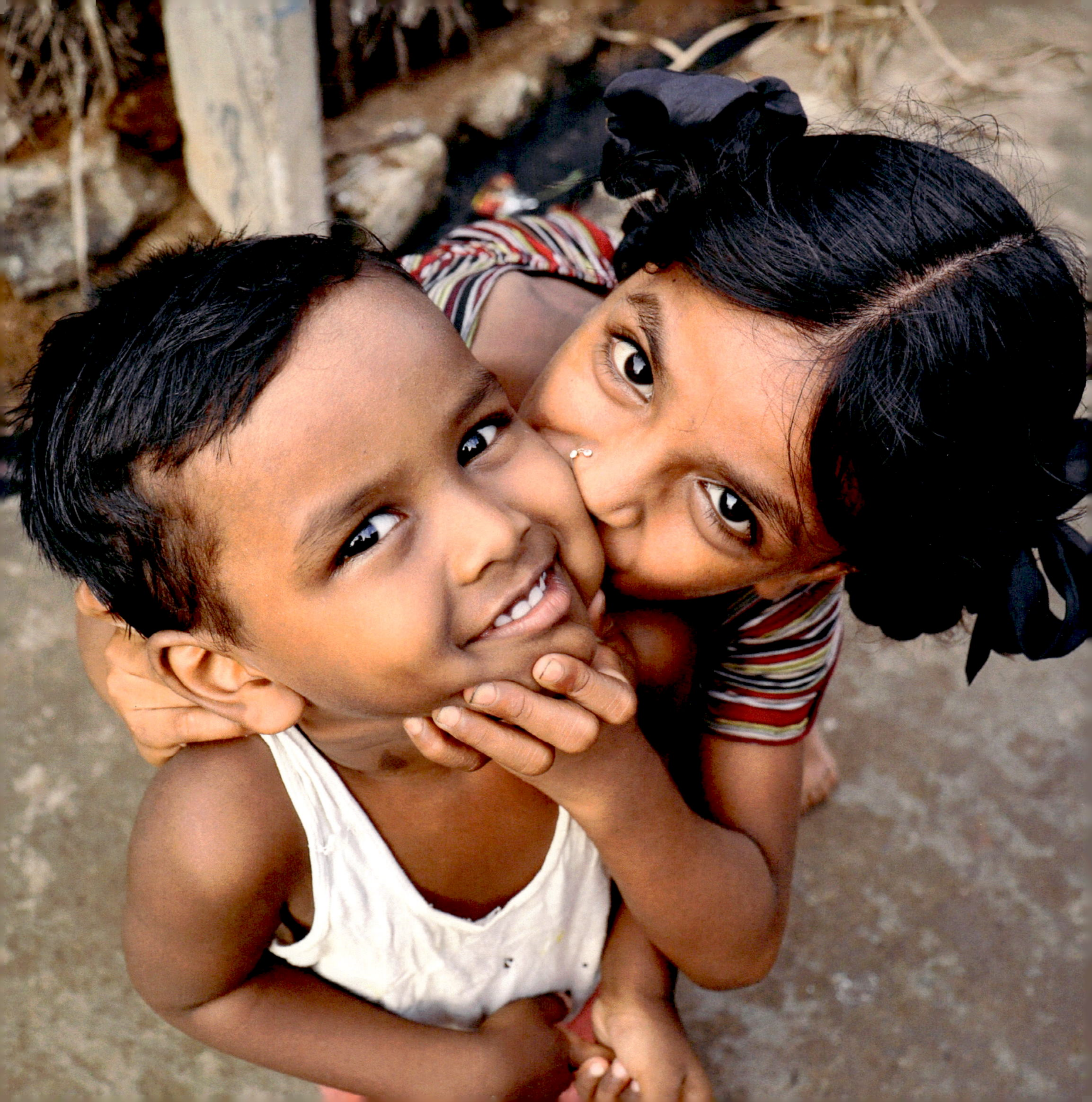

thank you:

To our families, friends, and many supporter's whose encouragement, love, and prayers have carried us through this incredible journey. We could not have done this without you.

To YWAM Kona, PhotogenX International, Paul & Susi Childers, Christian Fox, Layne Beckner Grime and Anne Hennighausen for providing the framework and facilitation of this program.

To Joseph Avakian for his design expertise, patience, and impeccable humor that kept us moving forward throughout the creation of this book and laughing every step of the way.

And a very special thank you to Mathu Thomason and Brad Robertson, for counseling us through some very challenging times. You encouraged us to keep fighting the good fight - to be a family that refuses to quit on each other. We are eternally grateful for your love, counsel, and a swift kick in the you-know-what.

Photo Credits: Scott Savage, Sarah Wallensteen, Lily Wang, Dawn Pfaff, Marisa Groff, Nathaniel Lynch, Hilary Haddow & Sarah Haberly

Writing & Editing: Sarah Wallensteen, Hilary Haddow & Dawn Pfaff

Design: Scott Savage, Marisa Groff, Lily Wang, & Nathaniel Lynch

Graphics: J. Eric Albrecht & Carrie Davis

Printed in China by onthemark www.onthemark.net

Dawn Pfaff | 34 | San Jose, California

"Traveling the world has taught me many things, most of all this: God is big and we are small. The world is big and we are small. But no matter how small, every single human being - past, present and future - is an intentional creation formed from the depths of God's love. Lou Engle said it best, 'God had a dream about you and then he wrapped a body around that dream.' "

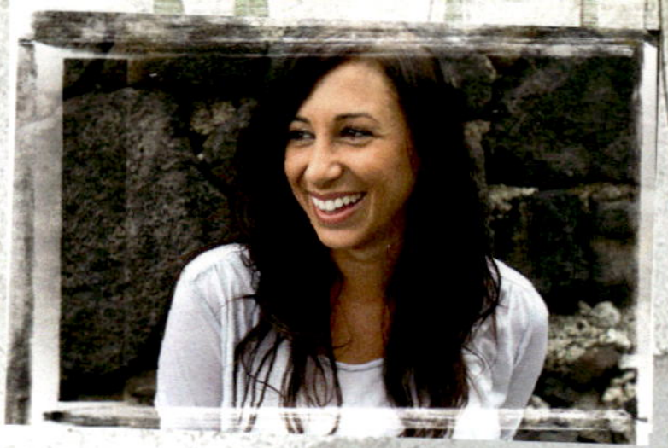

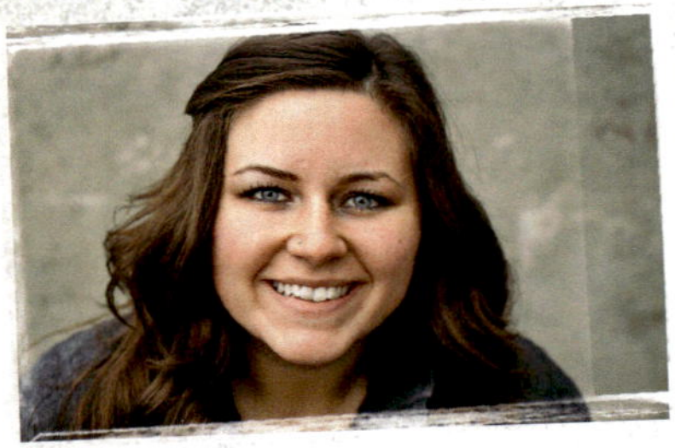

Hilary Haddow | 24 | Tacoma, Washington

"The countless new friendships we made around the world are ones that will be forever imprinted on my heart. As well as the families and individuals that helped reshape my ideas on the depths of family."

Lily Wang | 27 | Xia Men, China

"There is nothing more fascinating than our fellow humanity. Take time to listen to one another, whether it be a stranger, your own family member, or a homeless person living on the streets. When you give of yourself for others you will in turn become who you were created to be."

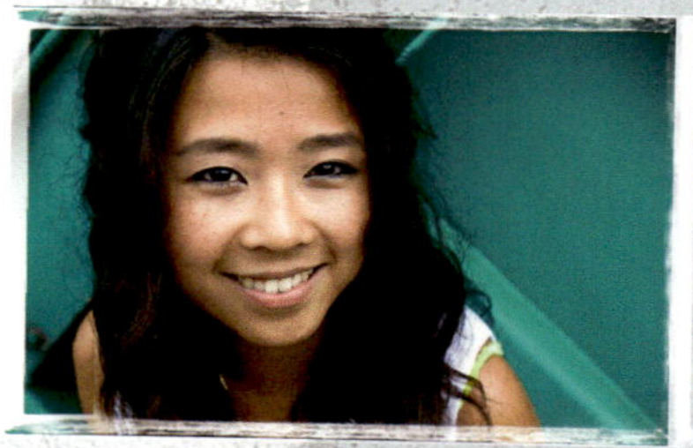

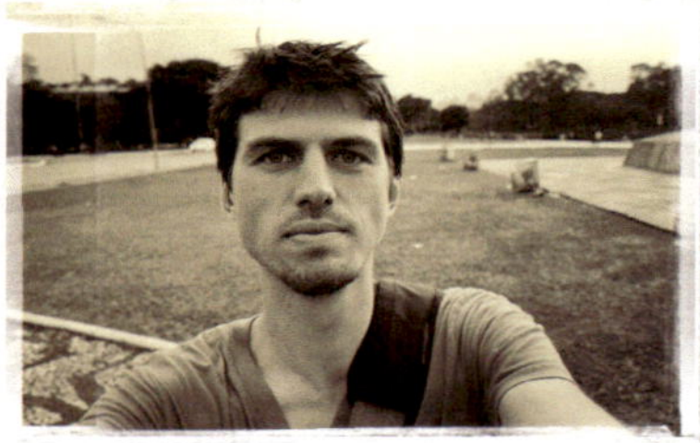

Scott Savage | 28 | San Diego, California

Hope alone is not enough to create change, but with patience, love, and gratitude we must fight to see our hopes become reality. Though If we lose hope we lose our chance to succeed. It must be kept alive through the greatest gift we have: our ability to serve others.

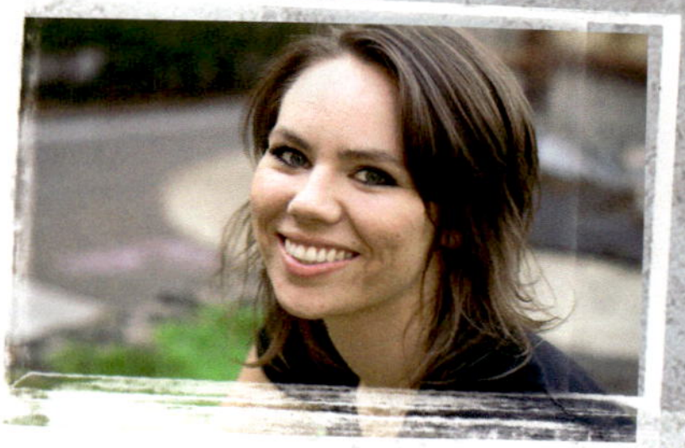

Melissa Haberly | 25 | Mt. Vernon, Washington

"For me, track was the beginning of letting go. I had to let go of my ideas of love, family, commitment, surrender, and dependence. In that, I've learned to truly embrace what it looks like to risk. Only then can you begin to really embrace people, families, communities, and culture - to embrace the world and all its potential."

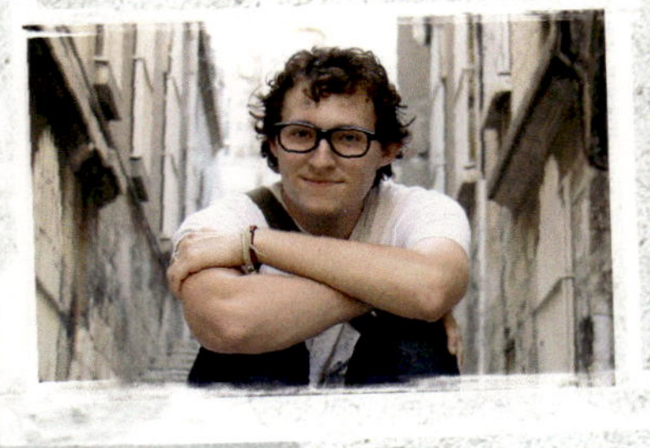

Nathaniel Lynch | 21 | Seattle, Washington

"Through track I learned how to embrace the differences within a community and have come to recognize that we are so unique around the world, but at the same time all so similar."

Marisa Groff | 22 | Lancaster, Pennsylvania

"Travel is more than just the seeing of sights; I have been changed by the people I've met along the way. They have taught me to never give up, to forgive always, be selfless, and to live a life of intention. We need to slow down and find joy in the simple things. There is so much beauty around us that goes unnoticed."

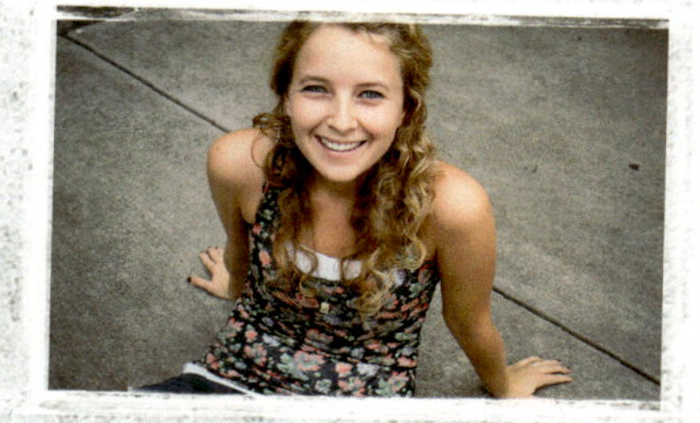

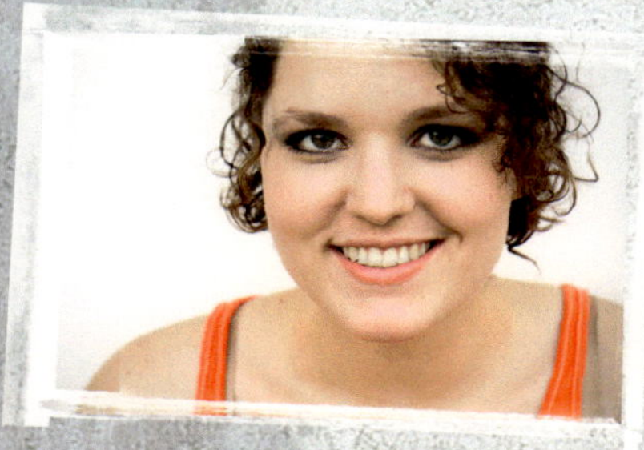

Sarah Haberly | 23 | Mt. Vernon, Washington

"The track taught me that family is not simply blood relatives, and home does not lie within walls or borders. My family is now amongst the nations, and home is my contentment and security in God, no matter where I am."

Timothy Euken | 21 | Kaneohe, Hawaii

"This track has meant to me the beginning of a lifelong journey towards something greater than myself. I see injustice issues not as numbers anymore, but as faces, and I can't deny those faces the voice they deserve."

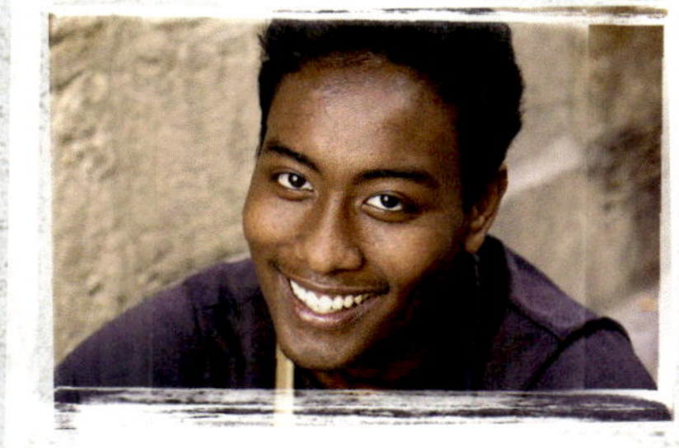

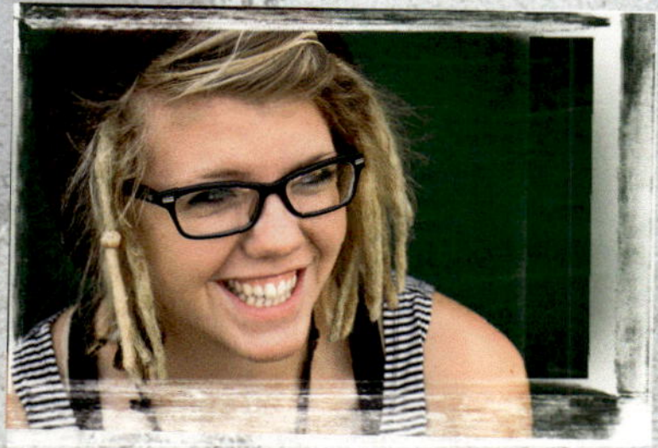

Sarah Wallensteen | 21 | British Columbia, Canada

"The world, with its vast array of people and cultures, is absolutely stunning. I have learned and experienced the beauty found in our differences. In so many cases we let our differences divide us, but in reality they should bring us together. We have so much to learn from each other if we would just stop and listen."

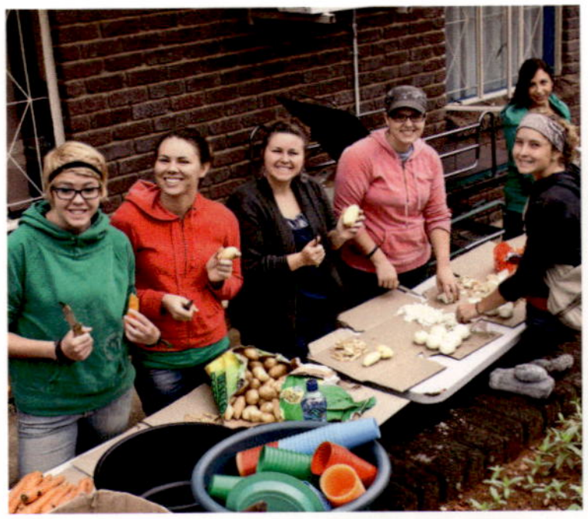
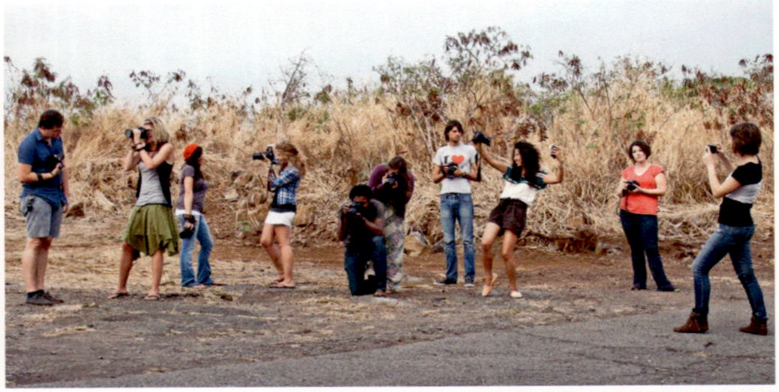
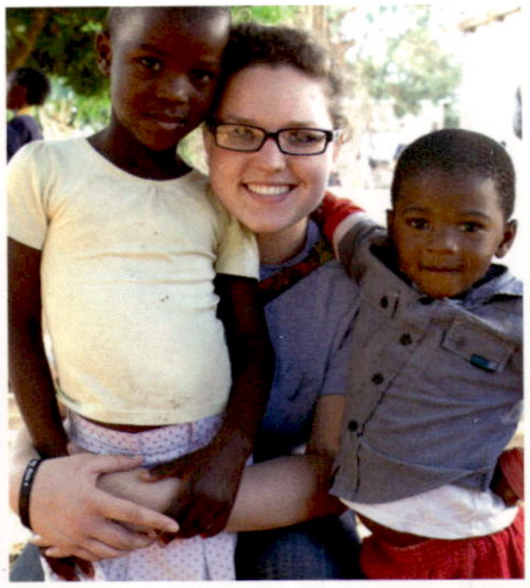
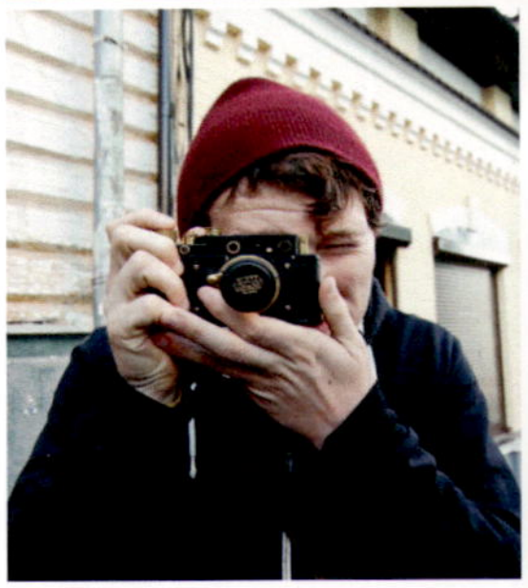
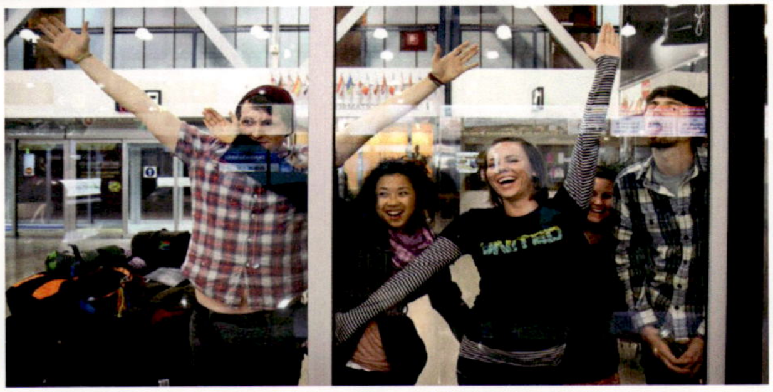
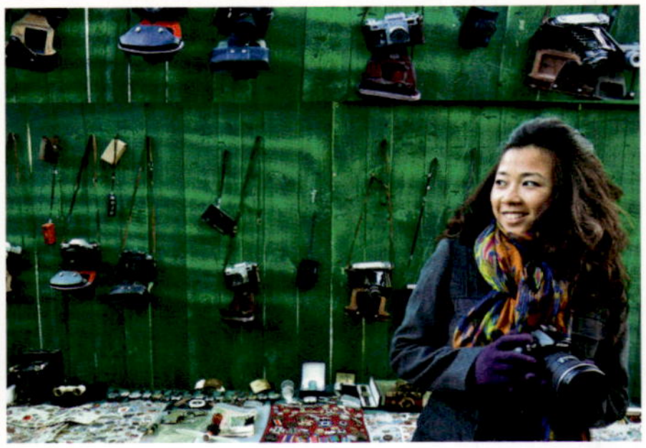
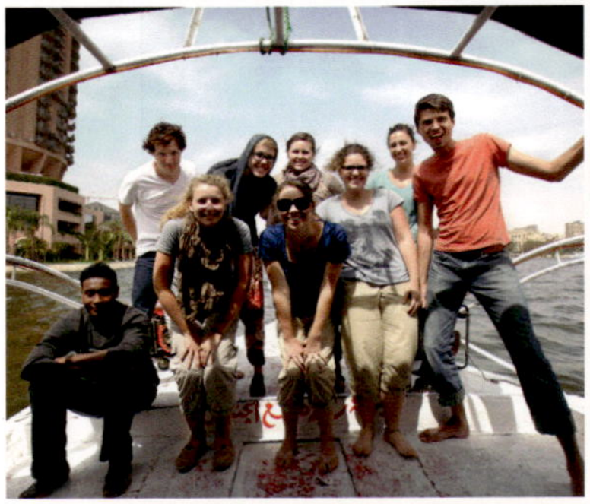
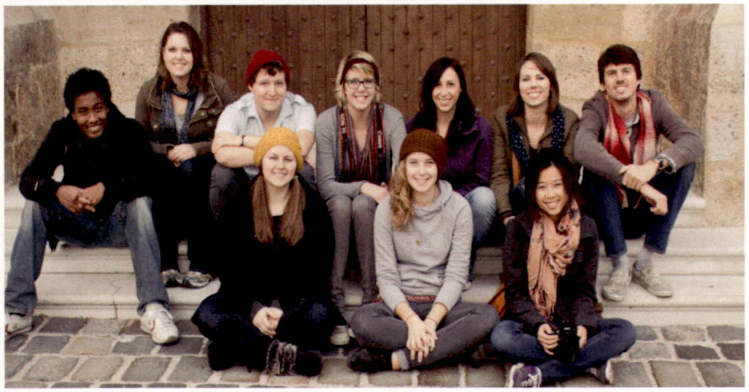
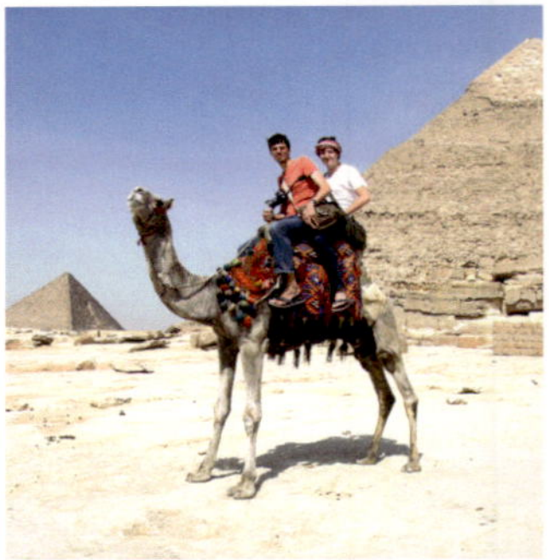
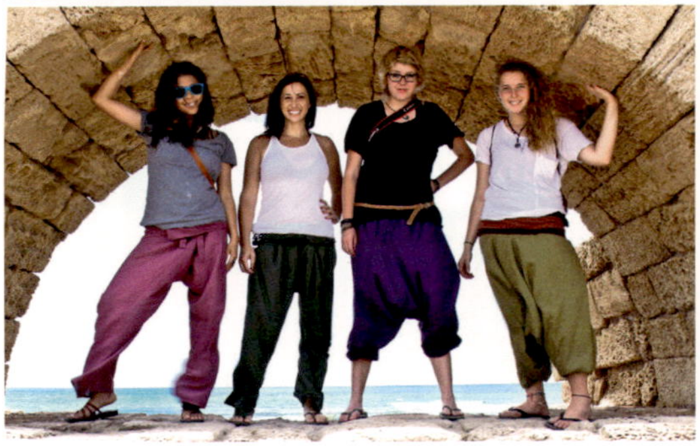
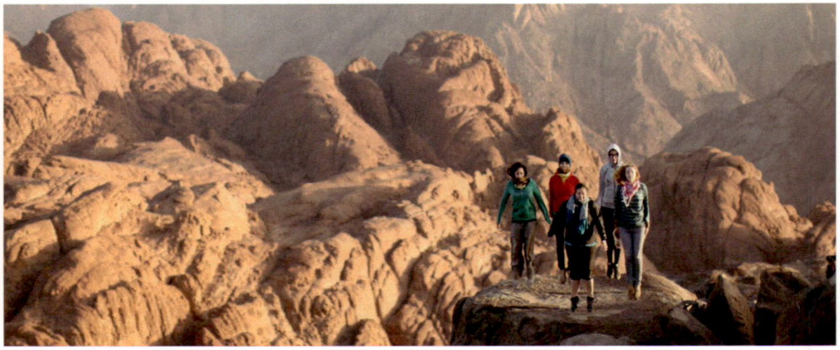

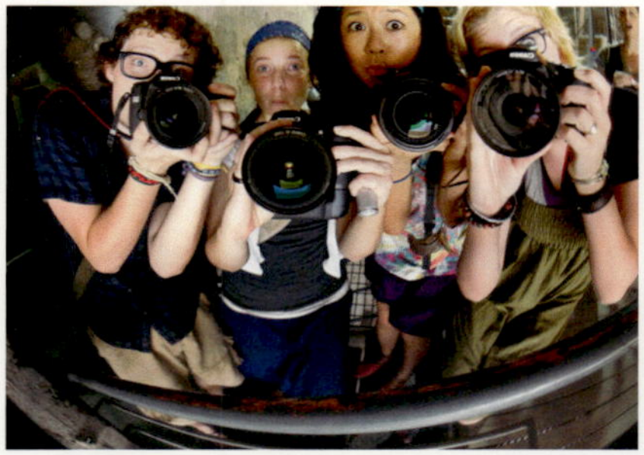

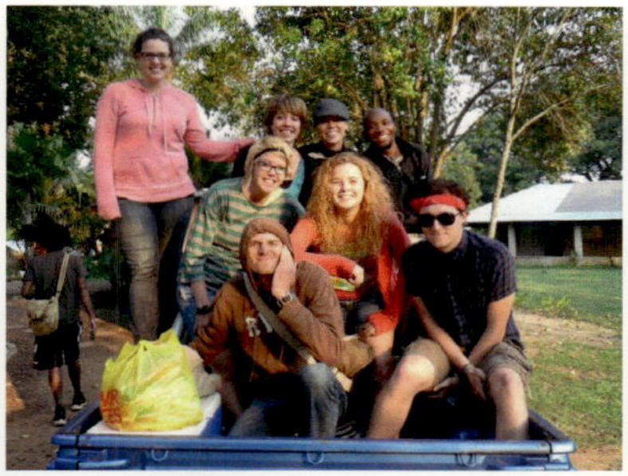

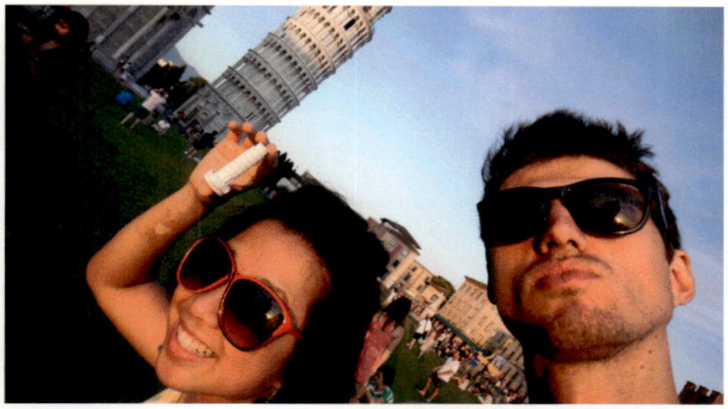

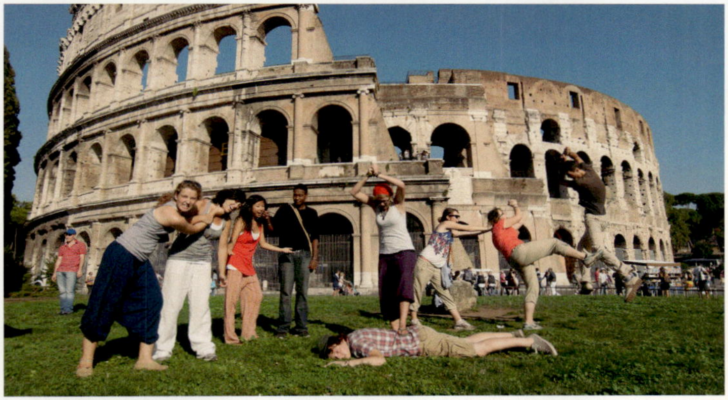

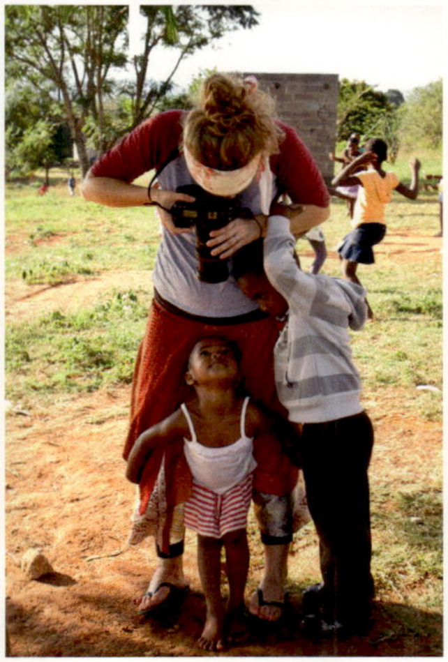

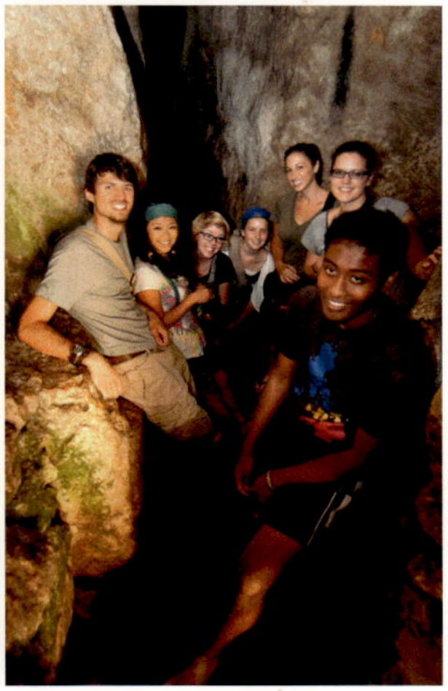

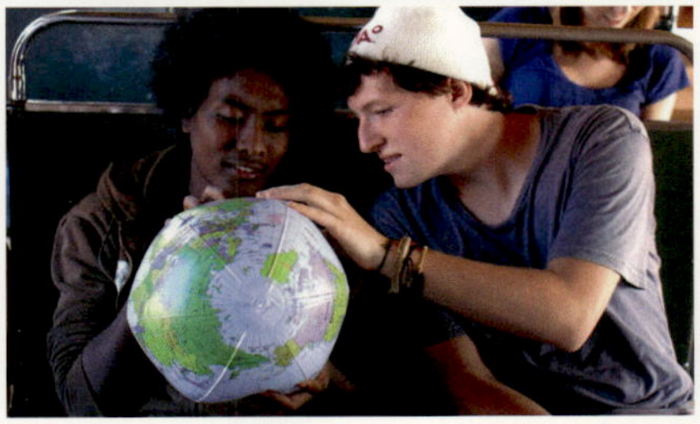

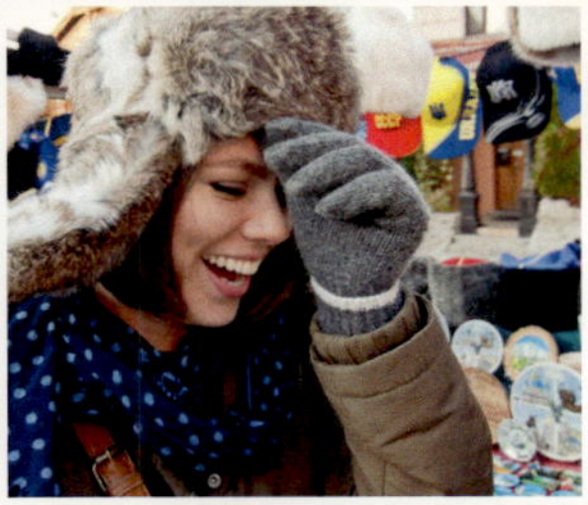

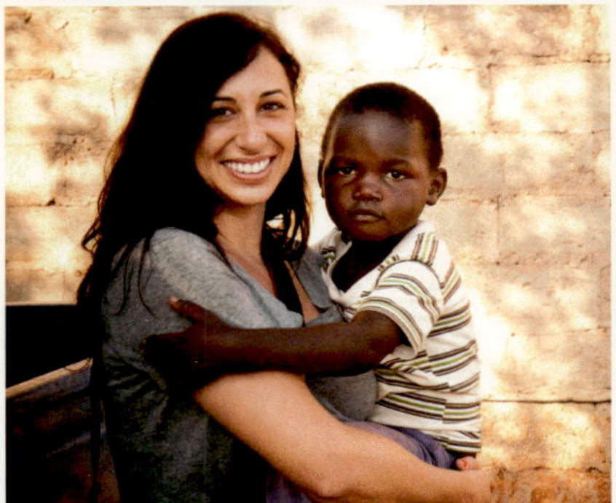

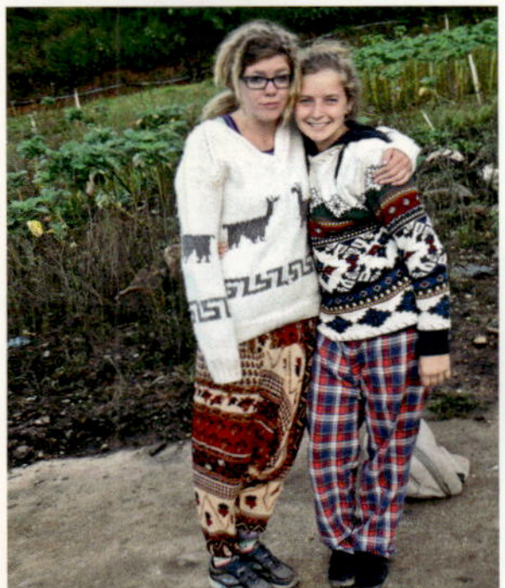

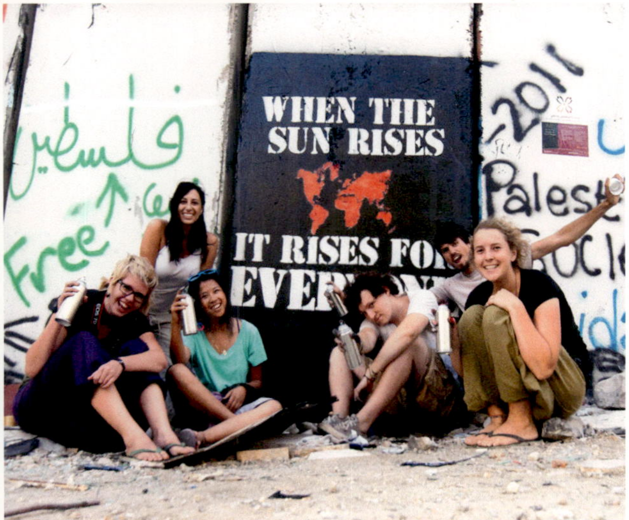
WHEN THE
SUN RISES
Free
-2011

References

All web sources accessed 25 April 2012

[1] "Orphan Estimates." *Childinfo.* United Nations Children's Fund, Jan. 2011. Web. <http://www.childinfo.org/hiv_aids_orphanestimates.php>

[2] Merida, Tony, and Rick Morton. "The Scope of the Worldwide Orphan Crisis." *New Hope Digital.* New Hope Publishers, n.d. Web.

[3] Meintjes, Helen, et al. "Child-Headed Households in South Africa: A Statistical Brief." *Children Count.* Cape Town: Children's Institute, University of Cape Town, Sept. 2009. Web. <http://www.childrencount.ci.org.za/uploads/brief_child_headed_households.pdf.>

[4] Foy, Henry James. "UNHCR Refugee Statistics: Full Data." *The Guardian.* The Guardian, 14 June 2010. Web.

[5] Pike, John. "The World at War." *Global Security.* Global Security, 4 March 2012. Web.

[6] Mercer, Phil. "Australia's Aboriginal Suicide Rate Sparks Concern." *BBC News.* British Broadcasting Corporation, 8 May 2011. Web.

[7] "Elder Abuse and Neglect: In Search of Solutions." *APA.* American Psychological Association, n.d. Web.

[8] "General Comment 4: The Right to Adequate Housing." Treaty Body Database Committee 11.1 (1991). *UNHCHR.* United Nations Organization, 13 Dec. 1991. Web.

[9] Bell, Julie Reed, and Seth Borenstein. "2012's World Gone Wild: Quakes, Floods, Blizzards." *MSNBC.* Microsoft Corporation, 19 Dec. 2010. Web.

[10] "Haiti Earthquake Facts and Figures." *Disasters Emergency Committee.* London Web Limited, Oct. 2011. Web.

[11] Barrionuevo, Alexei, and Liz Robbins. "1.5 Million Displaced After Chile Quake." *NY Times.* New York Times Digital, 27 Feb. 2010. Web.

[12] Jingjing, Han. "China to Mourn Quake Dead, Public Entertainment to be Suspended." *Xinhuanet.* Xinhua News Agency, 20 April 2010. Web.

[13] "China Earthquake Death Toll Jumps to 400." *CBS News.* CBS Broadcasting Inc., 15 April 2010. Web.

[14] "Natural Disasters Claimed 295,000 Lives Last Year." *ENS-Newswire.* Environment News Service, 3 Jan. 2011. Web.

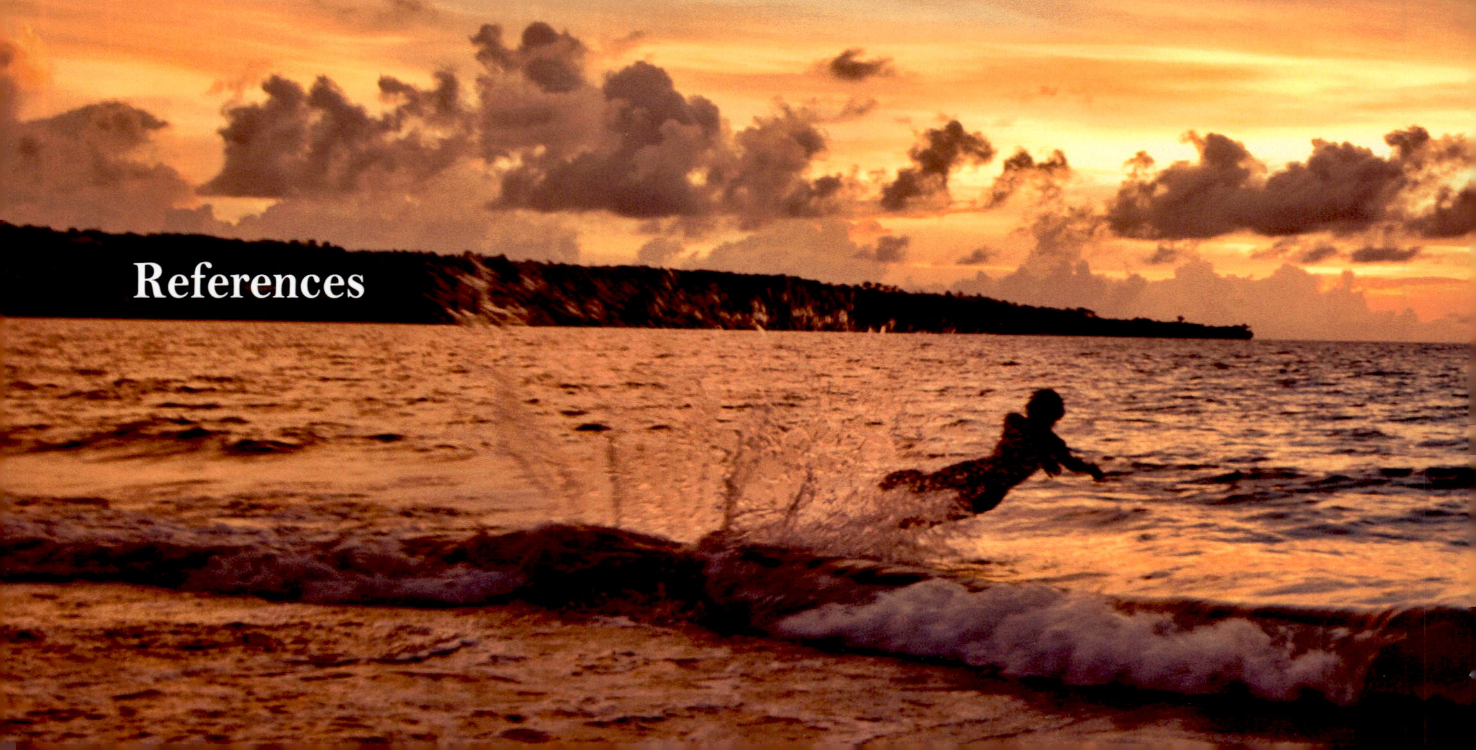

[15] "Pakistan Floods Still Claiming Lives, Six Months On." *BBC News.* British Broadcasting Corporation, 28 Jan. 2011. Web.

[16] Chagas, Marcos. "Flood: Rio's Tragedy Expected to Reach at Least 1,500 Deaths." *Brazzil Mag.* Brazzil Magazine, 26 Jan. 2011. Web.

[17] Yuasa, Shino, and Tomoko A. Hosaka. "Japan Earthquake and Tsunami Death Toll Exceeds 10,000." *Huffington Post.* Huff Post News, 25 March 2011. Web.

[18] Tutton, Mark. "10 Million at Risk from East Africa Drought." *CNN.* Turner Broadcasting System, Inc., 8 July 2011. Web.

[19] "Top 5 Worst Natural Disasters of 2011." *Global Post.* Global News Enterprises LLC, 30 Dec. 2011. Web.

[20] "Top 5 Worst Natural Disasters of 2011." *Global Post.*

[21] "Top 5 Worst Natural Disasters of 2011." *Global Post.*

[22] "Top 5 Worst Natural Disasters of 2011." *Global Post.*

[23] "Sex Trafficking." *I Stop Traffic.* Artists United for Social Justice, n.d. Web. <http://www.istoptraffic.com/home.html>

[24] "International Housing Statistics and Research." *Habitat For Humanity.* Habitat For Humanity International, 15 Oct. 2009. Web.

[25] "Statistic of Child Abuse." *Haltnow.* Humanity Against Local Terrorism, Jan. 2010. Web.

[26] "Rights of the Child." UNICEF General Assembly (29 Aug. 2006): 14-22. Web. <http://www.unicef.org/violencestudy/reports/SG_violencestudy_en.pdf>

[27] Jackson, Kenny. *Get Married for Christ's Sake – The Christian Singles Call to a World-Changing Marriage.* Creation House Books, 2011. Print.

[28] "The World Factbook: AFRICA: Swaziland: People and Society." *CIA.* Central Intelligence Agency, March 2012. Web.

[29] Sanchez-Padilla Elisabeth, et al. "High Prevalence of Multidrug-Resistant Tuberculosis, Swaziland, 2009–2010." *CDC.* Centers for Disease Control and Prevention, Jan 2012. Web.

[30] "Swaziland Statistics." *UNICEF.* United Nations International Children's Emergency Fund, n.d. Web. <http://www.unicef.org/infobycountry/swaziland_statistics.html>

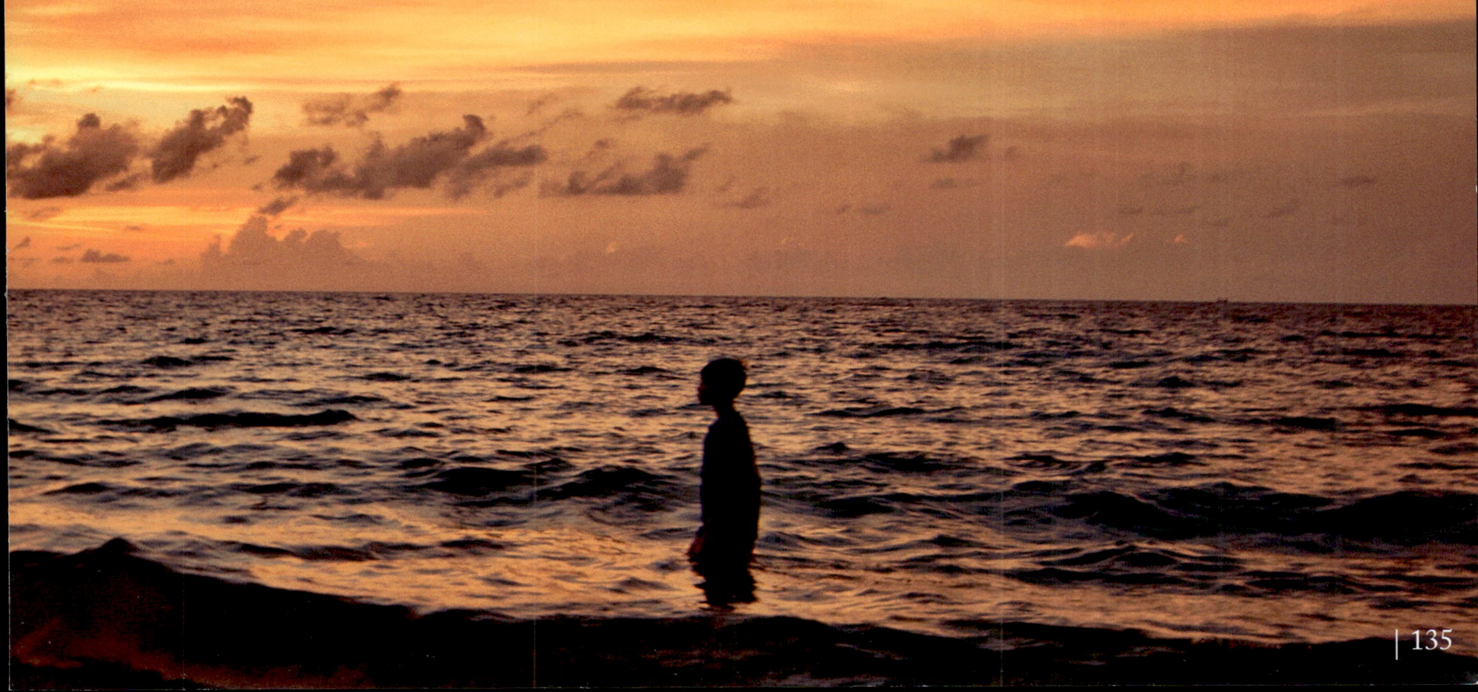

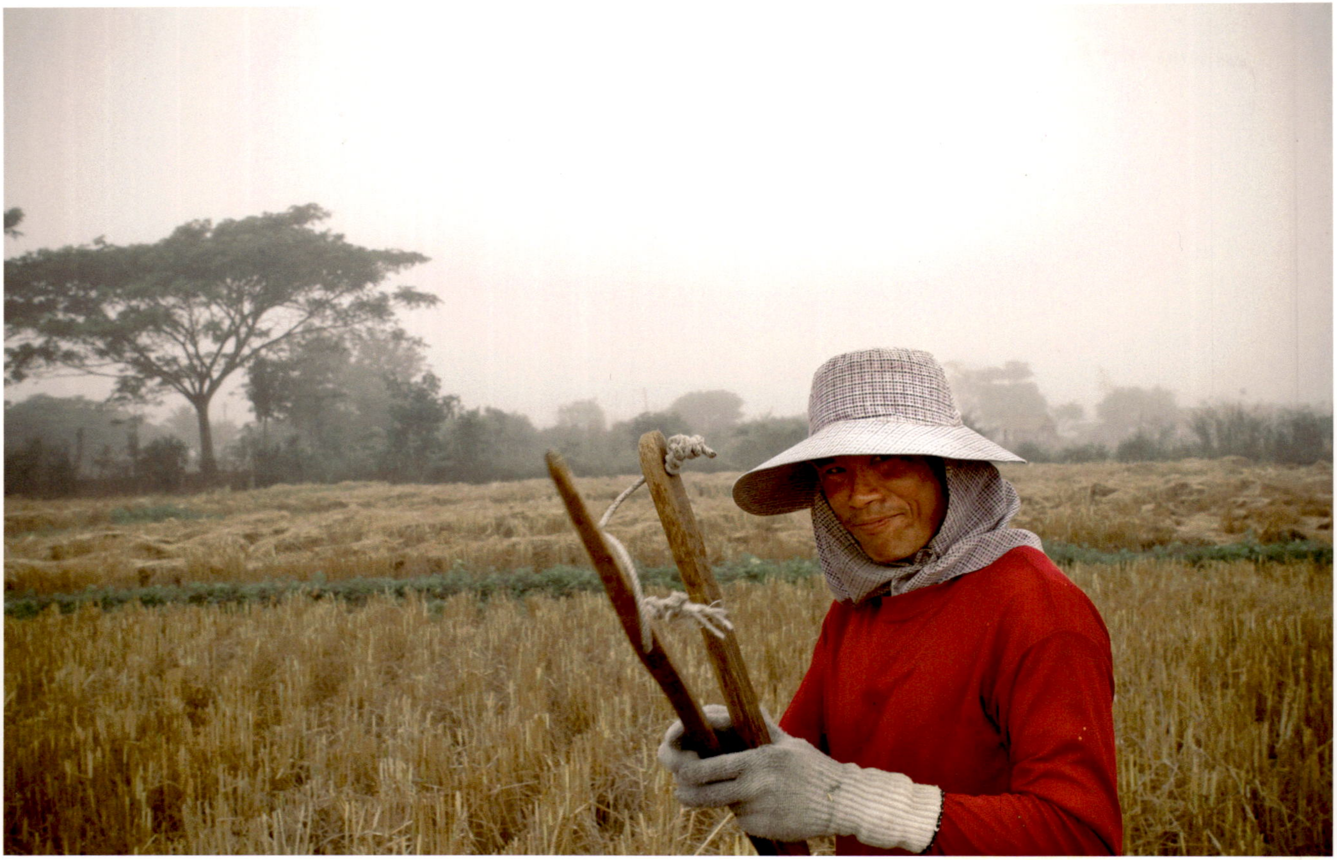

Broken: a call to restore the house of Humanity was created by students of the "PhotogenX Around the World Track" (a degree program of University of the Nations and PhotogenX International). The University of the Nations is a global university with campuses in 142 countries, offering over 600 courses in more than 100 languages. The Track program trains students in photojournalism and worldview while experiencing the nations of the world firsthand. For more information, visit:

www.photogenx.net
www.uofnkona.edu
www.ywam.org